Wines of France

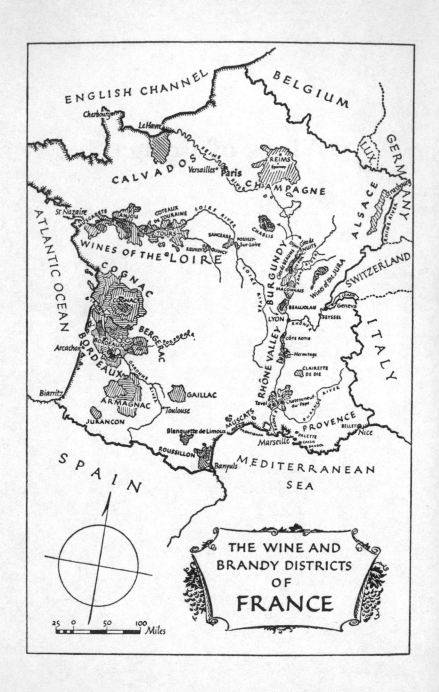

ENGLISH CHANNEL

BELGIUM

Cherbourg

Le Havre

CALVADOS

Versailles Paris

REIMS
Épernay
CHAMPAGNE

GERMANY

LUX

St Nazaire

COTEAUX
DE TOURAINE

LOIRE RIVER

CHABLIS

ALSACE

Strasbourg

MUSCADETS

ANJOU

TOURS

SANCERRE

POUILLY-
Sur-Loire

Côte de
NUITS

Dijon

RHINE RIVER

WINES OF THE LOIRE

REUILLY
QUINCY

CÔTE BEAUNE

BURGUNDY

Wine of the JURA

ATLANTIC OCEAN

COGNAC

COGNAC

MÂCONNAIS

SWITZERLAND

BEAUJOLAIS

L. GENEVA Geneva

BERGERAC

DORDOGNE

LYON

SEYSSEL

BORDEAUX

BORDEAUX

Arcachon

CÔTE RÔTIE

RHÔNE

Biarritz

GARONNE RIVER

Hermitage

CLAIRETTE
DE DIE

GAILLAC

RHÔNE VALLEY

DURANCE RIVER

ARMAGNAC

Toulouse

JURANÇON

Tavel

Châteauneuf
du Pape

Blanquette de Limoux

MUSCATS

PROVENCE

BELLET

Nice

ROUSSILLON

MARTIGUES

PALETTE

CASSIS
BANDOL

Marseille

SPAIN

Banyuls

MEDITERRANEAN
SEA

ITALY

25 O   50   100
                    Miles

THE WINE AND
BRANDY DISTRICTS
OF
FRANCE

Wines of France

by Alexis Lichine

IN COLLABORATION WITH
WILLIAM E. MASSEE

LONDON
CASSELL & COMPANY LTD
1958

CASSELL & CO. LTD.
37/38 St. Andrew's Hill
Queen Victoria Street
London, E.C. 4

and at

210 Queen Street, Melbourne; 26/30 Clarence Street, Sydney;
24 Wyndham Street, Auckland; 1068 Broadview Avenue,
Toronto 6; P.O. Box 275, Cape Town; P.O. Box 11190,
Johannesburg; 58 Pembroke Street, Port of Spain, Trinidad;
Haroon Chambers, South Napier Road, Karachi; 13/14 Ajmeri
Gate Extension, New Delhi 1; 15 Graham Road, Ballard Estate,
Bombay 1; 17 Chittaranjan Avenue, Calcutta 13; P.O. Box 23,
Colombo; Macdonald House, Orchard Road, Singapore 9;
Avenida 9 de Julho 1138, Sao Paulo; Galeria Guemes, Escritorio
454/59 Florida 165, Buenos Aires; Marne 5b, Mexico 5, D.F.;
25 rue Henri Barbusse, Paris 5e; 25 Ny Strandvej, Espergaerde,
Copenhagen; Kauwlaan 17, The Hague; Bederstrasse 51,
Zurich 2.

First published in Great Britain 1952
Second Edition April 1953
Third Edition September 1956
Fourth Edition February 1958

Printed in Great Britain by
Lowe and Brydone (Printers) Limited, London, N.W.10

TO

C. C. Philippe & Seymour Weller

two good friends, two wine-lovers

CONTENTS

vii

APPENDIX

MAPS

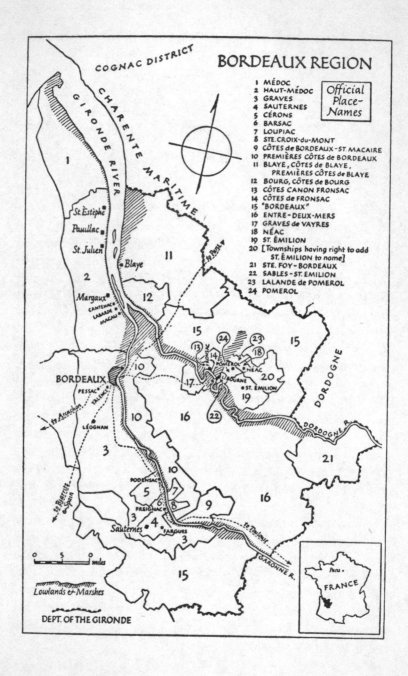

BORDEAUX REGION

COGNAC DISTRICT

Official Place-Names

1 MÉDOC
2 HAUT-MÉDOC
3 GRAVES
4 SAUTERNES
5 CÉRONS
6 BARSAC
7 LOUPIAC
8 STE. CROIX-du-MONT
9 CÔTES de BORDEAUX-ST. MACAIRE
10 PREMIÈRES CÔTES de BORDEAUX
11 BLAYE, CÔTES de BLAYE,
   PREMIÈRES CÔTES de BLAYE
12 BOURG, CÔTES de BOURG
13 CÔTES CANON FRONSAC
14 CÔTES de FRONSAC
15 "BORDEAUX"
16 ENTRE-DEUX-MERS
17 GRAVES de VAYRES
18 NÉAC
19 ST. ÉMILION
20 [Townships having right to add
   ST. ÉMILION to name]
21 STE. FOY-BORDEAUX
22 SABLES-ST. EMILION
23 LALANDE de POMEROL
24 POMEROL

CHARENTE MARITIME

GIRONDE RIVER

St. Estèphe
Pauillac
St. Julien
Blaye
Margaux
CANTENAC
LABARDE
MACAU

BORDEAUX
PESSAC
TALENCE
LÉOGNAN

to Arcachon

to Biarritz & Spain

PODENSAC
PREIGNAC
Sauternes
FARGUES

to Bayonne

FRONSAC
POMEROL
NÉAC
LIBOURNE
ST. ÉMILION

DORDOGNE R.

to Toulouse

GARONNE R.

0   5   miles

Lowlands & Marshes

DEPT. OF THE GIRONDE

Paris
FRANCE

The Wines of France

THE greatest wines on earth come from France. The wines of this century are the greatest in the history of man. We are now living in a Golden Age of wine, thanks to the one Frenchman in every seven who earns his living making wine, and to his father, and to his father's father, as far back in time as there have been men tending vineyards on the sunny soil of France.

France not only makes the best wine, and more of it, than any other place on earth, but also drinks more per man, because a Frenchman knows a good thing when he tastes it. The 1,800,000 French wine-growers drink more wine than any other group, and it is a wonder that they let the rest of the world have any of it. The economics that forces them to do so will also, according to some, force them to stop tending some of the great vineyards in a decade or so—a reason for taking advantage of what there is while it still exists.

The most elementary details about wine history and wine drinking form a basis for understanding the wonders that wine possesses. In the excitement of drinking wine these simplest elementals are often forgotten. It may prove useful to know how wines became part of France and to understand the basic things a Frenchman considers when he drinks wine or thinks of it—things so simple and habitual that he may be almost unaware of them.

1

Nobody knows how or when vines were first tended in ancient Gaul, though it is supposed that they were brought in from the Near East by Phocæan traders some centuries before Christ. There is a feeling among winegrowers that everybody stopped whatever he was doing and took to planting vineyards. In those bad old days when the Romans invaded Gaul, there were vineyards in many parts of France.

With the growing power of the monks during the early centuries of this millennium, more vineyards were planted. From Cluny, in the wine country of Burgundy, bands went out to establish monasteries and vineyards, forever linking the history of the Church with the history of wine. Many of the great vineyards were planted by ecclesiastics, and nearly all of them belonged to the Church at one time or another. There is probably not a hill, slope, or plain in France where vines can grow that has not been planted at one time or another, and it is through the trial and error of the past twenty centuries that today's vineyards have gained their greatness.

French winegrowers would have you believe that the main purpose of the Crusades was to bring back new varieties of vine. Perhaps among them were the Pinot, from which all great Burgundies are produced, and the Gamay, which produces an enormous quantity of wine, but only one of any quality, the Burgundy known as Beaujolais. They also state that wine has always been the major produce of France and still is. In 1350 the equivalent of one million cases was exported from the port of Bordeaux. In 1790 six million were shipped, while in 1955 the equivalent of four and a half million cases are being exported.

With the French Revolution, vineyards began to pass out of the hands of the Church and the aristocracy and into the hands of the French people, who were more or less pleased with this state of things until the last half of the nineteenth century, when some zealous winegrower imported American vines to see how they would do on French soil. They did well, completely destroying nearly every vineyard in France. On the American roots was a burrowing louse called the phylloxera, which was fatal to French vines. Today almost all French vines are grafted to American roots, which are resistant to the phylloxera.

The wines of France are as varied as they are good. Nowhere else is there such a variety of countryside or such a variety of wine—a special wine to go with every change of scenery. East of Paris is the Champagne country; the vineyards of Burgundy lie just south of it and extend all the way down to Lyons. Along the Rhône valley are other great vineyards, flanked on the southeast by those of Provence, and on the southwest by a range of lesser wine districts extending to the Pyrenees. Southwest of Paris are the wines of the Loire Valley, and the great vineyards of Bordeaux below that; far over on the eastern borders are the Alsace wines, and below them those of the Juras. To the north and southeast of Bordeaux are the wines that are distilled into the fabulous brandies of France, Cognac and Armagnac.

All these districts produce wines that are distinctive, but not all are great. By far the largest quantities of wine come from the vineyards of the Midi, that vast stretch of land in southern France just west of the mouth of the Rhône. Here the wines are rated by the degree of alcohol they contain, and they are shipped all over France in tank lorries that look exactly like petrol lorries. To this quantity is added the immense amount of wine produced in the French departments and protectorates of North Africa, particularly Algeria. These wines are the ones most commonly drunk in France, where the average consumption per capita is forty-two gallons a year.

A Frenchman drinks wine because he does not drink water. This is partly a relic of the days when much of the water in France was dangerous to drink. And from those days also comes the much-scoffed-at story that water contains little frogs that get into your stomach and grow there, eventually causing you to die a horrible death while making croaking noises. Now everybody, including the Frenchman who tells you about the frogs, will deny the truth of the story; but the fact remains that hardly anybody drinks water in France.

Bottled water, of course, is something else, and vast quantities of Perrier, Vichy, Badoit, Évian, Vittel, and dozens of other spring waters gush down French throats daily. But these waters are drunk for health and are free of frogs; some of them are said to be full of all sorts of good things to ward off *foie* trouble. At least, they don't harm you, and you can never tell about tap water.

In France, *foie* trouble is the favourite disease, as popular a conversational topic as ulcers in other countries. One of the standard Franco-English conversations is that of a Frenchman explaining to an Englishman or an American what liver trouble is, and that all Frenchman don't have it, and the Englishman explaining what ulcers are, and that all Englishmen or Americans don't have them.

Foie trouble comes from eating and drinking too much, and every Frenchman can give you a long list of foods that are very bad for the *foie*: eggs, fats, butter, spinach, shellfish, sauces. This explains why the French never eat eggs for breakfast, though they are perfectly all right for lunch and dinner—perhaps the classic example of Gallic logic. But a Frenchman will add that one thing never bad for the *foie*—not in a million years—is wine. Sauces, yes, even though sauces are the basis of French cooking. But wine, never. The fact is, of course, that drinking wine makes it possible to eat rich food, because wine cuts grease, and a sip will leave your mouth perfectly clean and ready for another bite of whatever happens to be bad for the *foie*. Wine is not bad for the *foie*, but wine makes it possible to eat enough to get *foie* trouble.

Wine and food go together, with or without interesting effects on the liver, and it is impossible for the French to think of one without the other. Most Frenchmen drink wine every day. It is rarely a great wine, and usually a quite ordinary one, but it is almost always drunk with food. And there are practically no hard and fast rules as to which wine goes with what, though one rule seems to be that the great wines are not drunk with everyday food, or the other way round. And even the French, who drink wine from habit, also drink it for fun. One thing that makes wine more fun to drink is a series of laws that have made it possible to get what you ask for.

Before the depression few of the vineyards outside of the Bordeaux region were properly listed, nor was nomenclature controlled, and a famous name was often attached to an inferior wine. Probably more wine was fraudulent than genuine. But in the middle 1930's a series of laws began to be passed called the *Appellations d'Origine*, carefully defining which vineyards had the titles to which names, and what variety of grapes were to be used. Also, Burgundy wine-growers began following a Bordeaux system whereby the grower of the grape made and bottled his own wine, putting his name on the label and personally vouching for its genuineness.

As a result, it is now possible to buy honest wines from every well-known wine district in France. With this guarantee of authenticity, one can gain accurate knowledge about wine from drinking it, something that was hard to do before, since you never could be sure of what you were getting.

People have been led to feel that the simple enjoyment of a bottle of wine is out of the question, and that wine-drinking must be surrounded by ritual and pretence. Any advice, suggestions, or rules about wine are not necessarily wine salesmen's talk, and the best of them should add to your pleasure, giving you greater value for what you spend in effort, time, and money.

There is one pretension about wine which might not be thought of as a pretension at all. It is the matter of descriptive adjectives, the jargon of wine. Through the years these words have become almost meaningless through constant use and abuse, and yet they are used throughout the world to describe wine. You can think of them as clichés, or you can think of them as shorthand terms for a variety of subtle but definable taste sensations. Everybody is born with a tongue in his head, and the tongue can recognize what the terms stand for even if it is hard to put into words exactly what the tongue recognizes. One man's tongue may recognize wider degrees of distinction between the terms, but anybody can get to tell the terms, and the wines, apart.

It is not difficult to tell two wines apart. The wine from one vineyard is not the same as the wine from another, and your tongue can distinguish the difference, but you need to taste the two wines against each other. The greater the wine, the sharper the distinctions. It is easier to make distinctions when the wines are from different districts, and it is not too difficult to distinguish between the wines from the same vineyard and the same vintage, but from different barrels. This is no particular credit to one's discernment, but merely an indication of how widely wine can vary. Wines are living things. Each has its own distinctive character, and most of them are good to drink. The enjoyment is there for everyone, sparkling in the glass. The difficulty comes in trying to talk about it.

The more you know about wine, the more pleasure you can get from it, for knowledge of wine helps you to buy good bottles. Real wine knowledge comes from drinking. The more wines you taste, the more you will enjoy them. It is disappointing, for example, to drink a great red Burgundy or red Bordeaux when the wine is too young, just as it is disappointing to keep an old wine until it is far past its prime. White wines, except sweet ones (which can live for a generation), should be drunk when young, rarely older than ten years, preferably when only three or four; and yet many such wines are kept until they are musty, flat, brown, and unpleasant, a characteristic called maderization, after Madeira wine, whose colour they take. On the other hand, some people turn their noses up when a great red wine is only slightly past its prime, ignoring all the good things it contains, merely because its freshness and strength have waned.

The greatest distinguishing factor between exceptional wines is soil. The earth is what gives a wine its character. Each wine-grower thinks his land is best, perhaps because he knows it best. No group is more chauvinistic than wine-growers, a man from Bordeaux scorning Burgundies as sun-cooked wine, the Burgundian scorning the wine of the Bordelais because of its light feminine qualities. These prejudices spread, for almost everybody in France is friendly with or related to a vintner and acquires his loyalties.

Wine is a work of art, for it is not only the soil but the man, who makes the wine. Wine-making is a matter of judgment, not only as to the time when the grapes should be harvested, but as to how long the wine should ferment, how long it should stay in the barrel, how it should be treated if it gets sick, when it should be bottled. It is a wine-grower's saying that when it comes to wine, as much depends on toil as on rain.

Wine has a great appeal to the eye, both for its colour and for its clarity. Many a painter has become excited over light gleaming on wine or the shimmering reflection of wine on a tablecloth. Each wine has its own hue—the yellow-green of a Chablis, the straw of a Meursault or Montrachet, the gold of a Sauternes—and its hue is a characteristic as distinguishable as any other.

But the art of wine can be detected best through the most elusive of our senses, smell and taste. It is one's nose that gives an understanding of what a great wine can be. What you smell is the evaporation of esters and ethers, those elusive chemical components which the wine contains, a collection called "bouquet" because there are so many different ones in each wine. Some people speak of bouquet as the first full smell of the wine. The later smell is called the aroma, and is more lingering. When a wine is too cold, or when a bottle is first opened and before the air has had a chance to evaporate some of the wine, its bouquet is hard to identify. One of the outstanding qualities of young wines from some varieties of grape is "fruitiness," an odour that may remind you of freshly picked raspberries, or violets, or truffles.

Because the alcohol increases this evaporation, many wines also have the taste of these fruit and flower smells. Fruitiness is also a taste characteristic of young wines. Equally, many wines have a lingering taste in the mouth, the aftertaste. It is quite distinct from the "original taste," just as the bouquet is distinct from the aroma. Some wines have a tendency to fill the mouth, a characteristic usually defined as "body" imparted to them by alcohol and tannin. Wines heavy in body are pleasantest to sip; of those light in body it is more pleasing to take several swallows at once. Some wines are so full in body that you have the feeling that you could take bites of them and chew, a quality called *mordant*.

In great wines a balance of qualities is needed, body being poised against acidity, which gives the wine freshness. If a wine is too acid, it tastes sharp; if it is not acid enough, it tastes flat and flabby. What holds the qualities of a wine, so that it will live long enough to develop all its characteristics to the full, is tannin. A wine too strong in tannin will taste heavy and bitter. When all these qualities are integrated, the wine is in balance, which is often called the quality of smoothness. A well-balanced wine is always a good one and can often be a great one.

Edward VII has been quoted as saying: "Not only does one drink wine, but one inhales it, one looks at it, one tastes it, one swallows it . . . and one talks about it." Sometimes wine can be confusing because it contains so many different things, all bidding for attention. But of one thing you can be sure: good wine is good to drink.

Bordeaux:

The Largest Great Wine District

BORDEAUX is a seaport sixty miles from the sea, a fan-shaped city on a curve of the Garonne, capital of the province anciently known as Gascony or Guyenne, and its fame was made by the wines from the vineyards surrounding it. These produce and export more good wine than any others in France. An English possession for three centuries, the city returned to the French crown in the middle of the fifteenth century. The stamp of the English remains in *claret*, their name for the red wines of Bordeaux, a corruption of the French *clairet*, which used to mean a light blend of red and white wines.

Bordeaux is the fifth largest city in France. Its 260,000 people talk about wines the way Newmarket talks about horses, and wine remains its most valuable export, as it has been for a thousand years. The city, reached by a steel bridge spanning the Garonne, sprawls out from a great riverside square dominated on the quay side by two ugly columns whose principal ornaments are the behinds of four fishes, up near the top under the crowning sculpture. The square is often filled with travelling fairs and circuses; each spring there is a flea market that lasts for a week, and a gaudy trade fair is held in the month of June. Downstream from the square begins the Quai des Chartrons, a shabby row of waterfront buildings, owning space in which is a mark of distinction, for they contain the cellars and offices of the greatest merchants in the Bordeaux wine trade. In summer the offices are all closed, for the merchants go to Arcachon, over on the Atlantic side of the estuary, and visiting buyers must go to the beaches to do business with the merchants baking in the sun.

On the square is the Hôtel Splendide, which has a nightclub in its basement. The hotel is the Bordeaux headquarters for the visiting wine buyers, and boasts of a wine card that lists over two hundred wines of Bordeaux. A couple of blocks away, near the market, which is an open, circular dome of iron girders and glass whose side walls are hanging awnings vertically striped in red and white, is one of the strangest restaurants in the world, the Chapon-Fin. Built in the nineties, it is made to look like a grotto. It has a rock garden and pool in the back, glass-covered, trellised terraces along the side. The whole is encased under a glass dome, and it is here that the owner of Château Haut-Brion must come if he wants to taste any of the fabulous wine of the 1906 vintage that his vineyard produced. Equally famous among visiting buyers is the Restaurant Dubern, which you enter by passing through a marvellous delicatessen, and there one can get such Bordeaux specialties as *cêpes à la Bordelaises*, huge mushrooms cooked in olive oil with tomatoes. One of the favourite restaurants of the *bordelais*, called Chez Catherine, is a modest and relatively inexpensive eating-place, on a side street. The name on its front is Restaurant Riche, however, and among the specialties are mussels and baby crabs, the former having partially devoured the latter and having been caught before digestion was complete.

Wine is a big business in Bordeaux, complete with brokers, exchange quotations, and speculation on the various vintages and growths. The brokers are called "courtiers,"

11

and in the old days, when strangers needed protection from marauders, they used to accompany visiting buyers to the vineyards. They still do. At one time things were so bad that the banks of the river were walled to keep out river pirates. All the wine of Bordeaux is sold through brokers, who act as go-betweens for grower and buyer, certifying that the wine bought is genuine and in good condition.

The broker is much more than a necessary evil, for most of the wine is bought directly after the harvest, kept in the château during its two years or so in barrel, and delivered to the buyer after the bottling. Many of the wine châteaux sell the wine in barrel after fermentation is complete, but the broker is still necessary to ensure that the wine lives up to its expectations. Most of the brokers specialize in wine in barrels, but some are concerned with the wine only after it is bottled. There are about five hundred brokers, some of them of English families who have been in the business since the eighteenth century, when a man had to get letters patent from the king before he could set up shop. As one of them says, Bordeaux is smothered with brokers.

The shippers buy from the brokers and send the wines of Bordeaux all over the world. The great bulk of their business is in regional wines, those which carry the names of the district or commune, but not those of particular vineyards, for they are a blend. The five greatest districts are the Médoc, to the north of Bordeaux; Saint-Émilion and Pomerol, twenty miles east, which produce red wines; Graves, to the south of the city, which produces both red and white wines; and Sauternes and Barsac, which produce the greatest sweet white wines in the world. The shippers also sell regional wines from the lesser districts and wines from various communes, such as Saint-Estèphe or Margaux, in the Médoc.

Bordeaux wines are also sold under other labels, usually misleading. "Graves Supérieur," for instance, is a name often tacked on wines that are merely regional and are sold at prices higher than ordinary Graves, being often more expensive than château-bottled Graves. Such wines give the buyer no cachet of authenticity and are often of poor value.

The same type of label is one saying "Haut-Sauternes," which is popularly supposed to denote a superior Sauternes —that is, a sweeter one—and these wines often command prices higher than the château-bottled wines. The Committee of Place-Names has done much to dispel many myths that had no foundation. Among these was the relation of Haut-Sauternes to Sauternes. Pierre Bréjoux, Chief of the Technical Section of the Committee, states: "There is no appellation Haut-Sauternes. The word Haut is theoretically forbidden. It is tolerated, however, as long as shippers supply Sauternes in the event that their customers request 'Haut-Sauternes' labels. The wine, however, must be from the district of Sauternes." There is a myth about Sauternes, particularly on the part of the trade: a belief that there is such a thing as a good dry Sauternes. All good Sauternes is sweet, and a dry Sauternes is a poor one. In an average year a good château-bottled Sauternes is a sweet wine with a dry finish, less full-bodied and not so sweet as the same wine in a good year, when it is characterized by a rich, luscious taste, a much-desired quality that makes for high prices. The better the vintage, the sweeter the wine.

Many poor vintages of Sauternes are dry, and to insist on a dry regional Sauternes is to demand a poor wine. The château-bottled Sauternes can be pleasant in off years, but they are never dry, and taste pleasantly soft and on the sweetish side. Sauternes is not synonymous with white wine, but denotes a small and precisely defined district that specializes in sweet wines.

The doyen of the Bordeaux shippers is Louis Eschenauer, Uncle Louis to everybody in the Bordeaux wine business, a man criticized by many for his wartime activities, but the man whose intervention is responsible for saving the bridges of Bordeaux, the city's lifeline. Uncle Louis thinks that the Château Latour of 1870 is the greatest wine the world has ever seen, mostly because 1870 was the year of his birth. He thinks wine baskets are an abomination. He won't let anyone but himself handle the bottles in his private cellar. His firm's tasting-room is next to his office; he has to pass through it to talk to his assistant.

Like such powerful colleagues as Cruse et Fils, Frères; Calvet; Barton et Guestier; Kressmann; de Luze; Lalande; Delor; and Sichel et Fils, Frères, Uncle Louis has regular hours when he will see the brokers, usually between ten and twelve and between two and four. The brokers appear with their samples, which look like medicine bottles, each with a gummed label on which is printed in ink the name of the wine, its vintage, its alcoholic content, and its price. If he likes the wine, Uncle Louis will buy it, and when the wine is ready it will be delivered to his cellars, which are under the building that houses his office and the packing plant.

The regional wines are aged in barrels or stored in glass-lined concrete vats. The wines are cleared, filtered, bottled, corked, capped, labelled, wrapped, and crated in the various drab rooms of the building above, and there is a carpentry shop where the cases are made, a cooperage where the barrels are made, and a blacksmith shop where the hoops are made.

The workers' lunches are heated in a fireplace in the blacksmith shop and are eaten on barrel tops as often as not. One of the favourite dishes is *chabrot*, a soup bowl containing the last few spoonfuls of soup, into which a glass of wine is poured. Each worker gets a ration of one ordinary bottle of wine daily and an additional two or three bottles of a better wine every month, a custom still common throughout France, the theory being that it makes him less likely to tipple the wines he's handling.

14

Most shippers also buy château-bottled wines, those bottled by the grower himself; and sold under the precise name of a château or vineyard rather than under the more generic name of a region, district, or township. Like stocks on an exchange, their prices fluctuate with demand. Many of the châteaux are castles in name only, not comparable to the noble edifices in the château country of the Loire. The title *château* was adopted over a century ago to lend distinction to that system whereby the owner guarantees the authenticity of the wine from his vineyard. All the great wines of Bordeaux are château-bottled, and all are classified according to greatness.

A great wine is usually defined as one that is true to type, excellent year after year, and long-lived. Such qualities as being distinctive, consistent, and long-lived may seem at first to be arbitrary, but they are not. A great wine should be expected to reflect the outstanding qualities of the soil from which it comes, and to do so whenever the weather gives it a chance, year in and year out. A wine has characteristics that take years to develop (balance, bouquet, and finesse are three), and if a wine cannot live long enough to reach its prime, it is not considered great. That is why those who make their living from wine think of wines as individuals and constantly personalize them. This sometimes sounds ridiculous to people not concerned about wine, but a grower is quick to point out that all wines are filled with bacteria that give each wine a life of its own. The great wines of Bordeaux often live for half a century. Many take twenty years to develop, and some are still drinkable after fifty years and more.

The wines of Bordeaux were not thought of as great until the middle of the eighteenth century. During and after the English occupation much of the wine was shipped to northern Europe, but it was then simply known as the wine of Graves. It was so poor that in the sixteenth century the

French passed a law that no wine could be exported from the port of Bordeaux until all the local wine had been sold. At that time, when all wines were drunk young, those from outlying districts were preferred, and the law made it so difficult to get them that the English stopped buying claret and switched to Port, Sherry, and Madeira.

It was not until the days of Louis XIV that Bordeaux came to be appreciated in France at all, and the Sun King himself thought it terrible. It was the custom to send momentarily obnoxious nobles away from the court, and many were banished to Bordeaux. Among these was the Duc de Richelieu, who loved Burgundy and only learned to like Bordeaux after his friends foisted on him a bottle with a fake label. It became his favourite, and this was the beginning of its popularity.

By the beginning of the nineteenth century certain districts and vineyards stood out as superior, but by the mid-century six growths were considered supreme; the châteaux of Yquem in Sauternes; Haut-Brion in Graves, and Margaux, Latour, Lafite, and Mouton in the Médoc. And there was much argument over which vineyard deserved second place.

In 1855 Parisians decided to hold an exhibition, and they sent down to Bordeaux for samples of its best wines. This was as much excuse as the town fathers needed to set up an official classification of the wines. The growers from Médoc and those from Sauternes seem to have run the show, for these were the only two districts classified. But even amid the storms of jealousy and politics it was felt necessary to mention Haut-Brion, one of the greatest vineyards, but unfortunately in Graves.

The sixty participants in this race of thoroughbreds, set up by the classification of 1855, will all have earmarks of greatness, since they were born on great soil, but their care or breeding will, each year, distinguish those that will finish near the top. Yet many a wine in the third or fourth classification may show its excellence, vintage after vintage, when great care has been devoted to the vine and the wine. The listing followed closely the commercial evaluations of the wines, and it has been compared by Henri Binaud, president of the shippers' association of Bordeaux, to a stud book. He said in a lecture at Vintner's Hall, London, that "the competition of quality between them can be compared to a very open race. As on a race-course, though the horses with the most regular form and the noblest pedigree have a greater chance to win, and in fact often do win, it also happens sometimes that there reach the post before them, in some races, competitors whose form is, on that occasion at any rate, superior to their own." As it has turned out, some of the horses have stumbled and others are showing far greater strength than their classification a hundred years ago even dreamed of. The form sheet has served a useful purpose but it is time for a change.

Today's prices are not always an accurate valuation of the wines, for promotion and speculation may make an expensive wine out of one that is merely good, not great. Shippers have been known to overpraise wines they hold in large quantities. The wine world has been embarrassed by a succession of amazing years and seems to be somewhat afraid that the drinking public will get to expect surpassing greatness even when vintages cannot supply it. Hence it sometimes plays down a good vintage, such as '48 and '50.

Nobody knows more about the wines of Bordeaux than a Catholic priest, the Abbé Dubaquié, who was with the Wine Station of Bordeaux for over twenty-five years and is now its honorary director. The Wine Station acts as adviser and testing laboratory for the growers of Bordeaux, and the Abbé has saved many vintages from failure and others from mediocrity. The Abbé believes that a man who drinks beer or water exclusively does not give great wines enough credit, that the palates of some people are made of wood or maybe cement, that wine should be part of a meal, and that you cannot taste wines unless you have already learned to taste food. Wine characteristics come out only when the food is discreet, he says; too rich foods destroy the taste of the wine, and chances are that all Bordeaux people will not go to paradise, because they eat and drink too much and concentrate on wine. At times, he says, the Bordelais have been known to stop a meal to have another go at the bottle.

The Abbé insists that drinking wine is a sensation firing the imagination, one of the greatest things in creation. Knowing wine depends on having drunk enough small ones, in contrast to the great ones, he says, and many French do not know wines because they drink *vin ordinaire* all the time, great bottles very rarely.

To know wines, the Abbé suggests starting off with a small but typical wine of the Médoc and drinking enough to know it. Then he suggests trying one of the lesser wines from Saint-Émilion, followed by a lesser Burgundy, the two having some resemblance. Or drink only red wines for a while and then begin tasting dry white wines. Tasting is a matter of learning, says the Abbé, because you must compare wines, classifying them by your own standards, which nobody else can do for you. After that it is time enough to begin drinking the great wines, especially when a great bottle is preceded by a lesser one of the same type. Learning about wine is one of the pleasantest educational pursuits known to man.

The Abbé says that no specific classifications of wine can be made, for wine is not arithmetic. There are no sharp standards of measurement, just as there are none for paintings or the perfumes of flowers, and he points out that the rose has one smell, the lilac another. The only standard is your own taste.

Many of the good wines of France are lost in the blending vats of the shippers, according to the Abbé. Many Bordeaux wines that could be distinguished are lost in the vats of commerce, in the "big sauce." Ordinary wines and poor vintages should be left to the "big sauce," he says, for there is a chance to make something mediocre out of what would be merely bad.

The wine trade lives on *coupage*, blending being its only contribution to wine production. The disinterested wine experts, particularly those in the Church, have been fighting the custom of blending ever since the 1600's. Blending may improve the quality of bad wines, but it also destroys the great wines. The system of chopping off the peaks and filling in the valleys is particularly common in Burgundy, where sugar is often added during fermentation to increase the alcoholic content, thus often destroying the individuality of the wine.

In Bordeaux more than in any other wine district of France vintages may be relied upon as being authentic, especially in château-bottled wines. In great years one may assume that all the wines of such a large district are good. In intermediate or poor years, however, one may often find great wines only through careful selection, for they may depend upon when a particular château harvested. Generally speaking, the consensus in the Bordeaux trade concerning the vintages of the last twenty-five years is as follows:

1926 *Small yield. The wines were hard and rather slow in maturing. Spotty in many cases, some wines unattractive, lacking softness and fatness. Some of them are harsh. Others have reached good maturity.*

1927 *Very poor year. Should be avoided.*

1928 *Exceedingly slow in maturing. Many of the wines have recently become ready for drinking. Most of the wines of this great vintage were drunk before they were allowed to prove their greatness.*

1929   *Considered as the first great year since* 1900. *These wines matured rapidly, and little of this vintage remains. Now past its peak, and from here on it will lose in quality. In the thirties '29 clarets were considered the greatest of the century; today this is no longer true. The white wines are superb if well kept.*

1930, 1931, 1932   *The less said about these wines the better.*

1933   *These small wines were good and pleasant when young. They reached their maturity a long time ago and have declined rapidly.*

1934   *A very abundant yield, producing excellent wines, which matured much more rapidly than the '28's.*

1935   *A very mediocre vintage.*

1936   *A small yield, of very little interest today.*

1937   *The red wines had a great amount of tannin and are slow in maturing. Most are now ready. This vintage produced some great wines that will last a long time. The white wines are exceptionally great, surpassing all expectations.*

1938   *Average, on the whole. Some pleasant rather short-lived wines were produced, especially in the reds.*

1939   *Small wines, of no interest today.*

1940   *A fair year. The wines rested too long in barrel, as there was a wartime shortage of bottles. Many are "seché," or tartly over-dry.*

1941   *A very poor year.*

1942   *The white wines were better than the red. Very pleasant, with no remarkable greatness. Because of low prices they were good values, but are now on the decline.*

1943   *Many excellent wines were produced.*

1944   *Light wines. The best have been ready since 1950, pleasant for consumption in France.*

1945   *Some consider this vintage to be the greatest of the century. Some of the white wines suffered from hail. The exceptional quality of the great growths has taken ten years to declare itself. Many not yet ready.*

1946   *A small year, mediocre in quality in red and white.*

1947   *A very great year in red wines. These wines have matured faster than the '45's, and are all now ready. Excellent body and bouquet. The whites are still greater than the '45's.*

1948   *Good red wines. Because it came between the great '47's and the '49's, its prestige is handicapped.*

1949   *A very good year. The soft red wines have matured quickly and are apt to disappoint those who wait too long to drink them. The white wines are exceptionally good.*

1950   *Wines matured very rapidly; typical of a dependable year without extraordinary greatness.*

1951   *Pleasant wines, quick maturing, none great.*

1952 & 1953   *In Bordeaux a rivalry existed between '52 and '53, two very great years. While many great '52's surpass many '53's, on the overall picture future wine-lovers will unhesitatingly choose '53. This is true of the Médoc. In St. Émilion and Pomerol, on the whole, the contrary is true.*

1954   *This vintage suffered from the shortcomings of vintage charts. The wines are maturing quickly; they will be pleasant and drinkable in 1956. The year was condemned in the early summer of 1954 when the weather was bad. Good weather during the harvest was unsuccessful in re-establishing the reputation.*

1955   *Developing remarkably. While some care must be taken in choosing from certain of the lesser classified growths, it will definitely be a great year.*

Note: In February '56 a freeze affected many of the great vineyards of St. Émilion to the extent of destroying practically all of the 1956 crop. Sauternes and Barsac less badly affected and the Médoc in spots will average about a 25% loss.

21

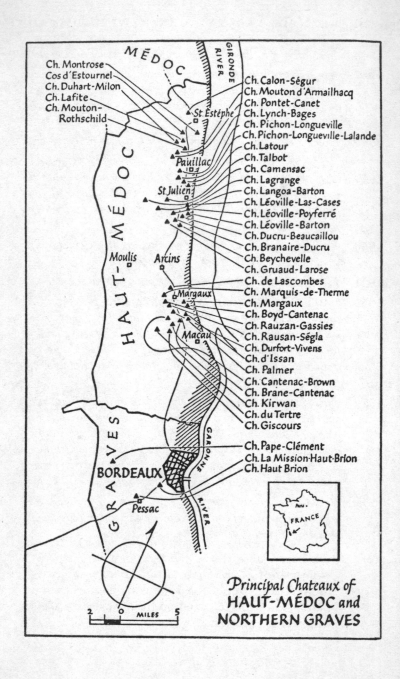

Ch. Montrose
Cos d'Estournel
Ch. Duhart-Milon
Ch. Lafite
Ch. Mouton-Rothschild

MÉDOC
GIRONDE RIVER

St. Estéphe
Pauillac
St. Julien

Moulis
Arcins

Margaux
Macau

HAUT-MÉDOC

GRAVES

BORDEAUX
GARONNE RIVER
Pessac

Ch. Calon-Ségur
Ch. Mouton d'Armailhacq
Ch. Pontet-Canet
Ch. Lynch-Bages
Ch. Pichon-Longueville
Ch. Pichon-Longueville-Lalande
Ch. Latour
Ch. Talbot
Ch. Camensac
Ch. Lagrange
Ch. Langoa-Barton
Ch. Léoville-Las-Cases
Ch. Léoville-Poyferré
Ch. Léoville-Barton
Ch. Ducru-Beaucaillou
Ch. Branaire-Ducru
Ch. Beychevelle
Ch. Gruaud-Larose
Ch. de Lascombes
Ch. Marquis-de-Therme
Ch. Margaux
Ch. Boyd-Cantenac
Ch. Rauzan-Gassies
Ch. Rausan-Ségla
Ch. Durfort-Vivens
Ch. d'Issan
Ch. Palmer
Ch. Cantenac-Brown
Ch. Brane-Cantenac
Ch. Kirwan
Ch. du Tertre
Ch. Giscours

Ch. Pape-Clément
Ch. La Mission-Haut-Brion
Ch. Haut Brion

FRANCE

Principal Chateaux of
HAUT-MÉDOC and
NORTHERN GRAVES

2   0   MILES   5

The Médoc

THE Médoc begins just north of Bordeaux. It is a narrow strip of land, rarely more than a dozen miles wide, stretching along the left bank of the Gironde. While the district extends for sixty miles, right down to the spit of land where the river joins the sea, the best wines of the plain are grown in the communes of Cantenac, Margaux, Saint-Julien, Pauillac, and Saint-Estèphe, all in that section nearest Bordeaux which is called the Upper Médoc. Ancient French wine-growers taught the Romans the use of wine-barrels instead of amphoræ. From the men of Flanders they learned how to reclaim the land from the encroaching sea. These reclaimed lands were made into vineyards that look like nothing more than gravel beds on the well-drained, slightly sloping soil overlooking the wide, placid Gironde.

These wines of the plain grow on both sides of the vineyard road connecting the insignificant crossroad towns with Bordeaux, between the pine copses encroaching from the Landes. The vines share this narrow strip of soil with the wide meadows, the orchards, the farms, and the vineyards of lesser fame. On a drive north from Bordeaux over the rolling country, the first place of fame is Macau, renowned for such wines as Château Cantemerle and also for its artichokes. Like the wines, the artichokes are classified in growths, but they are not the only produce of France that have *crus*, as classifications by quality are called.

Across the river and far to the north is the Cognac country, and along the inlets are the famous oyster beds where the flat *marennes* come from. These have *crus*. Over to the east, in Périgord, the truffles have *crus*, and so do the sardines, the tins of which have to be turned over every few months like champagne bottles ageing in the cellars. The cider of Normandy, cheeses, and practically everything else grown in France is classified. The chicken from Bresse is famous, not merely for its flavour, but also for being the only animal to have an *appellation contrôllée*, which is sure to make the *poulardes* both happy and proud. The French love for classification is not limited to wine.

No wines have been classified so much or so often as those of the Médoc, the business starting back in the fifteenth century and continuing to this very day. The most famous classification is the outmoded one of 1855, when sixty Médoc vineyards were included. These were divided into five *crus* or growths. Later seven more were rated "exceptional" and placed right after the five original *crus*, and now hundreds of others have been classified into "bourgeois," "artisan," and "peasant" growths. And the "bourgeois" growths have been divided into two parts.

All this wine categorizing is an attempt to standardize something that varies endlessly. The most important factor influencing the wine is the ground on which the vines are grown, one parcel being obviously better than another. Yet all the wines of Bordeaux have a certain recognizable taste, one that is delicately flowery, light in comparison with the fuller tastes of the hill wines of Burgundy and the Rhône.

The care given these great vineyards is another determining factor of quality; hence, many wines which may have officially been classed in the third or fourth categories may be brought up to such a peak of perfection that they may well rival or surpass those that are in a higher classification.

This super-care or, in many cases, lack of it, depending on the standards, the financial ability, or the avarice, of the present owners, has created mutterings often heard in Bordeaux, that the 1855 classification is obsolete.

An example of how great soils may be desecrated by lack of care is visible in one of the oldest vineyards in the Médoc, in the village of Cantenac where the Benedictine monks, who were to the Médoc what the Cistercians were to the Clos Vougeot in Burgundy, built their priory. For many generations they had tended their vines with religious care. More recent owners were less meticulous and when, in 1952, the author acquired Château Cantenac-Prieuré, part of the vineyard had to be replanted so that it could regain its former greatness. The vineyard is now called Château Prieuré-Lichine. Bordeaux merchants and wine-lovers throughout the world have learned that one should never think of a wine in the fourth class as being nothing more than a fourth-rate wine. Far from it. Many a fourth growth is sold on the Bordeaux market at prices comparable to those paid for second growths, and certain third growth wines will fetch higher prices than some seconds. Be this as it may, the chances of the much needed changing of this hundred-year-old classification are remote.

One of the choicest Médoc soils is in the vineyards of Château Margaux, only a dozen miles from Bordeaux, which perhaps gained its distinguished position because its gravelly sand is so well drained. The estate of Château Margaux consists of nearly 600 acres, of which only about 200 are vineyard. Of those usually planted in vines, some 50 acres are now resting, while another small portion is given over to the makings of a white wine called *Pavillon Blanc* that is not considered great enough to carry the famous château label.

The château itself sits in its vast park at the end of a cobbled drive guarded by a wrought-iron gate. It is a great rectangle of a building, the centre of its front façade boasting four columns making a roofed porch modelled after the Parthenon, of all things. The interior is strictly Empire, however, and here lives the owner, M. Ginestet, who began buying Margaux back in 1934 and completed the purchase just in time for Christmas 1949. When he began buying, the wine had slumped in quality, but replanting and continuous care have re-established its greatness.

Near the château, which is pictured on the label, are the buildings where the wine is made—great low sheds called *chais*, built around a courtyard that opens out on the vine-yards and their short-staked, knee-high roots. The central *chai* contains the presses and the enormous vats, almost ten feet high and six across, typical of Bordeaux wine-making, where the grape juice ferments for a week or two before being barrelled, the time depending on the amount of sugar it contains. When the fermentation is complete, the new wine is drawn out of the oak vats into new oak barrels, which are trundled into the adjoining *chai* and lined up in long rows on their sides, resting on heavy timbers.

This *chai*, about the size of a small auditorium, is presided over by the *maître de chai*, the cellar-master in charge of the vine-growing and wine-making. He is the most important man at a wine château, and makes the final decision as to when the grapes shall be picked, how long the grape juice remains in the vats, when it is to be barrelled and bottled, how the wine is to be treated, and so on. This *chai* of Château Margaux is one of the biggest. Its tile roof is held up by great columns; the whole interior is whitewashed and spotless, and big enough for the great banquets held every year or so, at which as many as fifteen hundred people have been served.

The cellar-master keeps his new wine in this *chai*. Nowadays the wine of Médoc is bottled the second spring after the harvest, though until recently it was not bottled until the second summer. Barrel time has been shortened at the demand of the shippers, the shorter storage time reducing the cost somewhat and enabling the merchants to sell the vintage sooner. There is little resistance to this practice by the proprietors, but some objection, for any negative qualities in the wine can be detected and perhaps cured in the cask, whereas once the wine is bottled, nothing can be done to it.

The new barrels sit with glass stoppers in their bungs, and a curving glass tube called a *pipette* is lowered into the barrel, allowed to fill with wine, and then removed and drained into your glass. At any one time there are usually three vintages in the *chai*, and it is customary to taste them all, starting with the most recent.

Across the courtyard is the darker, smaller *chai* where the older wine is kept, the barrels tightly closed with cane-wrapped bungs turned down. It is the Bordeaux custom to tap these barrels for tasting through a small hole drilled in the barrel end and stopped with a wooden peg. The peg is pulled with a wine-grower's tool that is a combination plier and hammer, but the wine does not spurt out, because of the vacuum in the tightly sealed barrel. The claw of the tool is jammed under the crossboard braced over the barrel end, and leverage on the hammer handle exerts pressure on the barrel end, squirting wine through the hole and into your glass.

The château makes on an average a hundred and fifty *tonneaux* of red wine in a normal year, and a dozen of white, a *tonneau* being a term for four barrels and containing the equivalent of ninety-six cases. At Margaux each vat used to be barrelled separately, perhaps to check the quality of wine from the replanted vines, though it is more customary in Bordeaux to blend the wines of a given year together when they are being put in barrel.

As far as vintages go, the first years of the forties were poor because the vines were new, but by 1943 Margaux had one of the best years since the twenties. 1945 was still better, though the great quantity of sugar made for difficulties. By 1947 the vines were old enough to make a magnificent wine, perhaps a shade better than any other of the three great vineyards of Bordeaux. The improvement was so marked that the wine merchants of Bordeaux could not quite believe it, and settled it all by shaking their heads and saying: "Fantastic!"

Adjoining Château Margaux is the vineyard of Lascombes. To the eye, there is no definite demarcation between the two; the vines are the same, the soil is claimed to be similar, and yet Margaux is a first growth, Lascombes a second; due to world demand, Margaux oft-times sells much above the price fetched by its neighbour. Here is an example where ownership and management have influenced the tricky nuances of nature. In the nineteenth century Lascombes enjoyed high praise. At the outset of the war, the vineyard fell into the hands of a Parisian shipper who reserved its output for his own clientele, thus incurring the antagonism of the Bordeaux trade. Owned since 1952 by a group of wine-loving Americans and the writer, Lascombes is creating a minor revolution in an area not always as aware of the times as it ought to be. Rapidly regaining and even surpassing its previous greatness, the château makes a present average of ninety *tonneaux* of red wine in a normal year. The vineyard, by selective exchanges and purchases, has been consolidated and improved. Many experts agree that the 1953 vintage shares with Château Lafite the honour of that particular year in the Médoc.

A dozen miles up the road is the cluster of buildings called Saint-Julien. Saint-Julien has given its name to the best-known of regional bottlings, red wines drunk more often than those of its greater château bottlings, because they are more plentiful and cheaper.

Beychevelle, adjoining Saint-Julien, is said to get its name from the call of those ancient mariners who used to sail up the Gironde in ships loaded with timber to swap for wine, and who shouted *"Baisses les voiles"* as they struck their sails because of the changing wind and current off the vineyards. The corruption of words was no trouble at all to succeeding generations of Bordelais, and you cannot mention the vineyards in Bordeaux without being told the story, often with gestures.

Just above the town is the big, rambling château of Léoville, shared by Las-Cases, whose *chais* and vineyards are on the right of the road, and Poyferré, whose *chais* and vineyards are opposite. The half of the château belonging to the owner of Las-Cases has a new roof, perhaps to make it easy to tell the two apart. Poyferré used to be listed the better of the two. Its '29, for instance, is considered one of the greatest bottles made in the Bordeaux region that year, and is today soft, round, and aged, but should be drunk before 1960. The '34 has been called magnificent, but still has not reached its peak. It seems to be the consensus that Poyferré has slipped recently, though its wines of '43 and '45 are called great, even better than those of its twin. The wine of Las-Cases is better, however, for '47, with a fine body slow to develop because it is so hard, originally tasting somewhat musty in the cask because of trouble with insects during the growing season, a characteristic that disappeared when the wine was bottled in the summer of 1950. Its vineyard is entered through an ugly stone arch that appears on its label, the stone of which has been eaten away on its river side by the hard winds and rains blown up from the water. Nearly a hundred and fifty acres are in production, producing 170 *tonneaux* in '53, and while the quantity is increasing through the fifties due to new planting quality is likely to go down because of the many new vines.

While the Léovilles are classified as second *cru*, Beychevelle is officially fourth, though the Bordeaux merchants state it should be a third, and often sell it for the price of a second *cru*—a slight confusion often met with in the world of wines. In a fine year, when the alcoholic content is over twelve per cent, Beychevelle has great finesse, but when the percentage is lower, its wines are too light. A good year for Bordeaux means a great year for Beychevelle, the '28's and '29's being magnificent, the '34's and '37's very good. 1943 broke the rule, however, being not up to its standard. 1945 re-established it by being very fine, while '47 is big, soft, round, and *mâché*, which means it is so full that it can almost be chewed. 1948 has a fine bouquet, though not so great as the previous year, while '49 only gradually acquired finesse because the grapes were picked late. (*Finesse* is an untranslatable term that means something like "supreme delicacy," or "fine breeding," or "exceptional elegance.") 1953 Beychevelle is outstanding.

The vineyards of the great Château Latour border on those of Léoville Las-Cases, though it is in the neighbouring commune of Pauillac, a regional name that rarely appears on a bottle of regional wine. In June 1950 a new promotional order of owners and shippers was created for boosting the sale of Médoc wines. Château Haut-Brion, from Graves, was the only wine from outside the Médoc that was included as a member. At their headquarters in Pauillac one of their chief activities is the holding of dinners at which the members wear long medieval robes and call themselves Compagnons du Bontemps, "good-time companions." *Bontemps* are small wooden pails that hold the egg whites used in fining, symbolized by the members' white-topped hats. Shouting their slogan, "Par le Bontemps, pour le Bon Temps, toujours Médoc," the Compagnons organized Bordeaux's first large wine auction in March 1951.

The château of Latour was burned down at the end of the Plantagenet period when Talbot, the last English commander, was defeated there. All that remains of the old château is a domed water-tower hulking above the famous vines, a caretaker's small, ugly house covered with ivy, in a grove of trees, and an old stone crenelated gateway that guards the entrance to the *chais* and appears on the label.

A fabulous treasure is supposed to be buried somewhere about the place, and the cellar-master, who is as fond of garlic as he is of the wine, will let you look for it, providing that you don't hurt the vines. The *chais* are among the handsomest in the Médoc, being built round a court planted with rows of vigorously pruned plane trees. The new wine is kept in a long low *chai* with small windows looking across the vineyards to the river. Production at Latour is small: less than 110 acres, all planted in vines, none resting. Dead roots are torn up and replaced each year. In 1949, 78 *tonneaux* of wine were made, about the average, but in 1945 there were only 50 *tonneaux*, a very small yield.

Constant care is one of the secrets of great wine according to most cellar-masters, says Latour's *régisseur*, or manager. One aspect is meticulous cleanliness, particularly the scrubbing of the new barrels before the new wine is poured into them. While ageing in the barrels, some of the wine may evaporate, necessitating refilling the barrels frequently to keep the wine sound. This refilling is called *ouillage*, and it is done so often at Latour that the outsides of the barrels between the two centre hoops are stained red with the wine. One visitor insisted that each barrel was painted with a red stripe, and perhaps the symmetry is helped somewhat by wiping the barrels with a cloth after each refilling. In Bordeaux the new wines rest in barrels laid with the bungholes up, stoppered with glass bungs.

The wines of Château Latour have an extremely long life. The '37's—like so many clarets of that year—are only now ready to drink, while the '47's will not be ready until the 1960's. The '47 is not so soft and supple as the '45, which is round and fat, slow in maturing, a hard or *corsé* wine that should be splendid and will become a great bottle. The '48

B* 31

has an excess of tannin, and it will take years for it to get rid of this harsh and bitter taste, but the '49 is conceded to be nothing short of wonderful. Latour makes very great wines year after year, but when the vintage is not up to standard, it is sold to the shippers to be bottled as a mere Médoc not bearing the Latour label. One of its greatest years, the one that can be drunk today if you can still find it, was 1929, when it was heralded as the greatest Médoc, followed in that vintage by Mouton, Lascombes and Léoville-Poyferré.

Across the road from Latour is Château Pichon-Longueville, half of which is owned by a group of Bordeaux brokers and whose wine is bottled as Château Pichon-Longueville Comtesse de Lalande, after a former owner. Its wine, classed as a second *cru*, has a character similar to that of Latour.

Above Pauillac is the other great first *cru* of Médoc, Château Lafite, one of its neighbours being the first vineyard of the second *cru*, Château Mouton-Rothschild, the latter never having recovered from the shock of being classified a second. The two are owned by rival branches of the Rothschild family.

The name of Château Lafite has lost an *f* and a *t* through the years, though one of the early owners had two of both. It is maintained that the name refers to the old French word *lafitte*, meaning "knoll" or "height." In any case, the château is on a rise, an architectural jumble of towers and terrace and dramatic cellars. Great light wines are produced in nearly every good year, classics being '29, '45, '47, '53, while '34 was supreme. Called exceptionally good are '37 and '49. Experts refer to the 1950 vintage as one having considerable "choix"—you can choose between "highs" and "lows". Lafite is definitely one of the highs. Château Lafite and Château Lascombes are generally ranked outstanding among the '53's, leading vintage so far in this decade.

The Château Mouton-Rothschild, near by, has been in the Rothschild family since 1868, and the family has spared no pains in keeping the superlative quality of this wine on a par with the four first growths with which it deserves to be classified. The château is a series of low, Spanish-looking buildings, with the most decorated *chais* in all of Bordeaux. The new wine is kept in a long, low *chai* with indirect lighting and a mammoth cut-out of the vineyard shield, bearing rams. Underneath are cellars lit with hanging wrought-iron hoops holding clusters of tiny electric candles, birthday-cake size.

Its wines claim some of the highest prices paid by the Bordeaux merchants, and noted for the fact that they develop considerably with age, therefore being hard to classify when young. The vintage of '47, which is considered the outstanding wine of the year, is extremely slow in maturing, resembles the '28. The 1948, however, is definitely on the light side, and has little of the Mouton characteristic. 1950 is disappointing today, with a small bouquet, the wine being uninteresting. The 1952 is a great year for Médoc and especially for Mouton. 1953 is also decidedly outstanding in all Médoc wines. The Mouton 1945 is superb, and with time will be referred to as the epitome of very great claret. It resembles the '29, a classic of all time, developing slowly, big, full, and velvety. In 1943 this great vineyard did not live up to expectations and was surpassed by Margaux, Cheval-Blanc of Saint-Émilion, and Haut-Brion of Graves.

For some reason, the fifth *crus* around Pauillac are particularly well known, Mouton-d'Armailhacq and Pontet-Canet being better known than many of the second, third, and fourth *crus*. Mouton-d'Armailhacq is owned by the Rothschild who has the other Mouton, so good promotion may account for its exceptional fame.

Another fifth *cru*, Château Pontet-Canet, belongs to the

fine shipping house of Cruse, the best-known château wine that is not château-bottled. Château Kirwan is also a classified growth that is not château-bottled, as is Château Léoville-Barton. These are the only three wines of the Médoc that are not château-bottled.

Pauillac used to be an important port in the old days, sailing vessels mooring in the yellow, silted water to load wine cargoes. Today most of the wine goes to Bordeaux for shipment, and the quay is the more or less exclusive property of fishermen, whose tall tales of fabulous wines challenge the stature of their fish stories.

Above Pauillac is Saint-Estèphe, the last town in Haut-Médoc, whose best and most famous vineyard is that of Château Cos-d'Estournel, the vineyards of which are easily seen from those of Château Lafite. The vineyard boasts of a surrounding wall littered every few feet with Chinese pagodas; during the war the Germans mounted anti-aircraft batteries in each pagoda and they were damaged but are now rebuilt. The vineyard produces about 100 *tonneaux* a year, with about 150 acres in vines, and another 100 resting.

Château Montrose and Château Calon-Ségur round out the gamut of the Saint-Estèphes. In general, these wines are harder, more *corsé*, or full-bodied, than those of the townships of Margaux, Saint-Julien, and Pauillac. In that part of the Médoc north of Saint-Estèphe and running down to the mouth of the Gironde, most of the wines are lesser *crus*. Many of the wines are excellent, some comparing favourably with the classed growths and surpassing many of the lesser vineyards in that section of the Médoc nearest Bordeaux.

If Médoc is complicated from the standpoint of endless classification and the great number of its wines, its fame is justified by the wide range of wines it produces, extending from small to great. The efforts needed to discover them make for pleasant adventures.

Saint-Émilion & Pomerol

THE red wines of Saint-Émilion are grown in an area not much more than a mile square, on the high plateau and slopes above the valley of the Dordogne. The old town, some twenty miles east of Bordeaux, is reached by driving across that wedge of vineyard formed by the branching of the Gironde and called Entre-Deux-Mers. Much of the lesser wines of the Bordeaux region is shipped from the small port of Libourne, just downstream from Saint-Émilion, whose shippers are looked down upon by their colleagues of Bordeaux, as are the wines from the minor districts of the *côtes* of Blaye, Bourg, Fronsac, Néac, Graves de Vayres, Canon Fronsac, and Lalande de Pomerol to the north of Entre-Deux-Mers. Of these, Fronsac and Néac are the most important.

Saint-Émilion stands at the head of a cleft in the plateau, the road turning away from the river and running up the valley floor between two steep, vine-covered slopes to the heights, dominated by a detached steeple. The church is down below, a series of great caverns carved out of the rock, and what would be its roof is the plateau itself, now the flagged terrace of the local restaurant, where you can sit at small tables covered with check tablecloths, under a canopy of vines, and look out over the valley while you eat your lunch. One of the specialties of the house is lamprey, caught in the rivers below and cooked with the red wines of

Saint-Émilion; and the wine list has a long range of local wines to choose from, to be drunk with a speciality of the town, a kind of macaroon that is not sweet.

Saint-Émilion is one of the loveliest wine towns in the world. It was a halting-place for Breton pilgrims on the way to the shrines of Spain, and a nunnery and hospital were built there to care for the sick trying to reach the sacred places to be cured. Bits of the Romanesque buildings remain: a great moat, the side wall of an ancient church, and part of the hospital. In the forecourt of one of the cloisters a local shipper of sparkling wine has set up shop, using the crypts beneath to store his barrels.

In the lower town, near the entrance to the old church dug out of the rock, is the cavern where St. Émilion, the hermit, lived beneath the crumbling remains of a small

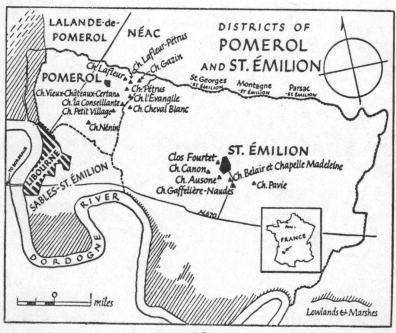

chapel. Beside the carved niche where he slept is a block of stone, and if you sit on it, lean far back, and make a wish, it will come true. Also beside the niche is a shallow well full of hairpins; if a girl throws in two and they land on the bottom in the form of a cross, she will be married within the year.

The town and most of the surrounding farmhouses are built of stone quarried out of the soft rock of the plateau. Some of the old quarries were used as burying-places, but those near the vineyards are used as wine cellars in which the local wine matures slowly and superbly in the cool dark.

Coming up the valley cleft to the town are the vineyards of Château Ausone on the left, the château itself being on the edge of the plateau. Contrary to Bordeaux custom, the wines are today allowed to mature in the great fermentation vats during the first winter after the wine harvest. Another break with custom is that during the following spring wines are put into old barrels instead of new ones. Local wine-growers feel that both practices hurt the wine, and Château Ausone is now thought to be inferior to Château Cheval-Blanc, the other *grand cru* of Saint-Émilion.

The owners of Château Ausone's less than eighteen acres, which are rotation-planted and yield an average of twenty-five *tonneaux*, are also proprietors of the thirty-two acres of Château Belair, which is the adjoining vineyard and a producer of lesser wine. The barrels of wine from both vineyards are kept in the same cellar, also contrary to custom, where they remain three years before the bottling, according to the cellar-master. Château Ausone's '49's seem to be characterized by hardness and bitterness, which are likely to disappear with time. The '37 was very hard, and not ready to be drunk until 1955; the somewhat softer '45's have also become drinkable, while the '47's are not likely to be ready until the 1960's. Both vineyards are extremely old. Ausone was planted by the Roman poet and local governor,

Ausonius, who gave the wine its name. Belair is even older, the original vineyard being made by gouging in the rock trenches that were then filled with earth and planted.

Farther down the steep slope are the vineyards of Château Gaffelière-Naudes, while across the road and reaching all the way up to the top of the terraced plateau are the plantings belonging to Château Pavie. The qualities of these wines place them among the first half-dozen of the principal Saint-Émilion growths. Just behind Château Ausone, farther back on the plateau, are Clos Fourtet and Château Canon, whose superlative wines are rated immediately after the two *grands crus*. All these growths vie with each other for first place, in 1934 the accepted order being Gaffelière-Naudes, Château Canon, and Clos Fourtet. In 1943 and 1947 Cheval-Blanc led all the rest, followed by Clos Fourtet and Château Ausone.

Such classifications are likely to raise an argument from one or another of the proprietors or the Bordeaux shippers, but they are all agreed that Saint-Émilion wines are the heaviest of the Bordeaux. They are often called the Burgundies of the region, perhaps because many of them are slope wines, which seems to give them a Burgundy character. The bouquet of these wines is generally small in comparison with that of the Médoc wines, which experts feel is a further distinction.

Château Canon is owned by a man who boasts of never having smoked a cigarette in his life. He was a broker of Saint-Émilion wines for forty years, and is a figure in the local sales organization, La Jurâde, which is mainly concerned with giving, as often as possible, banquets at which only Saint-Émilion wines are served. Part of the *chais* are in an old quarry directly under the local cemetery. The nearly fifty acres of vines produce nearly an equal number of *tonneaux*. The wine is allowed to ferment for about ten days in the vats and then rests in barrel for three years. Like the others, the wine is hard, the 1937 vintage being only now ready for drinking.

Scarcely a mile from Château Canon is the great Château Cheval-Blanc, right on the border where Pomerol begins. It produced the greatest Bordeaux of '48. The château is reached by driving down a long avenue of pines into the court of a low, handsome château, *chais* on both sides, the vineyards all around. The wine is so famous that a local proprietor began calling his vineyard Cheval-Noir, but all he got for his trouble was a lawsuit.

The château owns about a hundred acres, only about seventy-five of which are planted, and makes some ninety *tonneaux* a year. The cellar-master has a short, silver pipette that he uses to draw the wine from the casks for your glass, and he delights in telling you about the trouble they had in 1949 when the vines blossomed three times. This happens every once in a while in all vineyards, a warm spell starting the blossoms, a cold snap stopping the flower, sometimes even killing those that have budded, and the whole growing order beginning all over again when the weather warms up. It is good for the wine if the vines blossom and fall within ten days, for a slow budding cuts down the yield and size of grapes.

In spite of all the trouble, the '49 will be a great wine characterized by fatness, softness, and a comparatively big bouquet, which the vintage has throughout Saint-Émilion. ("Fatness" means a big soft wine without much body, in contrast to a full wine, which has much body, owing to tannin.) The '48 is excellent. The '53 will be a very great bottle, '46 not good at all, and in 1945 half the vintage was pasteurized, that drastic practice often tried by the wine-growers to save the wine from spoiling when the wines are too light. 1947 was one of Cheval-Blanc's greatest years, when, according to some, the wine made was the greatest of all Bordeaux.

The wines of Pomerol come from the neighbouring commune, and are noted for their distinctive bouquet. One of the best vineyards, La Conseillante, is right across the road from Château Cheval-Blanc. In sight is Château Vieux-Château-Certan, not to be confused with the three or four others with Certan in their names, and Château l'Évangile, which is ranked just after it. The best vineyard of Pomerol, however, nearly everybody agrees, is Château Pétrus, deserving greater recognition, whose vineyards are beside those of Vieux-Château-Certan. The Pomerol wines are heavier and harder than those of Saint-Émilion, but the vintage analyses are similar. A characteristic of these wines is fatness.

The wines of Saint-Émilion and Pomerol, grown from a cross between the Merlot and the Cabernet Franc called Bouchet, were among the first wines of France to be known, and it is claimed that they were drunk in the times of the Druids, although some argue that the vine was brought to the high plateau by those same early traders who are supposed to have planted it all along the Mediterranean. However and whenever wine growing got started, the local vintners like to paint the picture of young and tempting Eleanor of Aquitaine gliding through the waters of the Dordogne in her gilded boat, surrounded by musicians and poets, and drinking the heady wine from the high plateau. It is a pretty picture, even without the macaroons.

Graves

THE vineyards of Graves run for some thirty-five miles along the western bank of the Garonne, in a strip rarely more than five miles wide, which starts just above Bordeaux and continues to just below Langon. The vineyards encircle both cities, as well as the sweet-vine districts of Sauternes and Barsac, and also that of Cérons just to the north, the wine of which is considered an intermediary between the often dry white wines of Graves and the always sweet wines of Sauternes.

Running parallel to it along the eastern bank of the Garonne are the vineyards called the *Premières Côtes* of Bordeaux, producing fair red wines in its upper half, fair sweet wines in the lower. Opposite Sauternes are the sweet-wine districts of Loupiac and Sainte-Croix-du-Mont, while across the river from Langon is the district of Saint-Macaire. All these districts produce good secondary Bordeaux wines.

The wines of Graves are both red and white, and its greatest vineyard is Château Haut-Brion, in Pessac, a suburb of Bordeaux. The highway, with its clanking tramway line, divides the vineyard. The red wines come from a plantation of 95 acres, most of which is on your right as you drive south. It is a large vineyard fenced with an iron grille and dominated by a concrete water-tank shaped like a mushroom. Along the back of the plantation is an old concrete shed that is a shooting range for the Army, and at its foot are the château and its park, the *chais* adjoining. Across from the towered château is a second section, where some red wines and all the white wine are produced.

Until the turn of the century Haut-Brion produced no white wine of any importance, but one day its former proprietor was having lunch with the owner of Château d'Yquem. He complained about the fact that he owned a tremendous vineyard, but produced no sweet dessert wines and had to buy them from other growers. The owner of Yquem agreed that this was a shocking thing, and had some of his vines sent to Haut-Brion the next day. When the plants began bearing, nobody was more surprised than Haut-Brion's proprietor to discover that the wine made from the Yquem vines was very dry. He was still forced to buy dessert wines from other people, but as consolation he became the owner of a white wine that has been called the greatest on earth. Also, he now had something to serve with the fish.

The white wine of Château Haut-Brion is mostly unknown because only some ten thousand bottles are produced each year, less than ten acres on the left side of the road being given over to the white grapes, half Semillon, half Sauvignon. In an attempt to improve quality and yield, a section on the right side of the road was torn up in 1932 and planted in white grapes. The yield increased, but quality fell, so the old plantation was allowed to rest for six years. When it was replanted, the wine had a different and finer quality, producing an unbelievable white wine in 1945. According to the *régisseur*, who has been at Haut-Brion for more than a quarter of a century, this is decisive proof that the soil is what makes the wine. Further experiment produced fabulous wines in 1947 and 1948, an even more sensational wine in 1949. The way of making the wine has not changed, except that today it is bottled earlier than formerly. In 1928 and 1929 bottling took place after three years in the cask; today it is done after eighteen months, and the '48's were bottled when barely a year old. Another couple of acres of white vines were planted in 1950, increasing the yield to a present twelve hundred cases.

Château Haut-Brion was producing Bordeaux's greatest red wine in the Middle Ages, when the English began calling it claret. In those days, and for several centuries after, the wines of Graves were the only ones known, and up to the beginning of the nineteenth century Médocs were known as Graves. Graves means gravel in French, and the great vineyards look like gravel pits. At Château Haut-Brion the gravel is as much as sixty feet deep, and the wines from many of the better vineyards in the Médoc have their distinctive taste because of their gravel and pebbly sandstone under-soils. To the north of Château Margaux, however, the Médoc soils contain more sand, one of the reasons why it was originally named a separate district, for such slight differences in soil make a difference easily detectable to the taste. The abundance of gravel at Haut-Brion is often given as the reason why its wines are good even in off years, the light surface reflecting any excess heat, the porous pebbles draining the vineyard quickly.

Talleyrand was once owner of Château Haut-Brion, and the success of his diplomacy at the Congress of Vienna after Napoleon's defeat, is often attributed to his cook. At fabulous dinners Talleyrand pitted his victorious guests against one another, and in the warmth of fine food and the glow of glorious wine they made expansive concessions to that wily representative of a defeated nation. Talleyrand's chief opponent at the Congress was another vineyard-owner, Metternich, one of whose proudest possessions was Germany's greatest vineyard, Schloss Johannisberger, in the famous Rheingau.

The red wines of Graves are unusually long-lived, Château Haut-Brion of '28 and '34 being just now about ready to drink. Many of the still older wines taste sturdy and vigorous today. A further distinction between the great Graves and the great Médocs seems to be that the Graves wines taste even better at the end of a meal, whereas the Médocs fall off slightly by then, an indication of the exceptional balance and bouquet of a Graves.

Proper making of the wine has much to do with its quality, of course, and cellar-masters must know precisely when to order the harvest to begin, for a day too late puts the wine out of balance, a day too early may mean that the grapes will not have reached their peak. By waiting, the cellar-master risks losing his harvest in a sudden hail, and by picking too soon, he may make an inferior vintage when others are making a great one. The Abbé Dubaquié says that cellar-masters possess an extra sense, purely animal, which tells them when to harvest, when to barrel, and when to bottle.

According to the cellar-master at Haut-Brion, each year's problem is not only when to catch the harvest, but also what to do with it once you have it. He is in favour of fast vinification, particularly in hot years. The grapes are hustled into the vat room, passed through an *égrappilloir* (a grape hopper that tears off the stems), and emptied into the vats by means of an endless chain of buckets. Some of the stems, the skins, and the pulp remain with the juice, and this residue is called the must. The alcohol in the juice dissolves the colour from the skins; the longer the must and juice remain in contact, the heavier and darker the wine. In 1945, when the grapes seemed to begin fermenting while still in the pickers' baskets, the juice and must were left in contact for only three days. It was only four days in 1947 and 1949, when the great amount of fermenting grape sugar changing to alcohol caused the wine to colour quickly. In 1944, when the alcohol was low, the contact lasted two weeks, and the wine was still too light. White wine, which should pick up no colour from the grapeskins, is pressed at once and then dumped into the vats, or *cuves*, to ferment.

When the wine has taken its colour, the must and juice are pressed, the juice going back into the vats for further fermentation. The pulpy must can be presssed a second time, though this second press is not mixed with the first, being made into a separate wine of poorer quality. When fermentation is complete, the wine is barrelled. Before being bottled, it must be fined. Fining is the process of removing particles from the wine, a fine liquid being put in the wine to collect the particles and drag them to the bottom. Egg whites are most commonly used.

Vintages for Château Haut-Brion follow the normal pattern, except that the wine is supposed to be better than most in poor years, greater than most in good years. The '43 is ready for drinking, pleasant and full of charm, round and well-balanced. The 1944 vintage was the best of all Bordeaux in that poor year. 1945 is the vintage of the century, perhaps the best of all the first growths. Like the 1906, softer than the '29, it can be drunk now, and will last for another thirty years. The 1946 was so bad that it was not bottled under the château label, and the same thing happened in '36, when the wine was sold to the shippers to be bottled merely as "Graves." 1947 is another great year, the wine being less "fat," less full and rich, than the great '45. It is more *nerveux*, which means strong and nervy, and has more finesse, or delicacy. At the same time, it is a harder wine, which will take longer to develop, needing at least ten years, like most of the Haut-Brions. Because the '47 and '45 are so great, 1948 is classed as only a good year, for it lacks fat. The 1949 is called very, very good, with finesse like the now drinkable '34, but lighter, and is rated by many local brokers as equal in greatness to the '45's and '47's. In 1950 Haut-Brion again proved its predominant greatness in producing in this vintage, known for its exceptionally large yield, a red wine which is not only better than most of its peers from the Médoc, but also one which will surpass in quality many a great wine of many better-rated vintages. All true claret lovers will easily understand why in 1855, when classifying the wines of the Médoc, the committee of experts could not overlook Haut-Brion from adjoining Graves and rated it as a first growth along with Lafite, Latour, and Margaux. Again, '53 is outstanding.

Across the street from Château Haut-Brion, is Château La Mission-Haut-Brion, no relation except in name, its wine being more like a Médoc than a Graves. All in all, there are some dozen vineyards in Bordeaux that have tacked Haut-Brion to their name. The name is more or less legitimate for those vineyards around Château Haut-Brion, however, as they were all part of the same domain at one time.

La Mission-Haut-Brion claims that it is responsible for getting St. Vincent into trouble. It seems that St. Vincent, the patron saint of wine-growers, had not been in heaven very long before he was attacked by a terrific thirst and a yearning to taste again the great wines of France, the Burgundies, the wines from the Rhône Valley, and the Loire, beady Champagne, and delightful Bordeaux. He applied to the powers that be for a leave of absence, presenting such a pathetic mien that his request was granted provided that he would come back on time. There is little doubt that he intended to, but when time was up, St. Vincent was still down on earth, busily tasting wine. They found him in the cellars of La Mission-Haut-Brion, drinking lustily, not just drunk, but hopelessly plastered and in no condition to make a journey anywhere, least of all where there might be danger of shocking cherubs and setting a bad example. St. Vincent was turned to stone on the spot, and you can see him there today, mitred cap awry, eyes bleary, and still clutching a rather dilapidated bunch of grapes.

The wine that caused all the trouble comes from a vineyard planted two-thirds in Cabernet Franc and Sauvignon, one-third in Merlot. No white wine is made, and the red vintages follow those of Château Haut-Brion.

Behind La Mission Haut-Brion, and belonging to the same owner, is Château La Ville Haut-Brion, a vineyard producing white wines exclusively. Across the railway line, which runs parallel to the road, is Château La Tour Haut-Brion, and next to it is Château Fanning-La-Fontaine, whose vineyards adjoin those of Château Haut-Brion as you leave Bordeaux. Down below Château Haut-Brion is Château Pape-Clément, planted by that pope who moved the papacy to Avignon, near which the vineyards of Châteauneuf-du-Pape are located. These vineyards produce only red wines, similar to, but not so good as, the great Haut-Brion.

Some ten miles south is a cluster of vineyards around the little town of Léognan, the best of which is Château Haut-Bailly, classed as an exceptional growth, a red wine equal to that of Château La Mission-Haut-Brion. Almost on a par with it, and right down the road, is Château Carbonnieux, which produces both white and red wine. Carbonnieux was once owned by monks who, to evade the Mohammedan edict against wine, shipped the wine to Turkey as "mineral water" of Carbonnieux. It was particularly hit by the frosts in 1945, which destroyed much of the vineyard. While only seven per cent of the wines were new in 1950, the percentage has increased, and that has lowered the quality of its wine for the years 1951-55. For the whites, fifty thousand new plants, called "feet" by vintners, were set in 1949. Over 20 *tonneaux* of white wine, and the same amount of red, are made each year, though 45 *tonneaux* of white were made in 1947. The vintages for both vineyards are rated good in '43, '47, and '49; but the white '48 is considered less good, with an aftertaste of sulphur.

Château Larrivet-Haut-Brion, near by, has similar vintages.

Over to the west of Léognan is the Domaine de Chevalier, which lost a third of its red-wine plantation—thirty-five thousand vines—in the 1945 frosts. Most of this has been replanted in Cabernet and Merlot rouge. It produces four *tonneaux* of white wine made from the customary Semillon and Sauvignon grapes. This very good wine is greatly appreciated in England. Its white wines are considered second to Haut-Brion. To the north of Léognan is Château Olivier, owned by Louis Eschenauer, also a producer of red and white. The wine, which is not bottled at the château, but in Eschenauer's cellars in Bordeaux, is one of the better-known white Graves. Vintages of both vineyards follow the usual run. Farther south is the handsome moated Château de la Brède, with a magnificent library, classed as a national monument, but the wines produced from its vineyards are small.

In the listings of the various Graves vineyards, some attempt at a descending order of quality has been made, though any slavish following of the list will arouse arguments, for weather changes or bad judgment on the part of the cellar-masters can completely upset the order. Wines and vineyards are hopelessly overclassified, and some of those classed as principal growths will often surpass those two classified as exceptional. Few of them, however, are likely ever to come even close to red Château Haut-Brion, which is also supreme as a dry white Graves in much the way that Château d'Yquem, the greatest of all sweet wines, is supreme in Sauternes.

Sauternes and Barsac

THE place where the sweet wines come from is south of
Bordeaux, twenty miles up the Garonne River, and,
like Bordeaux itself, surrounded by Graves. The nearest
sizable town is Langon, where you will find the good restaurant Oliver in a hotel on the shady side of the public
square. A small river, the Ciron, divides the district, Barsac
on the north and Sauternes on the south, together forming
an area not much larger than half a dozen square miles.

The town of Sauternes is the capital of the district, a few
plastered buildings with grey shutters and an ornamental
palm tree here and there straggling along its single S-shaped
street. Its wines are heavier, sweeter, and more luscious than
those from Barsac. The town hall is at one end, the public
washing-place at the other, and an odd-looking church is at
the centre bend. Tucked in a hollow and surrounded by
vineyards, it claims a population of 600, and even when you
tack on the populations of its two flanking villages, Bommes
and Fargues, the total is less than 2,000.

Less than a mile north of the town is Château d'Yquem,
its vines producing the greatest sweet wine in the world. A
rough road passes between two blocks of outbuildings and up
to the gates of the fortress-like château. Its crenelated walls
have lookout towers at the corners, the great ports swinging
wide to open on a gravelled courtyard. From the walls, you

49

can look east down the gentle vineyard slope to the river, and all around you, and less than a mile or two away, are most of the first great growths of Sauternes. On the north, Suduiraut; to the east, Rieussec; to the south, Guiraud and then Filhot, the first of the second growths. Sometimes next in quality comes La Tour-Blanche, the vineyard often classified right after Yquem, while also to the west are Clos Haut-Peyraguey, Lafaurie-Peyraguey, Rayne-Vigneau, and the two sections of Rabaud, now again united into a single domain. Particularly in Sauternes is it obvious that the soil has much to do with making a great wine.

The cellar-master at Yquem, who sports a large girth and a small beret, reminds you of a tourists' guide as he leads you from his office. Hung on the walls are various pipes, nozzles, and shiny glass tubes use in winemaking, brass and enamel now, though formerly silver-plated, for no metal

DISTRICTS OF BARSAC AND SAUTERNES

except brass or silver must ever be allowed to come into contact with the wine. The shiny red wine-filtering machines, the bottling and corking machines, trimmed in brass, the intricate bottle-drier and washer, along with the racks of hoses, give the place the look of a spotless equipment room in a fire-station. Round, iron-rimmed tables painted grey are used for the labelling operation, which takes place in a whitewashed room between two *chais*, one for the latest vintage, the other for the older wines, which mature for three years in the wood. The *chais* are dug down into the ground, the vineyards starting at window level. It is a not unusual practice in Bordeaux to dig down into the ground two or three feet for the *chais* floor. This makes for a more even temperature.

The some 220 acres of Château d'Yquem produce an average of 90 *tonneaux* of wine a year. Until 1921 the very best of the wine used to be bottled as a *crème de tête*, a sort of super Yquem, but now the practice is simply to eliminate all the wines that are not exceptional and sell them for bottling as Sauternes. Because the wines are strong and full of sugar, Sauternes are usually fourteen per cent alcohol, and often more. They can live for decades. So far this century, the wines made in 1900, 1904, and 1914, are exceptional, and so are the '21, '24, '28, and '37 vintages. The last decade was one of the best ever, '45, '47, '49, and '48 being outstanding, in that order.

Sauternes are what they are largely because of the way the grapes are picked. Harvest is not begun until the grapes have shrivelled on the vine, the grape water dried out by the late autumn sun. At this stage the micro-organisms cn the skin of the grape go to work, and the grapes rot. The effect of this Bortytis Cinerea, as it is technically known, on the must when in fermentation is called *pourriture noble* in Sauternes, noble rot, giving the wine its sweetness and its high alcoholic content. A vineyard is not harvested all at once, and often the pickers go over the vines a dozen times to find the properly rotted grapes. They are not picked bunch by bunch, but grape by grape, and the harvest sometimes lasts a couple of months. One year at Château Filhot the harvest was not finished until Christmas.

At one time the second-best Sauternes came from Château La Tour-Blanche, over near the hamlet of Bommes. This rating and reputation are not valid today. A former owner gave the vineyards to the State, and now there is a State-operated school there for boys who want to be cellar-masters. The school has nothing to do with the vineyard, however, merely using some of the buildings as classrooms twice a week. The vineyard is rented from the State, the tenant paying an annual rent of 5 *tonneaux* out of an average yield of 25.

La Tour-Blanche has its tower, but it is brown, with a red tile roof, and has no present function, even as a symbol. In spite of this, the 60-odd acres of vineyards go on producing good wines, the average age of the vines being thirty-three years, about two acres being replanted each year. The barrels are kept in a long *chai* opposite the school buildings. They rest on beams set on the fine, carefully raked sand floor.

The school, which was started some years ago by the Abbé Dubaquié, is not concerned solely with the wine of Sauternes, but with vineyards and wines generally. Today the professor is an engineer from the Agricultural Service of the Gironde, and one of his main concerns is sulphur.

Sulphur is the wine-grower's best friend. It is used for spraying the vines, and sulphur candles are burned in the barrels to kill unwanted bacteria. Its use was discovered long ago, when vineyard proprietors took to spraying those vines along the roadsides with copper sulphate. A mild poison, the spray kept people from picking the grapes and eating them. One particularly bad year it was noticed that the spray also kept insects from eating them, and the wine-growers have been using it ever since. August 1 is by law the last day the vines can be so sprayed. Sulphur is used in only the smallest quantities in the constant fight against harmful bacteria when the grapes are on the vine, and in the barrels being prepared for the wine.

Sulphur is also used in exceedingly small quantities as an antiseptic in the wine, destroying harmful germs, acting as a binding agent and preventing wines from refermenting. French law, however, is very severe on the excessive use of sulphur. The unpleasant smell sometimes given off by cheap Graves once the cork is pulled indicates that the wine-grower resorted to sulphur.

Sulphur is particularly important in Sauternes, according to the professor, because it prevents the yeast in the wine from growing and thus keeps the sugar in the wine from excessive fermentation, a special problem in sweet wines. He also has an idea that the sulphur helps prevent that curse of white wines, maderization. This is caused by oxidation in the wine, a sort of rusting, which turns the wine brown. The resulting colour is like that of the wine from the Portuguese island of Madeira, hence the name. It gives the wine a disagreeable, musty, flat taste. Small proprietors seem to have a tendency to sulphur too heavily, and occasionally sulphur can be tasted in the wine. This is a case in which shippers are useful, for by blending different wines and by treating them properly they can make the sulphur taste disappear from the regional Graves and Sauternes. This vice of over-sulphuring is particularly prevalent in Graves, says the professor, in an attempt to make the much drier wines taste more like Sauternes.

Most of the Sauternes follow the same pattern in their vintages, though 1943 was an exception, as a hailstorm ruined many vines. Château La Tour-Blanche suffered heavily, the storm wrecking the harvest in ten minutes.

Many of the others suffered too. The standard planting in Sauternes is 40 per cent Sauvignon, 55 per cent Semillon, and 5 per cent Muscadelle, these grapes blending their properties to make a great wine. Semillon does not produce much juice, but its quality is excellent, though some vintners have tried to stretch their harvest by planting 75 per cent Sauvignon, according to the owner of Château Filhot, the first of the second *crus*, whose wine is the driest of the great Sauternes. They deserve to be a first *cru*. Its fine wines are under-classified, in much the way as are those of Mouton-Rothschild in the Médoc.

In the commune of Barsac, honours go to Château Climens, rightly considered by many to be the greatest sweet white Bordeaux after Château d'Yquem. There are some 85 acres of vines, producing somewhat over 30 *tonneaux* in an average year. The vines are tied close to the ground and heavily pruned, which reduces the yield but heightens the quality. Here all the vines are Semillon. After the harvest, the wine is allowed to ferment for a couple of months, or until it stops itself, though other wine-growers often stop the fermentation after three weeks.

Vintages at Château Climens are much the same as those in Sauternes, although '24 was an excellent year, as were '34 and '37. The vines were frozen in 1945, so there was no harvest, but some 2,000 cases produced in 1949 may prove that to be the great year of the century. Rich, the epitome of finesse and lusciousness, it may turn out to be as great as the '29, when Climens surpassed Yquem, if not greater. Where the Yquem of 1947 is full and rich, Climens has lightness and finesse. Climens is truly one of the very great sweet white wines of the world.

Right down the road is Château Coutet, like Climens blessed with a rocky undersoil that drains excess water from the vineyards. Its planting is two-thirds Semillon, one-third Sauvignon and Muscadelle, its wine somewhat lighter, drier, and less distinguished than Château Climens. Its wine is classed by many immediately after that of Château Climens, but it is very much on the drier side.

When it comes to Sauternes, there is often an argument about the runners-up, which in some years may be even better than some of the first growths; but for well over a century Château d'Yquem has been consistently the greatest of all Sauternes, and there no one will dispute its fame. Average and some poor years produce pleasant wines in Sauternes because they are not over-sweet. But when people ask for a dry Sauternes, they are asking for a poor Sauternes, for this wine is characteristically sweet. Sauternes is the world's greatest dessert wine. The Marquis de Lur Saluces, owner of Château d'Yquem, and ambassador of the wines of France as president of France's Wine Propaganda Bureau, claims that Sauternes is also excellent with fish. Many wine-lovers disagree with him.

92 Miles to Paris

CHABLIS

Auxerre
Chablis

YONNE

RIVER

Avallon

NIÈVRE

CÔTE-D'OR

Saulieu

CÔTE DE NUITS

Dijon

Nuits-St.Georges

CÔTE DE BEAUNE

CÔTE D'OR

Beaune

SAÔNE RIVER

Chagny

CÔTE CHALONNAISE

Mercurey

Chalon-s.-Saône

DOUBS RIVER

SAÔNE ET LOIRE

MÂCONNAIS

SAÔNE RIVER

Mâcon

Juliénas
Moulin-à-vent
Fleurie

Pouilly-Fuissé

AIN

BEAUJOLAIS

LOIRE RIVER

RHÔNE

LYON

RHÔNE RIVER

to Marseille 195 Miles

BURGUNDY REGION

Paris
FRANCE

0   10   20
miles

Seyssel

Burgundy:

The Wine Democracy of France

THE old domain of the hearty dukes of Burgundy begins near Sens, an old cathedral town past Fontainebleau, seventy miles south of Paris on the national highway running down to the Côte d'Azur. The highway skirts the ancient realm until it crosses a rolling range of hills called the Monts du Morvan, past a bulging promontory from which juts the moated Château de Rochepot brandishing its turrets above the peaceful valley. It then swings through the town of Chagny, at the foot of the Côte d'Or, then on down through the lesser vineyards of Burgundy, Châlonnais, Mâconnais, and Beaujolais to Lyons. All in all, it is a distance of some 225 miles.

On the way you pass through Auxerre, a medieval town of ancient buildings with modern shop-fronts with neon signs. Here are the mossy black slate roofs typical of Burgundy, and the jumble of a fourteenth-century cathedral. A net is cast across its central portal, either to protect you from falling bits of the crumbling statues or to keep the pigeons from nesting there. The road to Chablis starts at Auxerre, swinging across the river and up east into the hills.

Below Auxerre is Avallon, and farther down are Saulieu and the Hôtel de la Côte d'Or, where Alexandre Dumaine serves some of the finest food in France and offers a wine list that is a model of good selections.

Burgundy is surrounded by great kitchens, and while the centre of gastronomy has moved south to Lyons, the contribution of Burgundy chefs to great French cooking will never disappear. Although *bœuf bourguignon* may be the most famous, *potée bourguignonne* is probably the most traditional, a stew made of salt pork, pig's feet, and vegetables. *Meurette* is famous, a stew of eel made with either red wine or white. *Coq au vin* is a Burgundian dish, and one of its variations is *coq au Pommard*, and there is also *poulet au Chambertin*. *Pauchouse* is a soup of eels, pike, trout, and any other fresh fish available, a sort of Burgundian *bouillabaisse* made with white wine. A like dish made with red wine is called *matellote*. And there is *quenelles de brochet*, ground poached pike served with a cream sauce, one of the world's great delicacies when well made. From the town of Cîteaux, out in the plains, comes a bland cheese made by Trappist monks, the perfect accompaniment to the wines. And the people of Burgundy spend their lives making great wines to go with these great dishes.

Wine-making began in Burgundy some twenty-five hundred years ago, though nobody is quite sure how the vineyards got started in ancient Gaul. Pliny says that Helvetius, the ancient Swiss, introduced the vine. Livy maintains that it was a Tuscan by the name of Aaron, while Justin insists that some "Phoceans" landed in a gulf at the mouth of the Rhône near Marseilles and planted vines almost the instant they waded ashore. At any rate, when the "Phoceans" founded Marseilles, about 600 B.C., a cup of wine was presented to their chief.

No matter who introduced the vine, the Burgundians took to it wholeheartedly, and by A.D. 600 the Roman conquest had so spurred them on that vines were being planted everywhere. The Burgundians were so successful at glorifying the grape that the last of the twelve Cæsars, Domitian, in A.D. 89, furious at their supremacy in a delicate art, ordered all the vines to be ripped up. They interfered with the growing of wheat, he said. The Burgundians rioted, and the edict was never enforced, though it remained on the books until the Emperor Probus re-established the liberty of planting vines in 281. But it took hundreds of years to get the vineyards going full tilt again, and with the break-up of the Roman Empire the Church began to take over. This created a tremendous moral problem.

Wine was wealth, almost as precious as gold, perhaps inspiring the concept of liquid assets so popular in modern economics. Along with oil, spices, fabrics, and works of art, it made up the riches of the ancient world. And when the Church began gathering wealth, wine was one of the things it was on the lookout for. But being intoxicating, and exceedingly pleasant to drink, wine was opposed to the austerity and privation, the penance and poverty, the mortification of the flesh, and the strict abstinence that marked the beliefs of many of the religious orders. Wine's delights weighed heavily on the consciences of medieval monks.

St. Bernard, the same who made life miserable for Abélard, and thus indirectly for Héloïse, believed in the wealth that wine could bring and in its restorative powers, but he did not believe wine should be drunk for pleasure. Cluny, in the heart of Burgundy, and for some centuries the greatest church in France, came in for some harsh criticism from St. Bernard, largely because the monks drank so much and obviously enjoyed it.

Life was so luxurious at Cluny, in fact, that many of the Benedictines moved out to set up sterner monasteries. One group picked the swampy area near Beaune, calling themselves Cistercians after the *cisteaux*, or bulrushes, all around them, and a group of St. Bernard's nuns established themselves near by.

One of the ideals of the Cistercians, established in 1098 under the motto "Cross and Plough," was successful agriculture. The sparseness of the hills of the Slope of Gold was a challenge, and the monks soon discovered that the only thing they could raise successfully was vines. They planted the Clos Vougeot, and the nuns planted Clos de Tart, following the lead of the peasants and of other orders in the vicinity.

The local peasants were descendants of the Burgundii, an invading Germanic tribe who in the fifth century had established a kingdom that extended from the Rhine to Lyons and included Geneva. In the fourteenth century the land was denominated a duchy, to be ruled by Philip the Bold. He married Marguerite of Flanders, thus extending his duchy to include all the land north of Paris, as well as Luxembourg and Flanders. The Burgundian dukes owned the major part of France, felt that they should be kings, and joined the English against the Crown during the Hundred Years' War. At the same time England held Bordeaux. The French King was forced to give up Paris, and it was Joan of Arc who turned the tide in the Battle of Orléans. Subsequently, shrewd and impious Louis XI broke the power of the Burgundian dukes, adding their lands to his realm. Local scholars today claim that Louis was successful because he was desperate at the loss of the two great wine countries, Burgundy and Bordeaux.

All the religious orders added to their holdings throughout the Middle Ages, the rulers of Burgundy giving the Church their most prized possessions, their vineyards, perhaps out of fear of seizure and to ensure a safe hereafter for themselves and their households. In 587 King Gontrand gave the Abbot of Bengine in Dijon all the vineyards surrounding the city. In 1162 Duke Eudes II renounced all rights to the Cistercian vineyards. And so it went. When the Republic seized the vineyards after the Revolution, most of them either were in the possession of the Church or had been at one time.

60

The coming of the Cistercians and their schools of agriculture was as tremendous an encouragement to wine-making as the Roman conquest had been over a thousand years before—so much so, in fact, that regulation was needed. The first such rule came from Charlemagne, who owned vineyards at Corton, and in 809 it was ordered that workmen could no longer tread the grapes with their bare feet; it was unsanitary.

But the main trouble came from the Gamay grape, perhaps brought back by a crusader from the Near East. The Gamay grape yields a vast amount of juice, but its quality is low, in no way comparable with that variety known as Pinot, from which all the great wines of the Côte d'Or are made. Today the Gamay is planted all over the world—in Algeria, Chile, California, South Africa, and Australia—and since the Middle Ages it has also been planted in Burgundy. It has been frequently outlawed, one of the most vehement maledictions coming in 1395 from the last Duke of Burgundy, Philip the Bold. He ordered the destruction of all vineyards planted with Gamay, the "disloyal plant makes a wine in great abundance but horrible in harshness." Anybody who disobeyed was to be put in the pillory. At the same time Philip prohibited the storing of wines not grown in the district.

The two greatest evils in wine-making are illustrated by the ancient prohibitions. The first is the substitution of an inferior vine for a noble plant. In Burgundy the Pinot Noir and Pinot Chardonnay are considered the noble plants, yields from which are small. Only supreme soils are planted with these aristocratic vines, all others being planted with the heavy-yielding Gamay. To increase the yield of great wines from the choice vineyards, they are often mixed with Gamay pressings, the result being called *passe-tous-grains*. These are often fobbed off as truly great wines.

The second great evil of wine-making is mixing great

61

wines with lesser wines from another district. This blending, or *coupage*, is popularly referred to as the *grande cuisine* in Burgundy. Cheap, raw Algerian or Rhône wines are often mixed with great wines to stretch them. This, too, is sometimes passed off as real Burgundy.

When a great Burgundy is blended, its greatness is destroyed, for the wine is the result of the soil from which it comes, and a reflection of it. Once the Prince de Condé decided that he would like to establish a vineyard on his lands north of Paris, near Chantilly. He bought vines from one of Burgundy's greatest vineyards. They were fabulously expensive, and when they failed to produce a good wine, he stormed down to Burgundy and complained to the man who had sold him the cuttings. The answer was: "But sir, first it was necessary for you to take the soil."

Not only princes have thought they could make Burgundy wherever they wished. There is more "Burgundy" produced outside of Burgundy than is produced within the province. Wine-growers in California, Australia, South Africa, Chile, and Spain all sell wines they call Burgundy. The soil is different, the climate is different, the grapes are often different, the way they are grown is different, and the vinification is different. But they still call it Burgundy, as if all wines from Burgundy tasted alike, looked alike, and smelled alike. They do not, for Burgundies do not constitute a type, and it is even hard to distinguish a characteristic family taste. They vary in every way in which wine can vary. In France, at least, Burgundy is merely the name applied to a large and varied region where grapes are grown. The region produces a wide variety of wines, red, white, and *rosé*. Some are magnificent, and others are poor. The soil, the grape, the climate and the men make them distinctive.

Destroying great wines by blending, or by planting poor plants in great soil so that a lesser wine is made, is inimical to the perfection for which wine-growers strive. The wines are reduced to the lowest common denominator. When such wines are fraudulently sold as great wines at double or treble their worth, the buyer can notice nothing to get excited about and dismisses them as a howling pretension. Such wines are.

All this fraud got started in a big way shortly after the Revolution, in 1790, when the vineyards passed into the hands of individuals. Always handicapped by lack of an outlet to the sea, men began to make a business of the dangerous overland hauling. With more stable times, these wine-shippers began to make Burgundy known, and when Napoleon praised the wines, shippers could no longer meet the demand.

Burgundy has never been plentiful, the great wines coming from an area of scarcely 12,000 acres, and the shippers felt the need of blending in order to make the greatness go further. This was profitable, for Burgundy had become a fabled name. It was so rare that few people had ever tasted the real thing, and imitations were accepted as genuine. To a dangerous degree the same condition persists today.

Fraud by shippers was helped by the confusion in wine names that exists in Burgundy, by the great demand for a small supply, by the complete lack of legal controls, and by ignorance. The practice of blending was even defended by some because by blending good years with bad, and great wines with mediocre ones, a certain year-to-year uniformity was achieved. It was not until 1936 that the first effective controlling law was passed.

Prior to that date the wines of Burgundy were almost entirely controlled by the shippers. A few growers tried to set up the system followed by the Bordeaux wine-growers, whereby the man who owns the vineyard bottles his own wine, putting the name of the vineyard and his own name on the bottle as a guarantee of an honest wine. The wine-growers called the system estate bottling. It was encouraged by wine-buyers outside the district because it enabled them to get great wines without going to the shippers, and it proved profitable in good years. But in bad years the wine-growers had no buyers for their wines, and the shippers boycotted them.

The wine-growers were desperate by the time the depression of the early 1930's fell on them, and they were further crippled by overproduction in the cheap wine districts of France and North Africa. To protect their wines and to fight fraud they organized committees to draw up laws that would govern the making and selling of wine.

The passing of these laws and similar ones for all the great wine districts of France has worked a revolution in wine. The laws are one of the great modern achievements in the realm of jurisprudence, forged not by legal experts, but largely by the growers themselves. Not only was science important in drafting the laws, but tradition was involved, for wine is a work of both art and nature, and it is not possible to measure all the characteristics of a great wine with precision.

One of the men largely responsible for setting up these laws in Burgundy, along with the Marquis d'Angerville, of Volnay, is Henri Gouges, a man who has spent most of his life fighting for the wines he loves. "The first thing we had to do was classify the vineyards," he says. "No owner wanted his vineyard classed below his neighbour's, so it was difficult. We examined over a million vineyard deeds in all of France, and allowed only 9,800 of them to be registered. In 1934, some 420,000,000 gallons of wine came from the vineyards being considered for classification, but in 1936, only some 150,000,000 gallons were produced from the vineyards finally approved for classification."

In addition, the committee on which Gouges served also had to define wine districts, deciding which vineyards should be entitled to which famous names. The kind of vines used had to be agreed upon, how they should be tied and tended, when they could last be sprayed, and the time when the grapes could be harvested. If new vines were planted, it was decided that four years must pass before the wine yield could be declared.

"The wine is checked periodically by our experts," explains Gouges. "Each commune must produce a wine with a minimum alcoholic content, and the amount of acidity must be checked, for the wine will deteriorate if acidity is slight. Also, there is a legal minimum for tannin content, an element that permits a wine to age well. The producton from each vineyard must be registered, but not just to see that the owner does not sell more wine than he makes. If a man produces more than the average for the permitted grape during a particular vintage, he may have a few vines from lesser varieties. That is not allowed. But most important is the soil. That was defined, and also the undersoil. If the soil did not meet the standard, the wine was given a lower rating. In Meursault, when the slope changes to flatland, the vineyard classification changes. The exposure to the sun also affects the ratings."

In addition to this, it was necessary to define the bouquet of a wine, that medley of smells which comes from evaporation of elements in the wine. Under the law, bouquet is divided into two parts, the bouquet that wine has when new and the bouquet wine gains with ageing.

Original bouquet is characterized by the smell of the grape, which probably comes from the oils it contains, imparting to wine the fruity taste of fresh grapes. Muscat grapes make wine most outstanding in original bouquet, as do the Sauvignon of Sauternes and Sancerre, the Chenin of Anjou and Touraine, the Blanc Fumé of the upper Loire, and the Traminer of Alsace. When young, these wines are noted for floweriness.

Original bouquet is also believed to come from the action of the grape yeasts in the musts, an important thing to Champagne-makers. This bouquet comes out in the smell from the foam of Champagne when it is poured.

Acquired bouquet begins, and develops, with the ageing of the wine, and nobody is yet sure just what reactions form it. It is a characteristic exclusive with wines of great origin, and here is where tasting is necessary. The men making the laws must be not only organizers, lawyers, and salesmen, with an advanced knowledge of soil and geography, but also wine-tasters, for wines with acquired bouquet can never be drunk young. Some of the Médoc growths do not have a great perfume when young; as one writer puts it, they reserve "the splendid impressions for tasters who know how to wait." When acquired bouquet is sufficiently pronounced to be noticed by the nose, a taster can tell what is going to happen to a wine.

Acquired bouquet is the product of reactions that often lead to maderization of a white wine. It is the taste called *rancio*, which adds to the greatness of Madeiras, Marsalas, and the French Château Chalon, in the Jura district, but spoils other white wines. It is a flaw in dry white wines of France, which have a tendency to maderize. Particularly is it unpleasant in the Montrachets and Meursaults of the Côte de Beaune. Maderization is more unpleasant in Graves than in Sauternes, for instance, because sweetness hides the unpleasant, flat, musty, brownish taste of maderization. Acidity seems to prevent maderization, and the drier the wine, the more unpleasant is the brownish taste.

The two bouquets, original and acquired, combine to produce a distinctive quality, quite noticeable in Sauternes, for instance. Wines possessing them show great nobility, having a combination of fruitiness and bouquet that comes out only with age.

All this has a great deal to do with classifying vineyards and establishing the limits of a wine region. Still another consideration must be taken into account in parts of Burgundy where it is sometimes felt necessary to add sugar to the fermenting must in order to build up the resulting alcoholic content. This process, called *chaptalization*, after the man who first devised it, means that inspectors must taste the fermenting wine and know how much sugar to allow the vintner to add.

All these distinctions are reflected in the classifications of the wines from any particular region. The local committees set the standards for the various wines produced, first defining the area of the region and then the minimum requirements for the vineyards and the wines; and the national legislature formulates the decision into the law called *Appellation d'Origine*.

The annual declarations of amount of production filed by each wine-grower are checked by the local tax authorities, and periodic checks are made to see that a wine-grower does not sell more wines than he produces. The local governing board watches for fraud. All such boards work under the control of a national board, and all wines produced under its control bear on the label the phrase: "*Appellation Contrôlée*."

Wines from a region come under regulations whose stringency depends on the "*Appellation Contrôlée*" claimed by them. In this way a set of rules defines regional wines. There is an *Appellation Contrôlée* of "Burgundy." Stricter rules define district wines. There is an *Appellation Contrôlée* of "Côte de Nuits." Still more precise are rules for commune wines. There is an *Appellation Contrôlée* of "Gevrey-Chambertin." Still more exacting regulations define specific vineyards, such as the *Appellation Contrôlée* of "Chambertin." The many varied wines from each of France's great wine regions are thus carefully defined by law. As a result a Chambertin is one wine, a Gevrey-Chambertin another. The wines are similar; their qualities are not.

Vineyard names are particularly important, though the vineyard itself is not often an *Appellation Contrôlée*. As an example, the wines entitled to the *Appellation Contrôlée* of "Pommard" must contain at least 178 grammes of natural sugar per litre, a miminum alcoholic content after fermentation of 10·5 per cent Pommard wines that include the name of the vineyard on the label, however, such as "Rugiens" or "Clos de la Commaraine," must contain 198 grammes of natural sugar per litre, and a resulting alcoholic content of 11 per cent. When the vineyard name is added to the label, it indicates a superior wine.

The laws are detailed and complex, but they make it a simple matter for the buyer to select genuine bottles, for the primary indication of all this attention is summed up in a single phrase on a label: "*Appellation Contrôlée.*" By controlling the use of place-names, and by setting up a series of minimum standards instead of establishing merely one, French experts have preserved the distinction of their greatest wines by law. And yet shippers circumvent the law.

Unfortunately, the mere fact that a wine bears on its label the wording "*Appellation Contrôlée*" does not automatically mean that it is above all possibility a fraud. A shipper has the right to use this statement under the place-name—it means that this place-name is covered by a detailed list of specifications as to the boundaries of the district or vineyard, the variety of grapes to be used, the planting and cultivation of the vine are also controlled as well as the maximum yield per acre and the minimum alcoholic content of the wine enjoying the right to the name "*Appellation Contrôlée.*"

The element of fraud is dependent on human nature. The integrity and honesty of the shipper in observing and complying with the regulations as prescribed by law is a factor that no laws can guarantee, expecially those like the *Appellation d'Origine*, which need an adequate policing force to guarantee their enforcement.

A still further guarantee of authenticity and usually of

excellence in Burgundy is the system of estate bottling, by which the wine is produced by the grower, the bottle bearing his name and that of the vineyard in addition to the township. Because estate-bottled wines are produced in small quantities, by growers whose holdings are usually small, frauds may be checked easily. Where a large shipper may be able to afford fines, a small grower cannot. What is more, the grower feels that his signature is that of an artist. Proud of his name and wines, he has little incentive to discredit either. Even so, a good wine depends on the honesty of the man who makes it.

The Bordeaux label is relatively simple, for a château-bottled wine invariably carries the words "*Mis en bouteilles au Château.*" The Burgundy equivalents, however, rarely carry the wording: "*Mis en bouteilles par le propriétaire,*" or "*Mis au Domaine,*" or "*Mise du Domaine,*" or something similar.

French law specifies that an estate-bottled wine, or "*Vin de la Propriété,*" is one of which the bottler is the proprietor of the vineyard. He holds a licence to bottle only his own wines and no others.

A "*négociant,*" or shipper, may buy many wines, bring them to his cellars, blend them as he wishes, and bottle them under his label. There are many good and honest shippers, and the quality of the wine will depend entirely on their integrity. A *négociant* must give his status on the label. Many are the shippers who own a vineyard or even several vineyards. Recent French law insists that a shipper may claim being a proprietor or "*propriétaire,*" in addition to being a "*négociant,*" only if the wine shipped is from the township where he owns a vineyard. The label may then state "*Propriétaire*" or "*Négociant et Propriétaire.*" But if the wine shipped is from Pommard and the shipper's vineyards are in another commune or another district, he must then label the wines shipped from Pommard as Pommard, and his name can be followed only by the word "*Négociant*" preceding the address of his place of business. If a shipper owns a pocket-handkerchief-size vineyard in Nuits-Saint-Georges, he may buy wines, good or bad, from any part of this township and still state "*Propriétaire et Négociant à Nuits-Saint-Georges*" on the labels of these wines. So, a shipper who is a grower as well may stretch the wines from his own vineyards with good or indifferent wines guided only by his conscience and no label can indicate to the consumer the various shades of a merchant's honesty and his fortitude in resisting temptation.

The *Appellation d'Origine* laws by no means eliminate frauds, but they do help to reduce them. Many small wines go to market with meaningless phrases that closely approximate the significant ones. A list of phrases appearing on labels, both accurate and fake, appears below. The wise wine-buyer knows that the wording of a wine label is not pretension, but simple common sense, often making the difference between enjoyment and disappointment.

BURGUNDY LABELS

Good Honest Labels of Estate Bottlings

Mis en bouteilles par le propriétaire	(bottled by the owner or grower)
Mise de la propriété	(bottled at the estate or vineyard—same as above)
Mise à la propriété	(bottled at the estate)
Mis au Domaine	(bottled at the *domaine* or estate)
Mise du Domaine	(not necessarily actually bottled on the estate, even though part of the vineyard's production)
Mis en bouteilles au Domaine	(the same)

Name (XYZ) followed by the word *Propriétaire*	(owner or grower)
Name (XYZ) followed by the word *Propriétaire-Récoltant*	(owner or grower)
Name (XYZ) followed by the word *Viticulteur*	(wine-maker or wine-grower)
Name (XYZ) followed by the word *Vigneron*	(wine-grower)

The last word applies often where an absentee owner has a crop-sharing agreement with a wine-maker, the latter getting one-half or one-third of the production in payment for his work in tending the vines and making the wines. French law provides that the wines sold by the *vigneron* under his name are just as much "estate-bottled" as those sold under the name of the vineyard-owner. Sometimes the same wine may thus be sold legally under two different names.

MISLEADING STATEMENTS

Mis or *Mise en bouteilles dans mes caves* (bottled in my cellars)

If the bottler is not the owner of the vineyard, this statement is meaningless, as all wines are bottled in cellars, and if the bottler is not the vineyard-owner, chances are that by making such a statement he is trying to parade as such.

Mis en bouteilles au Château XYZ

This, again, is meaningless in Burgundy if the so-called château bears no proprietory relationship to the vineyard producing the wine. This is sometimes done by shippers who maintain offices in some château and bottle in its cellars wine purchased outside. The wine may be good, but this statement carries no guarantee of authenticity except that of the shipper's reputation.

71

Although the whole of France follows the same general pattern when it comes to vintages, each district has its own deviations and characteristics. Because grapes are a harvested crop, local weather conditions affect them and the resulting wine. When a great vintage comes along, the wines are quickly bought up when too young for drinking. Some great wines may not be fit for drinking for five or ten years, or longer. Each vintage must be considered in relation to specific wines, those which are good in some vineyards being poor vintages in others.

Such considerations are concerns of those who buy the wines from the wine-grower. In Bordeaux, when you buy a château-bottled wine, you can be sure you are getting the vintage marked on the bottle. In Burgundy, wines may bear false labels of old vintages. It is best to buy estate bottlings of a reputable grower or wines of a reliable shipper. Good wines are never cheap. Good old wines cannot be.

When buying wines, it is necessary to decide whether you are going to lay away the wine or drink it up. A great '49 from the Côte de Nuits may not be fit for drinking until 1955, whereas a Beaujolais is at its peak two years after the vintage. To taste the greatness of an old wine, it is wise to buy an old Corton, or an old Côte de Nuits, rather than spend money for an old Beaujolais, which is probably past its prime. A great wine is glorious when old. A good wine can be a disappointment. Equally, it is more of a pleasure to drink young, honest wines than old, fraudulent ones.

RED BURGUNDY

1923　*Though a great year in Burgundy, this vintage has not held up. Any genuine wines of this year would have a tendency to be faded.*

1924　*Very average in quality. Bottles of this vintage will rarely be found.*

RED BURGANDY

1925   *A very poor year, but a few vineyards, such as Romanée-Conti produced light wines that were still beautiful in 1951.*

1926   *This year, considered very good by many wine merchants, developed wines that became hard with age and lacking in charm. The same is true of clarets. Wines of this vintage, if one can still find them (and this is practically impossible), are not worth the effort of the search.*

1927   *A very poor year.*

1928   *This year produced some magnificent wines, sturdy in quality, which have practically all been drunk up. The quantity was very small in the Côte de Nuits because of hail.*

1929   *A very great year. Genuine bottles of this vintage are impossible to find in Burgundy, and will be still harder to find at your wine merchant's.*

1930   *Poor year. Produced wines much too light.*

1931   *Poor year.*

1932   *Poor year.*

1933   *Very good wines, with an excess of tannin. Bottles of this vintage, however, are practically unobtainable.*

1934   *Genuine '34's are practically non-existent. If available, they would be magnificent. Very abundant crop.*

1935   *Pleasant when young, '35's have fallen off today and are now disappointing.*

1936   *Very average in quality. Not worth considering.*

1937   *Although heralded as a great year, its wines have a tendency to remain hard. Chances are that many wines claiming to be of this vintage in the average wineshop are not authentic.*

1938   *Produced some worth-while wines, many which were soft and pleasant. A good vintage on the whole. Wines of this year are rare.*

1939   *Poor vintage.*

73

RED BURGUNDY

1940 *Uninteresting, should be avoided.*

1941 *Lower than average.*

1942 *Many very good wines on the light side were made. These should have been consumed by now, as they are not holding.*

1943 *Rather light. Many good wines were produced. Genuine '43's are rare.*

1944 *Rather mediocre on the whole. On the light side. What the wines lack in quality was made up in quantity.*

1945 *A very great year. The wines are developing slowly. Many of the magnificent Côte de Nuits will not be ready for several years. A perfect vintage to lay down, as it will keep for a long time.*

1946 *Many good light and fruity wines were made.*

1947 *A very great vintage year, but many failures produced by excessive sugar. Discrimination should be used in purchasing these wines.*

1948 *Far above the average in the Côte de Nuits. The wines are maturing rapidly. This vintage suffered in reputation because it came between the great '47's and the great '49's. Some wines of the Côte de Nuits, however, were better in '48 than in '47.*

1949 *The wines should have a good lasting ability. Many consider the red '49's as the best year of the generation.*

1950 *An enormous quantity of fast-maturing light wine was made among the reds.*

1951 *Fair wines.*

1952 *Very great wines were made in both red and white. However, as a whole the reds have a higher average and are more dependable.*

1953 *As in '52, great wines were made. If anything, the whites have a shade of superiority.*

1954 *Despite terrible weather, a few very good wines can be found in the Côte de Nuits.*

RED BURGUNDY

1955   *Care should be taken in selection but many excellent wines produced. Generally Côte de Nuits, especially around Chambolle-Musigny and Gevrey-Chambertin, better than Côte de Beaune, with the exception of Corton. Pommard and Beaune hit by hail. Parts of the Beaujolais also had hail, other parts turned out very great wines.*

WHITE BURGUNDIES

1934   *An excellent year, though most of the wines are likely to be too old and have a tendency to oxidize if they have not maderized already.*

1935   *The white wines were better than the red. Most of them are much too old, however.*

1936   *White Burgundies of this vintage are uninteresting today.*

1937   *High in alcohol and sturdy, these white Burgundies may prove to be disappointing now. Many great bottles may still be enjoyed.*

1938   *Better than average. Unless the wine has been well kept, you may be in for a disappointment.*

1939   *Poor year.*

1940   *Poorer than average.*

1941   *Poor as a whole. Should be shunned.*

1942   *Many excellent wines were produced during this year. The tendency is for these wines not to keep for long.*

1943   *Very good wines. The advisability of buying white Burgundies of this vintage is dubious, as their quality may largely depend on the way they have been stored.*

1944   *Definitely below average. Of no interest today.*

1945   *Many excellent wines were produced. In general, white Burgundies of this vintage were not so good as the reds. Slightly on the heavy side, perhaps they lack*

WHITE BURGUNDIES

distinction. Most are too old today. No Chablis was produced.

1946 *Many good, useful wines were produced.*

1947 *This vintage was superb. No other white Burgundies of the past eighty years have rivalled the quality of the great '47's. Unfortunately, most are maderized today.*

1948 *Like the red wines, white Burgundies suffered in reputation through being classified as an intermediate year between the great '47's and the fine '49's.*

1949 *Especially good in Chablis. This vintage is excellent, though the quantity produced was rather small.*

1950 *Excellent. Pleasanter than the '47's as they are not excessive in alcoholic content. The yield was far above average in quantity.*

1951 *The frosts of April 29, 1951, ruined 85 per cent of the wines in Chablis and well over one-third of the vines in the section producing white wines in the Côte de Beaune. Average quality.*

1952 *Excellent wines, beautifully balanced. A great year.*

1953 *If anything, the great white '53's are better than their red counterparts. Spring frosts again destroyed 85 per cent of all the Chablis. The little that was made was very good.*

1954 *Less than average.*

1955 *'55 as a whole still better than its red counterparts. With great breed and finesse will be every bit as good as '53.*

White Burgundies should be consumed young. If a generalization must be drawn, one could state that these wines will be pleasantly fresh after a year and a half or two years, and should be fully matured within six years. After this time some white Burgundies may still prove to be great, but there is always the risk of oxidation diminishing their value.

Chablis:

Oysters and Growers

CHABLIS squats in a valley ten miles up in the hills behind Auxerre. A country road winds east past barren slopes topped with clumps of young birch and pine. The oiled macadam is a sandy pink because of the red-brown foot-thick skin of topsoil and the whitish dust from the porous yellow undersoil. On flat stretches the roadside is planted with cropped sycamores, and the lanes leading off to farms and settlements are marked with double rows of slim, tall poplars, with dark-green balls of the killing mistletoe in their higher branches. Damp and cold in winter, riotous in summer, it is like any countryside, until you round the flank of the last hill and drive across the slanting valley floor to a huddle of stone houses where eighteen hundred people live for the wine of Chablis.

A thin slate steeple rises above the sandy walls of split limestone and the black, mossy roofs. It faces east to the curving slope, shaped like an oyster shell, and here are the eight outstanding vineyards of Chablis. Bougros, Les Preuses, Vaudésir, Grenouille, Valmur, Les Clos, Blanchots, and recently La Moutonne are where the wines classed as *Grand Cru* are produced.

The vineyards classed "outstanding" occupy 90 acres. The next most important "first growths"—Vaillon, Les Forêts, Montmain, Mont de Milieu, Montée de Tonnerre,

77

Fourchaume, and Séchet—comprise fewer than 520 acres. Today only one-third of this land is being worked, while the remaining two-thirds are resting. An outstanding Chablis vineyard must rest for twenty years.

The road from Auxerre leads straight into the square in the centre of the town and continues on out to the foot of the slope. It crosses over a shallow stream, never more than ten yards wide, overhung with willows. Reeds line its banks, and ducks dip in the pools or skim through the shadows cast by the old stone walls. The stream is called Le Serein, meaning either "serene" or "evening dew," no one in Chablis is quite sure which. But Le Serein, which north of Auxerre empties into the Yonne, which then empties into the Seine, is very suitable for serene Chablis, a happy, quiet country town.

The square in Chablis is much more spacious than it used to be: one night in June 1940, when the vineyards were in bloom, a fleet of Italian bombers blasted the place. Chablis wine-growers are still trying to figure out the reason for this, for the town is so far off the beaten track that it has no strategic importance. They will tell you about the centuries-old houses that were knocked down, adding happily that no bombs fell on the vineyards of either the great or the first growths.

On the left side of the square is the Hôtel de l'Étoile, now repaired. The owner, M. Bergerand, a towel tied bandana-fashion round his neck, tall chef's cap atilt on his big head, big white apron clinched around his bulk, urges you to try the specialities of the house; a terrine of rabbit to be eaten with à glass of Chablis, *écrevisses*, which are crayfish swimming in Chablis, Burgundy ham in a reddish sauce laced with Chablis, slices of veal cooked in Chablis, chicken poached in Chablis, or a soufflé served in scooped-out oranges, to be followed by a coarse, leathery marc made from distilled Chablis. He'll be only too glad to tell you that oysters and fish aren't the only things that are good with

Chablis, and to give you his recipes, printed on little slips of paper, to prove it.

One of the best of the seventy-seven growers in Chablis is Michel, a birdlike little man who thinks his wine the best in the world, and takes you down into his cellars to prove it to you.

If you don't have a *tastevin*, the shallow, dimpled silver saucer about the size of a small ashtray that is used by the wine-taster when he tests the wine, the grower will take out some clear glass goblets. On the way to the cellars he will ask you which vintages and growths you want to taste, taking out of his pocket a *tastevin* wrapped in a handkerchief and polishing it.

Most tasters use the *tastevin* in Burgundy, though some prefer glasses either because they believe they can see the colour better or perhaps from habit. The *tastevin* is silver, so no foreign taste will be imparted to the wine; it is dimpled along the sides so that you can see the colour of the wine at different depths. Some *tastevins* have ridges along one side to reflect the shimmer of light through the wine. In the centre is a knob almost as high as the lips of the "taste" and in the old days you could stick a candle on it. This must have made the utensil hard to drink out of, and wine-tasters of other times could probably be identified by singed forelocks and smoke smudges on their foreheads. The grooves of the "taste" darken quickly because of the wine. The handle is a silver ring, often with a thumb-rest on its top edge, shaped like the rest for a cigarette on the side of an ashtray. Others are in the form of a snake, with a middle loop by which you can hold the "taste."

After unlocking the door to the cellar, the grower picks up a sort of crowbar from the top of a barrel and takes the pipette down from a hook near the light-switch. Curiously called "thief" in English, a Burgundy pipette is about a foot long and an inch thick, a glass tube tapered at one end and having a metal ring at each side of the other end so that it

79

can be held by the fingers. On the top of the barrel is the bung, a wooden stopper around which a disk of wadding has been pressed. Working it out with a few bangs of the crowbar, the grower gently lowers the pipette into the barrel, tapping on the rounded hole with his thumb. If the pipette does not fill fast enough, the grower sucks the air out of the pipette through the thumb-hole, then covers it with his thumb and pours some of the wine into your "taste."

Michel will wave at some barrels in the corner with his free hand. "That's Vaudésir over there, and this is Les Clos." Like any grower, he is happiest when talking about his wines. "In Chablis we often store the wine above ground, but in the rest of Burgundy it's always kept in the *caves*, the cellars. After pressing, the wine is drawn off into the barrels, where it remains until it's ready for bottling, which will be in eighteen months or two years for Chablis. Then it's bottled, and ages for another six months to one year, depending."

Wine has two ages: the life in the cask, and the life in the bottle—childhood and adolescence. Here they usually use a special size of barrel, smaller than in other places. The big ones used in Burgundy, which contain the equivalent of 288 bottles are called *pièces*. These Chablis half-size barrels are called *feuillettes*. On average all the wine from the *Grand Crus* and the *Premiers Crus* amounts to an equivalent of 53,000 cases. In addition, the lesser wines labelled Chablis and Petit-Chablis produce the equivalent of 120,000 and 150,000 cases respectively. Most of these 270,000 cases are sold in barrel for French consumption.

Michel will look around the *cave*, which contains perhaps thirty barrels against the walls, with another double row of twenty down the centre. "I would say that less than a quarter of all the Chablis drunk every year is genuine. Maybe less than ten per cent."

When tasting, you hold the "taste" in front of you, about

waist-high, so that you can see the wine's colour under the bare light-bulb. The silver sparkles under the wine, and a good wine picks up and adds to the sparkle. These Chablis in the casks are young, green wines, but they should be clear, free of floating particles, and not cloudy. The colour should be a pale yellow with a faint green tinge. The smell of the wine should be clean and fresh, with no unpleasant odour of wood or sulphur, nor any musty or vinegary smell. These green wines taste sharp and often acid, but you can recognize the traditional taste behind the roughness and the bitiness: a flinty, clean taste that is supposed to come from the Kimeridgian chalk in the vineyards. This particular chalk also comes to the surface in Champagne. Wines change in the cask, one tasting fine one week and bad the next, while another barrel will be the reverse. Because young wine works in the barrel, these differences are easy to distinguish, and vary noticeably from barrel to barrel, vineyard to vineyard, and vintage to vintage.

After looking at the wine and smelling it, you take a small sip and, holding it in your mouth, purse your lips as if to whistle, sucking in air and making a gurgling sound that tumbles the wine about on the tip of your tongue. Then you spit it out on the earthen floor. Both gurgling and spitting are somewhat scandalizing to a novice, but after a couple of *caves*, the rankest of amateurs is spitting like a master, with a certain nefarious delight. Some of the growers swallow the wine, because it is precious even when green and undrinkable, but a taster cannot, because the green wine in his stomach deadens his taste. Not only that, but green wine acts as a purgative, and a wine-taster samples as many as fifty barrels in a day, which would be disastrous if he swallowed the wine, to say nothing of the fact that he would be roaring drunk every night and would ruin his kidneys in a week.

Another typical grower, not only of Chablis, but of all

81

Burgundy, is Marcel Servin, who raises and bottles his own wine and owns parcels totalling seven acres in Les Preuses, Blanchots, Bougros, and Vaillon. Because he, like Michel, handles the wine himself from vine to bottle, he is called an estate bottler. His name as proprietor and the name of his vineyard where the wine comes from are on the label of the bottle. He is a wine-growing peasant of Burgundy, and is proud of it. His wine is his life.

Servin's place is down from the square in Chablis, just beyond, where the river crosses the road. Standing at his front gate, which is of sheet iron painted a grey in which there is a little blue—a colour that is typical of Burgundy and is on most of the metal and wooden shutters and gates— you can look square at the vineyards of the *Grands Crus*. The slope is a little less than a quarter of a mile away and faces somewhat west of south. Servin, his wife, and his son work in the vineyards or for the vineyards all the year round, getting up at dawn and going to bed at dusk.

The gates of Servin's place open on a court about the size of a tennis court. The house is on the right, two storeys high, the *chais* and store-rooms along the back and on the left, their black roof slates uneven and mottled with thick green moss. The door of the house opens into a low, flagged room with a sink in one corner, a wood stove beside it, and a table in the rear, backed by a sideboard. The indoors activity during the daytime takes place in this combination kitchen, dining-room, sitting-room, and office. It is typical of the Burgundian peasant, and though other houses will be a little bigger or a little smaller, only the details vary.

Servin is a stocky, moustached man in his fifties, who wears felt slippers in the house and wooden sabots when he goes out of doors, dressed in corduroys the colour of ripe olives when new and of dried ripe olives when old. Although many vineyard workers now wear rubber boots, Servin clings to the heavy wooden clogs that used to typify the peasant. His son is a polite, cheerful, smiling boy in his twenties. His wife is a light-haired, pretty woman. With them lives his father, who is ninety-one, has a hearty wheeze, is bent double from working among the vines all his life, and, with nine decades of acquaintance with it behind him, strains the hard, white wine of Chablis through his yellow moustache. On good days he still does some pottering about the vineyard.

With the coming of winter, the vineyards are ploughed and fertilized with manure and phosphates. Servin and his son guide the horses between the narrow rows, and by January usually have them ready for the pruning. Both roots and the vine tendrils must be pruned so that none of the energy of the soil or vine will be wasted on parts that will not produce good grapes. Pruning begins on January 22, the day of St. Vincent, the wine-grower's patron saint. Any sick or dead plants are ripped up and new ones planted. The vine used is the Pinot Blanc, called Pinot Chardonnay in Burgundy, Beaunois in Chablis; it is grafted to American roots, the only roots strong enough to resist the dreaded phylloxera, the tiny plant louse that lives on grape roots. According to the tradition of Burgundy, all the planting must be done by Easter, whether Easter comes early or late.

Servin is likely to reach behind him at this point in the story of his life and begin setting out glasses. His son, as if on signal, will come in carrying a dirty bottle. Servin will carefully break the wax seal on the bottle, carefully insert the tip of the corkscrew into the centre of the cork, and begin to twist its handle, which is made of a shiny grapevine root.

"The best moon for planting is a red moon, or that's what they say," he tells you with a grin. "If the vines are planted too soon, the grapes will fall. It is very important, the planting. A good vine should live between twenty and forty-five years, but things happen. And after every storm we must go out with baskets, for the earth washes down the slope to the bottom of the vineyard, and it must all be carried back. After every storm. It is heavy, carrying the mud."

On one occasion Servin held the bottle pressed between his knees, and the cork came out with a pop. Everybody was suddenly quiet, watching as he poured a few drops into the glass before him. It was clear and whitish yellow, faintly green. He began to fill the glasses on the table. "Nowadays everybody wants clear Chablis, with all the sediment strained out—the particles of grape, the lees as a result of fermentation, everything—but when you do that, it takes some of the good out of the wine. But the colour is what counts. They used to put white of eggs in red wines, and isinglass in white wines, and even blood, or milk, or gelatin. Now we use pills."

He tasted the wine, sucking in air, and then nodded his head and grinned. "After Easter, all through April and until the 20th of May, we have a holiday. Nothing much to do, no ploughing."

His wife laughed and, reaching behind her, picked up a willow stick about a foot long and a quarter of an inch thick. "I'll show you what we do on holidays." She put the end of the willow stick between her teeth, bit it, then tore a strand loose and following it with her finger, stripped it off; then she wrapped the sliver around the stem of the glass, twisting it, turning it back on itself to make it stay. "This is the way we tie the vines to the wires. We sit up all night making the strands, and spend all day tying."

Servin grinned at his wife. "In the autumn we pull up the rotted stakes, replace them with new ones, string wires across their tops, about three feet from the ground, and tie the vines to them. Then in June the vine flowers into tiny whitish blossoms along the slope, and after that it must be very hot, with lots of sun, because the blossoms should fall

84

in ten days; if they last three weeks, the grapes suffer. Before and after the flowering we spray every week with copper sulphate until Bastille Day, July 14, but after that we spray only after it rains. In June we begin the tilling, then in August we plough again. And once in June, once in July, and again in August we trim the vines. With this."

Out of his belt Servin pulled a short, hooked blade, perhaps four inches long, with a smooth wooden handle. His son reached into his belt and pulled out an identical knife. Mme Servin waved her hand at the knives. "Everybody in Burgundy carries the *serpette* in his belt. It's like the carpenter's hammer or the mason's trowel. But it's the women who do most of the trimming. You must be deft and fast. It's a woman's work."

Servin nodded at his wife. "Then in September, holidays again, hunting and fishing. Perhaps a trip to Paris to sell some wine to old friends. And in September we put the wines in bottle if we haven't done it during the spring holidays, and we cooper the barrels, and clean them, and let sulphur candles burn in them to kill the moulds. And then there's the wheat-planting. We have wheat for bread and feed. In October comes the harvest, and we must keep the cellar warm for three weeks while the wine ferments, and then in November we make new stays and clean the vineyards. There are no Sundays in Burgundy. Every day is work."

This is the life of the men who make the wines of Burgundy, gamblers all, working for a good year. Proud of their great wines, the growers resent the fact that so many poor wines are sent to world markets as great Chablis.

One of the great battles over Chablis was settled in the spring of 1951, when the French courts finally decreed that "Moutonne" can now be sold as a *Grand Cru*. Formerly the name was used as a trade-mark by one Long-Depaquit. Now the name can only be applied to wines coming from a small 5-acre section between Les Preuses and Vaudésir. A large part of this land is now resting, and the name is now restricted to wines coming from less than three acres.

In the town is the good shipping firm of J. Moreau et Fils, unique because it specializes solely in the wines of Chablis. The firm is now run by two brothers, the younger of whom was in charge of wines at the French Pavilion of the New York World's Fair of 1939. The firm owns two acres of Valmur, two acres of Les Clos in the *Grand Crus*, and twelve acres of Vaillon in the *Premiers Crus*.

As for vintages, great ones occurred in 1928 and 1929, wines impossible to find anywhere today. Those of '33, '34, and '37 are almost equally rare, and many of them are now too old. There were several great years in the forties, '43 being excellent though somewhat acid, while '46 was good. Because of the extreme heat in the summer of 1947, the wine was one of the greatest vintages Chablis has ever had. The wines were extraordinarily high in alcohol, many of them containing more than fourteen per cent. A criticism has been that full richness of these wines is not characteristic of the dry steeliness usually associated with Chablis. So remarkable are these truly great wines that they are already by the excellent '49. 1950 produced an enormous yield and good wines. But, like true Burgundians, the wine-growers of Chablis are uncomfortable when you mention a bad year like 1945. This was a good vintage in most Burgundy vineyards, but not in Chablis, where every vine was frozen and practically no grapes were harvested. In spite of this, many casks have been sold bearing the tag "Chablis '45," and many a bottle of "'45" was exported by dishonest shippers.

The frosts on the night of April 29, 1951, froze eighty-five per cent of all the great vineyards. Hence, in 1951, only a few barrels of Chablis were produced. The freeze of 1953 took up to five-sixths of the normal crop, Marcel Servin, for instance, harvesting twenty instead of 120 *feuillettes*.

CHABLIS VINEYARDS

Grand Crus, OR OUTSTANDING GROWTHS

Blanchots	La Moutonne
Bougros	Les Preuses
Les Clos	Valmur
Grenouilles	Vaudésir

Premiers Crus, OR FIRST GROWTHS	TOWNSHIP
Beauroy	*Poinchy*
Beugnon	*Chablis*
Butteaux	*Chablis*
Châpelot	*Fyé or Fleys*
Châtain	*Chablis*
Côte de Fontenay	*Fontenay*
Côte de Léchet	*Milly*
Fourchaume	*La Chapelle-Vaupelteigne*
Les Forêts	*Chablis*
Les Lys	*Chablis*
Melinot	*Chablis*
Mont des Milieu	*Fyé or Fleys*
Montée de Tonnerre	*Fyé or Fleys*
Montmain	*Chablis*
Pied d'Aloup	*Chablis*
Séchet	*Chablis*
Trœme	*Beines*
Vaillon	*Chablis*
Vaucoupin	*Chichée*
Vaulorent	*Poinchy*
Vaupinent	*Chablis*
Vosgros and Vogiras	*Chichée*

The Côte d'Or:

The Heart of Burgundy

BURGUNDY'S greatest wines come from the Côte d'Or. Geographically the Slope of Gold begins at Dijon, one of the main stops of the Paris-Riviera Express. The railway and National Highway 74 run parallel to the strip of vineyards down to Santenay, forty miles south.

The Golden Slope is a low and rolling range of hills, topped by brush and scrub, along the western edge of the great Burgundian plain, which spreads eastwards to the Juras and Switzerland. The greatest vineyards are of Pinot grapevines planted just above the point where the hill slopes meet the flatland, a strip rarely more than a mile wide and more often barely a couple of hundred yards across. Below these, and on across the railway into the plain, are vineyards planted in Gamay grape. All the vineyards look the same, but the wine is not.

The Côte d'Or's favourite proverb says: "If our slopes were not the richest in Burgundy, they'd be the poorest." It is pure accident that this poor earth provides the precise combinations of soil and sun to make the great wines.

Driving south along the Golden Slope, a stranger does not pass through all the famous vineyards. The first vineyard he is able to identify is probably Clos Vougeot, where there is a stone arch every few feet. Some of these arches are quite ornate, opening on to a slightly tilted field of grapevines. He would pass through Nuits-Saint-Georges, Beaune, and near Pommard, but he would have to take a rutted lane to see the great Montrachet vineyard. He might be surprised to find in a stretch of carefully marked plantations one that was singled out to have a wall around it, with small square arches opening into the vineyard, some carefully marked with neat metal plaques bearing the owners' names. Such walled vineyards are called *clos*. One parcel of greenery looks much like another, and there is little way of telling which are great.

Yet the stories about the great vineyards are rare and wonderful. There was the general who made his troops present arms when passing Clos Vougeot, a custom that persists; and Pope Gregory made a cardinal of the man who was clever enough to send him thirty barrels of the famous wine. One historian says the reason Burgundian cardinals never visited Rome was that they didn't want to be away from their vineyards so long. Erasmus said that the only good reason he could think of for going to France was to drink Burgundy in its own land. Rabelais says: "How good is God to give us of this juice!" And Dumas is said to have declared that Montrachet ought to be drunk kneeling, with head bared. Almost everybody has something commendatory to say about great Burgundies, and usually the same thing, several times.

Today the Côte d'Or is divided into two sections. The Côte de Nuits, to the north, produces three-quarters of all the great red wines; the southern Côte de Beaune makes the rest of the reds and all the great white wines. The red wines get steadily lighter in every way as you go south, and most of the whites are in the vineyards of Meursault and below. Some Burgundians insist that the Golden Slope should today be divided into three parts, the third being called the Côte de Meursault, in order to distinguish more clearly the white vines of the Beaune Slope from the reds. As usual, there's an old local saying about it, in rhyme:

La Bourgogne a trois côtes ou je ne suis qu'un sot,
Côtes de Nuits, de Beaune, et Côte de Meursault.

In the old days there actually was a third slope, the Côte de Dijon. Once most of Burgundy's wines came from the vineyards surrounding Dijon, and at the little town of Chenôve is the world's largest winepress to prove it. Officially it is called "the Duke's winepress," but long ago it picked up the name of "Big Maggie," after Marguerite, that lusty Duchess of Burgundy. She was the mother of Philip the Bold, a gay old girl mentioned tantalizingly and often in all Burgundian chronicles, but so discreetly that you would never suspect her tremendous prowess. Marguerite presided over the harvest festivals, which have been described as bacchanalia; she has been called "amiable"; it is said that she bestowed her favours on the fastest harvesters and best vintners; and after her was named the biggest winepress in the world.

The winepress and its memories are all that remain of the fame of the Dijon slope, and the suburbs have engulfed many of its vineyards. Dijon used to be famous for its food, but today it is known principally as the world's mustard centre, and mustard is a condiment that spoils the taste of great wine. They also make there an alcoholic currant syrup called cassis. A teaspoonful in a third of a glass of French vermouth, which is then filled with seltzer and ice, makes the famous vermouth cassis. More popular in Burgundy is the drink made by adding a teaspoonful of cassis to a glass of chilled white wine. It is called *rince cochon* ("pig rinse"), and is the Burgundian equivalent of fruit salts.

The wines became famous because of poor transportation in those days when only local wines could be drunk. But when the Cistercian monks began producing their wonders, no amount of civic pride could make the people of Dijon keep on drinking their own lesser wines. The vineyards declined steadily, and when the phylloxera destroyed the plantings in the 1870's, the vineyards were replanted in Gamay grapes. But even forgoing quality for quantity was a failure, for Midi and North African wines captured the cheap-wine market.

Recently many of the old vineyards have again been planted in Pinot, particularly around the little town of Marsannay. Burgundy produces no famous *rosé* wines, and it was believed that these vineyards might produce an excellent pink wine. The result was a *rosé* that is light and fresh, less high in alcohol than other *rosés*, sold mostly by restaurants in carafe. Although it can be shipped, it rarely is, for it is little known. The best *rosé* is made by the co-operative of Marsannay, and most of the wine sold by the shippers as a Burgundy *rosé* is made in that town.

To counteract this lack of fame, a fête in honour of St. Vincent was held in Marsannay in 1949. The *Chevaliers du Tastevin* climbed into their robes and presented a colourful pageant to publicize the *rosé*. It is thus that shippers perform a service for the less-known areas of the Côte d'Or. With their methods of promotion and distribution, they encourage people to try the lesser wines, where differences are not great, and fairly large quantities can boast of an average goodness.

The great vineyards of the Côte d'Or, however, are some half-dozen miles south of Dijon, where the Côte de Nuits begins. And a confusion at once arises because the various towns of the Golden Slope have long since added to their names that of the nearest famous vineyard. Gevrey, for instance, has become Gevrey-Chambertin, Chambolle has become Chambolle-Musigny. And the town name applies not only to the village, but also to the commune, or parish, surrounding it.

To get round such difficulties, Burgundians will give you a phrase: "*Respectez les crus.*" This means: learn the name of the best growths, or vineyards, and pay no attention to any other names.

In Bordeaux little attention is paid to the names of towns or communes or to the geographical listing of vineyards. The vineyards are listed in order of merit, as a group, for an entire district. There has never been such a list of Burgundy vineyards, and while the wines of each commune have been classified, the wines of the whole Côte d'Or have never been given in one master list.

It may be helpful to follow the Bordeaux system of listing for the outstanding wines of the Côte d'Or. In this tentative list, local prestige, world reputation, the soil, the year-to-year consistency of the wine, the grower, and the value of the wine in relation to its price have been taken into consideration. The list is a consensus of many experts' opinions, and because wine is a product of nature and of man's skill, any wine in the following list could jump up or down half a dozen places for any particular vintage. Many an argument can be started among wine-lovers by bringing up this list, but it has a value to the novice of wines, it is of interest to the amateur, and it can be a basis of soul-searching for the expert. If nothing else, it shows that many of the most famous Burgundies are not the best, that many Outstanding Growths rank below many First Growths. Any complete agreement with this list is entirely coincidental.

RED

VINEYARD OR CLIMATS	TOWNSHIP OR COMMUNE	PRINCIPAL OWNERS
Romanée-Conti	*Vosne*	Domaine de la Romanée-Conti, de Vilaine et Chambon (sole owner)

RED [*continued*]

VINEYARD OR CLIMATS	TOWNSHIP OR COMMUNE	PRINCIPAL OWNERS
Chambertin-Clos de Bèze and Chambertin	*Gevrey*	Pierre Damoy; Domaine Marion; A. Rousseau; de St. Quentin; Deschamps; L. Latour; Remy; L. Camus; Général Rebourseau; Domaine L. Trapet; Drouhin-Laroze; Jaboulet-Vercherre; etc.
La Tâche	*Vosne*	Domaine de la Romanée-Conti, de Vilaine et Chambon (sole owner)
Richebourg	*Vosne*	Domaine de la Romanée-Conti, de Vilaine et Chambon; Louis Gros, Charles Noëllat; etc.
Clos des Lambrays	*Morey*	Mme Cosson (sole owner)
Musigny	*Chambolle*	Adrien & Roblot; Domaine Mugnier; Comte de Voguë; Domaine Prieur; etc.
Clos Vougeot	*Vougeot*	See list of owners on page 120
Bonnes-Mares	*Chambolle*	Adrien & Roblot; Claire-Daü Mugnier; Drouhin-Laroze; Comte de Voguë; P. Ponnelle; Groffier; Domaine Alexis Lichine; Hudelot; etc.
Grands-Échézeaux	*Flagey*	R. Engel; Domaine de la Romanée-Conti, de Vilaine et Chambon; Louis Gros; Groffier; Jayer-Mugneret; Veuve Mongeard-Mugneret; L. Gouroux; etc.

RED [continued]

VINEYARD OR CLIMATS	TOWNSHIP OR COMMUNE	PRINCIPAL OWNERS
Romanée-St.-Vivant	*Vosne*	Charles Noëllat; Arnoux; L. Latour; G. Marey-Monge; etc.
Clos de Tart	*Morey*	J. Mommessin (sole owner)
Cuvée Nicolas Rollin	*Beaune*	Hospices de Beaune
St.-Georges	*Nuits*	Domaine H. Gouges; Morizot-Pelletier; Misserey; Hospices de Nuits; E. Michelet; Liger-Belair; etc.
Latricières-Chambertin	*Gevrey*	Drouhin-Laroze; J. H. Remy; Alexis Lichine; L. Trapet.
Corton	*Aloxe-Corton*	Prince de Merodé; L. Latour; P. Gauthrot; etc.
Bressandes	*Aloxe-Corton*	G. Yard; Jaboulet-Vercherre; Prince de Mérode; Arbelet; Comtesse Chandon de Briailles; Dubreuil-Fontaine; M. Quenot; etc.
Renardes	*Aloxe-Corton*	Prince de Mérode; P. Petitjean; etc.
Cuvée Dr. Peste	*Corton*	Hospices de Beaune
Clos des Porrets-St.-Georges	*Nuits*	Domaine H. Gouges (sole owner)
Les Porrets	*Nuits*	J. Jarot; E. Michelet; Hospices de Nuits; etc.
Mazys-Chambertin	*Gevrey*	Camus; A. Rousseau; P. Gelin; Tortochot; A. Lichine
Les Pruliers, Les Cailles	*Nuits*	Domaine H. Gouges; Gessaume-Bourgeois; M. Guy; Misserey-Rollet; M. Grivot; J. Jarot; Besancenot-Granané; etc.

RED [*continued*]

VINEYARD OR CLIMATS	TOWNSHIP OR COMMUNE	PRINCIPAL OWNERS
Les Caillerets	*Volnay*	H. Boillot; H. Bitouzet; Bouchard Père et Fils; Bouley-Duchemin; Marquis d'Angerville; H. de Chavigné & S. de Lavoreille; A. Clerget-Buffet; de la Grange; Veuve Fabregoule; R. de la Planche; Malivernet; etc.
La Perrière	*Fixin*	Jehan-Joliet; Bellote; etc.
Amoureuses	*Chambolle*	Adrien & Roblot; Domaine Mugnier; F. Grivelet; L'Héritier-Guyot; Gardey-Jouan; etc.
Clos St.-Jacques, Varoilles	*Gevrey*	Comte de Moucheron, Deschamps (sole owner of Varoilles)
Échézeaux	*Flagey*	R. Engel; Domaine de la Romanée-Conti, de Vilaine et Chambon; L. Gros; Groffier; Jayer-Mugneret; Mongeard-Mugneret; L. Gouroux, J. Bossu; R. Bossu; etc.
Beaumonts	*Vosne*	Charles Noëllat; Lamarche; Grivot; etc.
Malconsorts	*Vosne*	F. Grivelet; Massart; etc.
Clos de la Roche	*Morey*	H. Ponsot; A. Rousseau; H. Remy; A. Jacquot; Groffier; Marchand; Mlle Ory; Veuve Tortochet; G. Lignier; etc.

RED [*continued*]

VINEYARD OR CLIMATS	TOWNSHIP OR COMMUNE	PRINCIPAL OWNERS
Fremiet, Champans	*Volnay*	Marquis d'Angerville; F. Buffet; Mme François; C. Rapet; P. Emonin; M. Voillot; J. Prieur; R. Caillot; Bouchard Père et Fils, etc.
Les Suchots	*Vosne*	Lamarche; Mme Blée; Maitrot; etc.
Clos des Réas	*Vosne*	L. Gros (sole owner)
Chapelle Charmes, Griotte	*Gevrey*	P. Damoy; Belorgey; J. Camus; Drouhin-Laroze; J. H. Remy; L. Trapet; Veuve Tortochot, J. Coquard; etc.
Clos du Roi	*Aloxe-Corton*	Baron Thénard; Prince de Mérode; D. Senard; L. Petitjean; etc.
Clos du Chapitre	*Fixin*	P. Gelin
Rugiens, Commaraine Epenots, Jarollières	*Pommard*	M. Drouhin; J. Guillemard; Pothier-Rieusset; Verdereau-Carré; de Chavigné and S. de Lavoreille; Domaine Gaunoux; Comte Armand; Clerget-Buffet; Jaboulet-Vercherre; B. Gonnet; Domaine Lejeune; Mme B. de Courcel; M. Parent; Poirier; Goud de Beaupuis; etc.
Clos de la Maréchale	*Nuits, Prémeaux*	Domaine Mugnier (sole owner)
Didiers, St.-Georges	*Nuits, Prémeaux*	Hospices de Nuits

RED [*continued*]

VINEYARD OR CLIMATS	TOWNSHIP OR COMMUNE	PRINCIPAL OWNERS
Clos des Corvées	*Nuits, Prémeaux*	General Gouachon (sole owner)
Vaucrains	*Nuits*	Domaine H. Gouges; Michelot; J. Confuron; Misserey; etc.
La Grand Rue	*Vosne*	Lamarche (sole owner)
Santenots	*Meursault, Volnay*	Marquis d'Angerville; de Chavigné S. de Lavoreille; E. Bouley; Clerget-Buffet; Thévenot; etc.
Fèves, Grèves, Clos des Mouches	*Beaune*	J. Drouhin; L. Voiret; Bouchard Père et Fils; Carimontran; Champy Père et Fils; Chanson Père et Fils; L. Latour; J. Guillemard; H. Darviot; F. Clerget; Martin-Bourgeot; Goud de Beaupuis; etc.
Clos de la Boudriotte	*Chassagne*	Claude Ramonet; L. Jouard; E. Guillon; etc.
Clos St.-Jean, Morgeot	*Chassagne*	Claude Ramonet; L. Jouard; E. Guillon; etc.
Les Angles	*Volnay*	H. Rossignol, etc.
Clos Blanc, Pézerolles	*Pommard*	Jaboulet-Vercherre; Poirier; F. Clerget; Cavin; L. Michelot; Faivre; Lochardet; Grivot; etc.
Clos St.-Denis	*Morey*	Bertrand-Sigaud; J. Coquard, A. Jacquot; G. Lignier; R. Moine; A. Rameau; E. Seguin; etc.

97

OTHER WINES

Note: In buying wines bearing the commune name with no vineyard name, the important factor determining selection should be the integrity and honesty of the shipper.

WHITE

VINEYARD OR CLIMATS	TOWNSHIP OR COMMUNE	PRINCIPAL OWNERS
Montrachet	*Chassagne and Puligny*	See list of owners on page 161
Chevalier-Montrachet	*Puligny*	See list of owners on page 162
Clos des Perrières	*Meursault*	Mme Albert Grivault (sole owner)
Bâtard-Montrachet	*Chassagne and Puligny*	See list of owners on page 162
Perrières	*Meursault*	Ampeau; Joseph Matrot; Domaine Lafon; Lochardet; Maurice Ropiteau; Comtesse P. de Montlivault; Camille Chouet; Joseph Coche-Vincent; Grosyeux-Polet; J. Boulard; Cauvert-Monnot; Bruey-Mouchaux; etc.
Corton-Charlemagne	*Aloxe*	L. Latour; H. Pialat; Page; Naudin; A. Duc; L. Jadot; Jaffelin-Rollin; Louis Cornu; Rapet; etc.
Musigny-Blanc	*Chambolle*	Comte de Voguë; Domaine Mugnier
Ruchottes	*Chassagne*	Claude Ramonet
Charmes	*Meursault*	Battault-Rieusset; Boillot Buthiau; F. Boillot; J. Boillot-Georget; L. Bouzereau-Bachelet; X. Hanauer-

98

WHITE [*continued*]

VINEYARD OR CLIMATS	TOWNSHIP OR COMMUNE	PRINCIPAL OWNERS
Charmes	*Meursault*	Latour; Jobard-Morey; E. Jobard; Pierre Jobard; Latour-Boissard; L. Leger-Charton; Michelot-Morey; Michelot-Rocault; Michelot-Truchot; J. Monnier; R. Monnier; Monnot-Meney; E. Morey; L. Morey-Porcheret; René Morey; Comte de Moucheron; Nouveau-Desandre; Percebois-Marchal; Perronnet-Chouet; Perronnet-Latour; Veuve Ponsot-Morey; Veuve Renaudin-Bonny; Mme R. Renaudin; E. Ropiteau; E. Ropiteau-Tiercin; Rougeot-Floret; E. Sillot; Tiercin-Baillard; Mme H. Vasseur; Veuve J. Vasseur-Boillot; Veuve Vitu-Pouchard
Combettes	*Puligny*	Etienne Sauzet; Domaine Leflaive; etc.
Clos Blanc-de-Vougeot	*Vougeot*	L'Héritier-Guyot (sole owner)

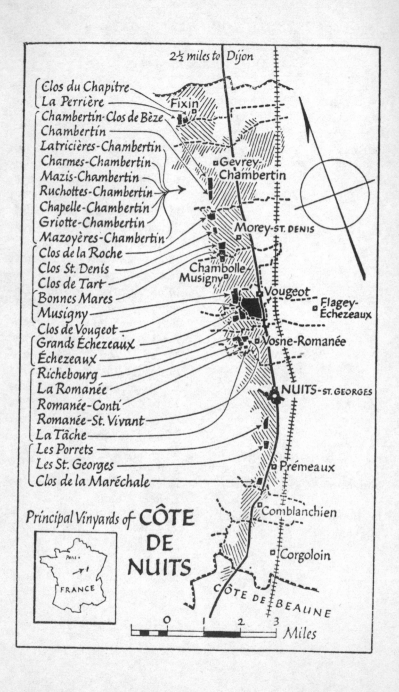

2½ miles to Dijon

Clos du Chapitre ——
La Perrière ——
Chambertin-Clos de Bèze ——
Chambertin ——
Latricières-Chambertin ——
Charmes-Chambertin ——
Mazis-Chambertin ——
Ruchottes-Chambertin ——
Chapelle-Chambertin ——
Griotte-Chambertin ——
Mazoyères-Chambertin ——
Clos de la Roche ——
Clos St. Denis ——
Clos de Tart ——
Bonnes Mares ——
Musigny ——
Clos de Vougeot ——
Grands Échezeaux ——
Échezeaux ——
Richebourg ——
La Romanée ——
Romanée-Conti ——
Romanée-St. Vivant ——
La Tâche ——
Les Porrets ——
Les St. Georges ——
Clos de la Maréchale ——

Fixin

Gevrey-
Chambertin

Morey-ST. DENIS

Chambolle-
Musigny

Vougeot

Flagey-
Échezeaux

Vosne-Romanée

NUITS-ST. GEORGES

Prémeaux

Comblanchien

Corgoloin

CÔTE DE BEAUNE

Principal Vinyards of **CÔTE
DE
NUITS**

FRANCE

0   1   2   3
Miles

The Côte de Nuits
and Its Regal Reds

THE Côte de Nuits vineyards begin near the village of Fixin and extend southward along the Golden Slope for a good dozen miles, down to a stone quarry just below Nuits-Saint-Georges, its biggest town, from which the Côte de Nuits takes its name. Within its carefully defined limits are some of the greatest vineyards in the world.

Making wine from even the greatest vineyards, however, does not always mean success. Too many things can ruin the wine. There are parasites such as the phylloxera and diseases such as mildew, which can destroy the vineyard. Insects are now and then so voracious that an entire crop is ruined. Back in the fifteenth century all men were ordered to go to confession and give up swearing so that the insects would go away, and in the following century insects were formally excommunicated and banished to the woods. Today copper sulphate is used to save the vine and its grapes.

There are dangers in the natural growing process. The vines pass through three crucial stages each season: wine-growers watch the grapes closely when the new shoots sprout, when the vine flowers, and when the grapes are ripe, just before harvest. At each step they can assess the possible quality of the vintage to come.

A late frost in April or May, a beating rain or high wind

during the summer, a drumming hail in August, or an early frost in September can undo the year's work. A wet summer may rot the grapes, a dry one keep them small. And yet weather quirks can upset all predictions. On the 6th of September in 1948 there was gloom all along the Golden Slope. Every wine-grower was convinced that the vintage would be bad, for the summer had been wet and cloudy. The grapes were small on the vines. But on the 7th the sun came out, shining bright and hot for three full weeks, and the grapes filled. The 1948 vintage was suddenly turned into a very good year, the fourth good one in a row.

Hail is the greatest danger. The great vineyards are parcelled into small sections, one man owning several in different areas, in the hope that hail will not destroy them all. Early hail is perhaps the most dangerous, for the stones break off the young sprouts. The vines may grow again, but not in time to produce mature grapes. The wine-growers call such small, green grapes as are produced *verjus*.

Quirks of weather and pestilence, though they occur in any vineyard, and to many other crops besides grapes, are particularly important on the Côte de Nuits. In the Côte de Nuits are grown grapes that cannot grow successfully in a more extreme climate. If they were planted farther north, the character of the wine would change, becoming thin and hard. And when Pinot varieties are planted farther south, the wine produced is softer and less robust. In much warmer climates, too much sun or rain destroys the delicate grape. You cannot grow the Pinot Noir easily in the Côte de Nuits, or grow it well anywhere else. It is in this tiny area that the Pinot produces its greatest wines. And only certain sections have the soil that can bring the supreme from the vines. This is why the great vineyards are so small, why the wine from one spot is good, and that from ten feet away only average.

On the Côte de Nuits the vineyards are called *climats*

(climates) for this very reason. Each one is slightly different in exposure, drainage, and soil, composing a different "climate." The name has spread to all the vineyards of the Golden Slope.

All the great *climats* face southeast on the Côte de Nuits, where the dawn sun hits the vineyards, drawing moisture up through the vines. The vineyards are on a slope so that the hottest noon sun strikes the plants at an angle. Farther south the vines would wither; farther north, the sun would not be hot enough. With such extremes in such a limited district, where a little too much or a shade too little can ruin a vintage, it is no wonder that the wine-growers talk about their vineyards in terms of music or of making love. They are talking about an art.

Nobody knows for sure why the vineyard of Clos de Bèze should be better than that of Charmes-Chambertin, just next to it, but you can taste the difference in the wine. It may be the tilt of the soil, the way the rain hits it, the composition of the soil itself; but part of it is the man who makes the wine.

A careful and conscientious wine-grower will make better wine than a careless, sloppy one, but the distinction is probably more subtle. Burgundians like to point to the fact that a race horse will run better for one trainer than another, that a great orchestra will sound different in the hands of various conductors. Just as children take on the mannerisms of their parents, a wine seems to pick up some of the character of the man who makes it. When Burgundians are tasting wines together, they sometimes joke about whether the picker during harvest was a virgin, a mother, or an old woman, for it used to be believed that such things made a difference. For generations, women were rarely allowed in the wine cellars, a pregnant woman never.

When all the minor differences in wine-growing and wine-making reach a conclusion in a particular bottle, that wine will have a character all its own, distinct and recognizable. Tasting one wine against another, anyone can tell the difference between a Côte de Nuits and a Côte de Beaune between a Chambertin and a Musigny.

FIXIN

The northernmost of the eight communes of the Côte de Nuits is Fixin, just above Gevrey-Chambertin. Its wines are similar to those of its famous neighbour, the vineyards having much the same exposure and soil. But out on the highway, at the lane that leads back to the town, a large sign boasts, not of the wines, but of a statue of Napoleon. Executed by Rude, the statue, called the *Awakening of Napoleon*, shows the great man just about to open his eyes, a dead eagle at his feet. It portrays the legend that Napoleon will come to life again almost any day now. It stands in a glade up in the woods behind the town, near a great avenue of pine trees leading to a Napoleon museum. The building is a replica of the house on St. Helena where he died, reproduced in two-thirds of its actual size.

The centre of tourist interest may well be this small museum, but the centre of local activity revolves around a circular building containing a circular pool, some fifteen feet across. It is the town *lavoir*, a laundry pool that is short of water these days, where the women of the town gather to wash their clothes and exchange gossip, some of the most ribald in the world. Near the *lavoir* is one of the oldest churches in the region, built in the eleventh century, with tombstones askew in the churchyard, and looking as if it had been excavated, not constructed.

The wines from the vineyards near Fixin have a deep red colour and a strong bouquet. Because of their high alcoholic content, they develop with age. When well made, they can almost equal the great wines of Gevrey-Chambertin. The wines from the Outstanding Vineyard, Clos de la Perrière, not quite 12 acres in size, are better than the wine from such First-Growth Chambertin vineyards as Charmes or Chapelle.

FIXIN

OUTSTANDING VINEYARD (*Tête de Cuvée*)

	acres
CLOS DE LA PERRIÈRE	12.–

FIRST VINEYARDS (*Premières Cuvées*)

CLOS DU CHAPITRE	11.25
Les Hervelets	9.+

Note: Names listed in capitals indicate vineyards whose wines are likely to be found exported.

GEVREY AND ITS CHAMBERTIN

The town of Gevrey-Chambertin lies nearly a mile back from the main road, on what is hardly more than a crossroad, with a few short side streets now and then breaking the jagged line made by stone walls and stone house fronts. The building line is the gutter, but over the walls or through the grilled gates there is now and then a glimpse of a large old house. Most of the houses belong to the winegrowers, and each has its wine cellar underneath, low and vaulted.

Many of the growers still sell their wines in barrels to the shippers, but some have taken to tending and bottling their own wine and sell it under their own label. This practice of estate bottling is called "*mise du domaine*" in French, and the phrase "*Mis en Bouteilles par le Propriétaire*," or a variant appears on the label.

It is at Gevrey where the "*Route des Grands Crus*," the road of the great growths, begins. Wandering south along the Golden Slope, the road passes through the greatest vineyards of Burgundy. Until recently, the vineyard road was little more than a wagon track rutted by the vineyard carts, muddy after a rain, dusty in hot weather. This spring, the departmental prefect ordered the widening and repaving of the road to encourage tourists to drive through the fabulous tracts. Far from being pleased at the improvement, vineyard owners were outraged, for it meant sacrificing a yard's width of precious vines, the equivalent of a barrel of wine for every few hundred feet of vineyard bordering the road. But today it is a lovely drive, with an old iron cross at nearly every turn to bring good luck. Down this road to the south, is the great vineyard that gives Gevrey its second name, the *Tête de Cuvée* of Chambertin. The phrase can be translated as "Outstanding Vineyard," or "Outstanding Growth."

Not too long ago practically every vineyard within the commune had Chambertin added to its name. To protect their greatest wines, the owners of the best growths formed an association in the 1930's and passed a ruling that limited the use of the name Chambertin to the two greatest vineyards, Le Chambertin and Chambertin Clos de Bèze, and those immediately adjacent to them. Latricières, Mazoyères, Charmes, Mazys, Ruchottes, Griotte, and Chapelle can also legally add Chambertin to their names.

All the confusion began shortly after the year 630, when Almagaire, Duke of Burgundy, gave some land to the local Abbot of Bèze. The abbot increased the size of the vineyard that was already there, and walled it. Some six hundred years later the adjoining field was made into a vineyard and called Champ Bertin, after its peasant owner. The two vineyards were eventually joined together and were finally bought by a man named Jobert. He followed custom by adding Chambertin to his name, and his efforts made the wine famous. Its fame rests on the less than 340 barrels produced each year by the two vineyards, now split up between some two dozen proprietors.

Chambertin is one of the greatest red Burgundies, and its vineyards are farther north than those of any of its peers. Along the Golden Slope, Chambertin is called "*Le Grand Seigneur*," and nobody disputes the title, perhaps out of respect for Napoleon, who called it his favourite wine.

Even without latitude and Napoleon, Chambertin would be a glorious wine. Burgundians talk of its *robe*, or deep, rich, red colour, and of its balance and fullness, all its various taste characteristics blending to make a majestic unity. Its tremendous nose—*bouquet* is too delicate a word—makes it a veritable Cyrano. When you have drunk Chambertin, you remember it.

On the way out of town on the Route des Grands Crus, the great vineyards begin just beyond the last house, which belongs to Mme Drouhin-Laroze, a vineyard-owner in Clos de Bèze, Latricières-Chambertin, and some of the lesser vineyards. On the right is Mazys, followed by Clos de Bèze, Chambertin, and Latricières—last but not least. On the left are Chapelle, Griotte, Charmes, and Mazoyères, the commune boundary separating these vineyards from those of Morey, to the south.

The two Outstanding Vineyards gain their greatness from the soil and its exposure to the sun, their honour and good name protected by the *Appellation Contrôlée*. Nearby vineyards that do not have the same blessings of soil and exposure, and are not allowed to add Chambertin to their names are Les Varoilles, Clos Saint-Jacques, Fouchère, Étournelles, and Cazetiers. Clos Saint-Jacques and Les

Varoilles must be sold with the name of the commune, Gevrey-Chambertin, preceding it. Almost as good as the seven permitted to add Chambertin to their names, and classed with them as "*Premières Cuvées*," or "First Vineyards," it is regrettable that these two, at least, are not also permitted to add the glorious vineyard name to their own. All have less distinction than the two greatest ones, rarely rising to the level of Chambertin or Clos de Bèze.

The largest and best producer of Clos de Bèze is Pierre Damoy, whose relatives own the second-largest grocery chain stores in France. He sells a good part of his wine to shippers, particularly in bad years, but recently he has gone increasingly into estate bottling, a practice that is slowly being extended all along the Côte.

Two of the best-known producers of Chambertin are A. Rousseau, one of the first to dare to go into estate bottling, and Dr. Marion, one of the greatest surgeons in France. His section produces the Chambertin of greatest finesse. Leon Camus is another large producer of excellent wines, but only a portion is estate-bottled. The good shipper, J. H. Remy of Morey-Saint-Denis, owns still another large section.

An English teacher at Chalon-sur-Saône, a man named Deschamps, rode the bus that travels along the main highway to be near his vineyards on the week-ends and on Thursdays, the French school holidays. He died in 1950, and now his widow continues to produce about one hundred cases of Chambertin each year, and also owns all of Varoilles, which gives some idea of how widely holdings are spread, how varied are the winegrowers. The Comte de Moucheron, for instance, who owns a château in Meursault, owns part of the Clos Saint-Jacques.

Many of the lucky owners of the *Têtes de Cuvées* also own parcels of first and second *cuvées*. The Chambertin of Rousseau, for instance, should not be confused with Rousseau

GEVREY-CHAMBERTIN

OUTSTANDING VINEYARDS (*Têtes de Cuvées*)

	acres
Le CHAMBERTIN	32.5
Le CLOS DE BÈZE	37.5

FIRST VINEYARDS (*Premières Cuvées*)

LATRICIÈRES	17.5
MAZYS or MAZIS	21.5
MAZOYÈRES	37.5
CHARMES	31.
RUCHOTTES and the CLOS DES RUCHOTTES	8.5
GRIOTTE	7.5
CHAPELLE	20.
CLOS SAINT-JACQUES	17.5
VAROILLES	15.
Fouchère	2.5
Étournelles	5.
Cazetiers	20.

SECOND VINEYARDS (*Deuxièmes Cuvées*)

Gémeaux	5.
Échézeaux	9.
Lavaut	24.
Combe au Moine	5.5
Carougeot	14.

Note: Names listed in capitals indicate vineyards whose wines are likely to be found exported.

Charmes-Chambertin, or with Rousseau Gevrey-Chambertin, the last being the generic term for all the wines of the commune. In this respect, it is interesting to note that some of the lesser vineyards are more famous than the two *Têtes*, largely because lesser wines are much cheaper in price and there are more of them. The two great vineyards produce only about 6,000 cases in a good year like 1947 or '48, the splendid wine of '49 being about half that in quantity. The quality of wine varies tremendously in the various communes along the Golden Slope, the two Outstanding Growths of Chambertin, for instance, being vastly superior to such generic wines as those sold simply as Gevrey-Chambertin.

Wine quality also depends enormously on the age of the vines, the older the better, although the yield decreases. New vines make small wines. Today the majority of the vines of the great Gevrey vineyards are in their prime, thirty years old, and the introduction of rotation planting will tend to keep their wines on a high level. The official yield for the commune is about 264 gallons to the acre; a fairly representative figure for much of Burgundy. This means that each acre yields about 100 cases of wine, when evaporation and loss in handling are taken into account. Of the great wines, most of them are drunk in the large cities of the world. In the village of Gevrey itself you can't find a bottle of the *Têtes de Cuvées* in either of the local restaurants and it is even hard to get one of the few bottles of the *Premières Cuvées*. Many of the growers rarely drink their own wines. They are too valuable.

MOREY-SAINT-DENIS

La Route des Grands Crus runs straight into Morey after passing the great vineyards of Gevrey-Chambertin. Morey is even smaller than its neighbour, with a shady square, and its few houses huddled round it like frightened children clinging to the skirts of the mother. On the right is a sandy stone wall in excellent repair, on which are the names of Clos des Lambrays and Clos de Tart, the great wines of the commune.

In the seventh century a nunnery was founded here, between the two monasteries of Bèze and Vougeot. Like the monks, the nuns started a vineyard, calling it Clos de Tart. Today the steep vineyard is owned by a shipper from Mâcon, J. Mommessin, while the neighbouring Clos des Lambrays, which had seventy-four owners in the early part of the nineteenth century, now belongs to one—big, burly, jovial Mme Cosson. This magnificent vineyard is a heritage from the late M. de Bahèzre, who spent the better part of his life reassembling the vineyard.

One of the least known great wines of the Côte d'Or is the Clos des Lambrays. Its 22 acres are tilled with exceptional care by Màdame Cosson, its sole owner, who believes in using small sticks of dynamite to shake the soil, thus allowing it to breathe. She produces a full-bodied, sturdy wine representative of the great qualities sought in Burgundy.

The wines of this commune are the forgotten wines of the Côte de Nuits, their magnificence almost unknown. There are intermediate years in wine, vintages overshadowed and forgotten because the preceding and following ones were so exceptional. The same thing happens to vineyards. Morey-Saint-Denis vineyards are intermediate because of their famous neighbours north and south, and yet its wines are among the best values in Burgundy, selling at lower prices than the much-bid-for wines of Gevrey or Chambolle.

Until the laws governing *Appellation d'Origine* were passed Morey wines went to market under the names of their neighbours—one reason why they are almost unknown. Morey long ago added Saint-Denis to its name, a

vineyard that is today only classed as a *Première Cuvée.*
The wine of Clos Saint-Denis is lighter than its peer, Clos de
la Roche, a full, rich wine.

The great wines of the commune, Clos de Tart and
Lambrays are strong, heavy, and sturdy. They take from

MOREY-SAINT-DENIS

Outstanding Vineyards (*Têtes de Cuvées*)

	acres
CLOS DES LAMBRAYS	22.
CLOS DE TART	17.5
BONNES-MARES (see Chambolle)	5.

First Vineyards (*Premières Cuvées*)

CLOS DE LA ROCHE	11.
CLOS SAINT-DENIS	5.
Calouère	3.
Les Chabiots	5.
Les Charnières	6.
Les Chenevery	8.
Aux Cheseaux	6.
Clos des Ormes	11.
Les Faconnières	4.5
Les Fremières	6.
Les Millandes	11.
Les Mochamps	6.
Monts-Luisants (white wine)	8.
Morey	8.
CLOS SORBET	8.

Note: Names listed in capitals indicate vineyards whose wines are likely to be
found exported.

ten to twenty years to mature, depending on the amount of tannin. Another magnificent vineyard is Les Bonnes-Mares, but as only a fifth of it is within the commune, the wine is usually associated with Chambolle.

It is here that the character of the wines of the Côte de Nuits makes a great change. That from the Clos Saint-Denis is a bridge between the sturdiness of the Moreys and the soft, elegant distinction of the Bonnes-Mares, Musignys, and other wines from the adjoining commune of Chambolle.

The vineyards are slightly farther south, the exposure to the sun is slightly different because of the steeper slope, the soil is slightly different in composition and drainage, and these infinitesimal variations make a pronounced change in the wines. It is in Morey-Saint-Denis that one begins to discover the wonder there is in wine.

CHAMBOLLE-MUSIGNY

Past the vineyard of Bonnes-Mares, the vineyard road swings right into the town of Chambolle, tucked under the highest mountain of the Golden Slope. Flanked on the north by a craggy outcrop, the town has the feeling of a mountain village.

The main street runs straight back to the wall and park surrounding the Château de Chambolle-Musigny, a large rectangular building in the massive nineteenth-century style, built over a splendid series of vast cellars and handsome vat rooms. The 1950 and 1951 vintages are managed by the author. The house was used as a barracks in the last war, first by the Germans, and then successively by the French and Americans. Near it is a modern structure whose owner also calls his building Château de Chambolle-

Musigny. The Mugnier family, who have owned the old château for nearly a hundred years, maintain that the owner of the modern building has no right to call his property Château de Chambolle-Musigny, which creates confusion.

Les Bonnes-Mares is north of the town. It produces wines softer than those from Morey, possessing a combination of delicacy and the more robust qualities of those to the north. One of the finest of Burgundies, still unknown and little appreciated, it overshadows all the wines of the other Côte, that of Beaune, with the exception of Corton, more famous than Bonnes-Mares, but its equal in quality.

As you drive east out of Chambolle toward the main road, the vineyards produce wines noted for supreme delicacy. The lane swings right and heads south, the crossing marked by an old stone cross, and on your right hand are the Musigny and the Petits-Musigny vineyards, producing wines known simply as Musigny. The vineyard road is downhill from these great vineyards, separating them from plantations that are only slightly less magnificent, the greatest of which is Les Amoureuses. The name means "Women in Love," and Burgundians feel that it is one of the loveliest vineyard names of the Golden Slope. Its wines are reminiscent of the bouquet and delicacy of the vineyard across the road.

Musigny has a glorious perfume and a lingering bouquet; it is truly one of the great wines of Burgundy, and the least masculine of them all. Its charm is feminine. The largest owner is the Comte de Voguë, related to the Champagne family that owns Moët et Chandon—an example of how families who work in wine have holdings in other districts. Other large owners are the Domaine Mugnier and, to a smaller degree, Mme Adrien, who also are proprietors in Les Bonnes-Mares and in Les Amoureuses.

The Domaine Mugnier was one of the largest owners of

first-class vineyards in the Côte de Nuits. In addition to its large holdings in Chambolle-Musigny, others include a section of Clos Vougeot and sections in Prémeaux of Nuits-Saint-Georges. It is one of the few Burgundy domains large enough to employ a *régisseur*. Most of its wines, beginning with the 1950 vintage, were estate-bottled, their care in the hands of a man trained in the art and theory of wine-making by Henri Gouges, one of Burgundy's greatest champions. Now, unfortunately, in the hands of a shipper, the wines have lost their reliability.

Below Les Amoureuses is a steep bank that drops down to a narrow plateau, then plunges down another hundred feet to the valley floor, dividing the slope into four levels in all. It is here that the Vouge River chooses to burst out of the mountainside, to wander down across the valley. Standing

CHAMBOLLE-MUSIGNY

OUTSTANDING VINEYARDS (*Têtes de Cuvées*)

	acres
Les MUSIGNY	25.
Les BONNES-MARES	34.

FIRST VINEYARDS (*Premières Cuvées*)

Les AMOUREUSES	13.5
Les Baudes	9.
Les Charmes	14.5
La Combe d'Orveau	12.5
Les Cras	10.5
Les Fuées	15.5
Les Gruenchers	7.5
Les Noirots	7.5
Les Sentiers	12.5

Note: Names listed in capitals indicate vineyards whose wines are likely to be found exported.

on the plateau above its mouth, you can look southeast and see the whole of the Clos Vougeot spread out below you. The main valley road bounds the walled vineyard on the east; the vineyard road bounds it on the west. Toward the back, the turrets of the château glint yellow in the sunlight, while the great vineyards of Musigny slant up the slope behind you. For many, here lies the heart of Burgundy.

It is in Chambolle-Musigny that you again notice the startling differences in the wines of Burgundy. The tiny plots produce wines of widely different character. It is in the Musignys that you find an outstanding delicacy, a contrast that is unexpected, and the wine is always a pleasant surprise.

VOUGEOT AND ITS CLOS

The river Vouge flows out of the hill near the vineyards of Vougeot, watering and naming them at once. From the vineyard road on the high land of Le Musigny, you can look across to the main highway running through its avenue of trees, the buildings of the town along its length, ending near the vineyard wall. The town now claims less than two hundred inhabitants, but there were many more working to dry the swampy lands when the monks moved in and began building their monastery in the twelfth century. They named their order, the Cistercian, after the reeds growing on the low land, and perhaps each one felt like a resurrection of Moses, an idea which must have been the root of many droll stories, in monk's Latin.

The Cistercians set out their vineyard on the slopes above their monastery, and its 125 acres then composed the largest in Burgundy. It still is the biggest of the first-class plantations. Once the monastery was finished, a great wall was thrown around the vineyards, and toward the back of the enclosed area it was decided to build a castle and a press house. The monk who was entrusted with designing it was so proud of his efforts that he signed the plans before taking them to the abbot, and that worthy resented the act. The plans were turned over to another monk for doctoring and were ruined. The abbot called in the architect, showed him the botched plans, and ordered the castle to be built as shown with all the flaws and errors intact, as punishment for his sin of pride in signing the plans. The architect is said to have died on the spot, out of mortification, but the abbot had no trouble in finding others to push the building through. The building is all that is left of the ancient monastery.

It was not finished until the fifteenth century, and has been constantly repaired ever since. Since the Second World War nearly ten million francs have gone into restoring the building, which had been used as a billet by the Germans during the occupation, and later as a prison camp by the Americans. At one point the disgruntled German prisoners tried to burn up the centuries-old presses, claiming they needed the wood for fires. The caretaker went hotfoot to the American commander, who slapped up a barbed-wire barricade around the massive machines. The press levers are enormous chestnut trees squared roughly with the axe, held in place by other squared tree trunks only slightly smaller.

The money for restoration came in through contributions to the *Chevaliers du Tastevin*, Burgundy's selling organization, made up of growers, shippers, and various dignitaries interested in wine. The order bought the castle for their meetings, and every other month they give themselves a big dinner, dressed up in red robes and square black hats, with silver *tastevins* dangling from a red and orange ribbon looped around their necks.

To hear Burgundians tell it, the wall around the Clos was almost as big an effort as the Great Wall of China, for it took more than a hundred years to build. Between eight and ten feet high, it is built of split stone. Along the rear section on the inside are espaliered fruit trees; along the short terraced drive to the castle itself is the tombstone of one Léonce Boquet, who united the vineyard into a single domain in the nineteenth century. Today the Clos is split up among more than fifty owners.

Rose bushes are planted along the drive, and as you walk up to the great doors and pull the vine root at the end of the bell-pull chain, the smell of the roses is in your nostrils. The caretaker's hound barks at the clanging and pelts across the yellow gravel of the court, waiting for the caretaker to open the gates and let you in. The great roofs of the older buildings to the back and on the right come slanting down almost to the ground itself, supported by heavy, timbered posts painted a purplish red, the colour of wine.

Across the court is the great room that used to be a storage shed for casks, where as many as five hundred members of the Tastevin can eat and drink, shouting out between songs and mouthfuls the slogan of their order: "Never in vain, always in wine." The pillars of the great hall are giant stone monoliths, tapering up some twenty feet to enormous beams and hanging on the pillars are the leather back-baskets formerly used for gathering grapes. Each basket is decorated with a painted coat of arms and dates of the most famous vintage years, the oldest being 1108.

From this walled earth comes another great Burgundy, a wine so superlative that it is a tradition for passing regiments of the French Army to salute the vines. When Napoleon once ordered some of the wine to be taken to him, the crusty guardian is said to have replied: "If he wants to taste this glorious wine, let him come here and drink it." It will always be one of the great Burgundies, magnificently full and perfumed, with a velvety robe and splendid balance.

But the wine varies enormously. Clos Vougeot is as large

as some of the vineyards that produce the great First Growths of Bordeaux, but there all the wine is blended by the single owner, here the wine is made by over fifty different owners. Also, the wine varies with the soil, and with its makers. Each man decides when his section is to be picked and when the grapes shall be pressed. In his own cellar he supervises the wine-making, decides when it shall be drawn off the lees, when it shall be bottled, and so forth. To see how any single wine can vary, all one need do is taste various bottles made by different men in the same year.

The wine also varies with the soil. Clos Vougeot used to be divided into three growths, the best on the sloping land up behind the castle, near the back wall. Centuries ago wine from this section was reserved by the abbot for gifts to crowned heads and princes of the Church. The farthest corner is called Musigny de Clos Vougeot, because it is nearest the Chambolle vineyards. This is owned by Louis Gros.

The top third of the vineyard also includes sections known as Garenne, Plante Chamel, Plante Abbé, Montiottes Hautes, Chioures, Quartier de Marci Haut, and the Grand and Petit Maupertuis. The middle section, whose wine is only slightly less glorious than that from the top, has always commanded high prices. The sections are: Dix Journaux, the *journaux* being an old vineyard measure; Baudes Bas; and Baudes-Saint-Martin. Even the wines from the lowest section, which are excellent in good years, sell for high prices. The sections are: Montiottes Bas, Quatorze Journaux, Baudes Bas, and Baudes-Saint-Martin. The various owners live up and down the whole length of the Côte d'Or, from Gevrey in the north and down even as far as Chalon and Mâcon, for being the owner of a slice of Clos Vougeot is a sign of true wine nobility. Every Burgundian aspires to that.

Wine from Clos Vougeot can be one of the greatest wines of Burgundy—yet much of what is produced is over-rated.

It is one of the most famous of the Côte de Nuits, as well known as Chambertin. Its wine has a distinct perfume, full and flowery, and often said to resemble that of violets. Like the other great Burgundies, it has been famous for centuries—eight of them. The toast of kings, the pride of princes, it has outlived them all. As long as wine is made in Burgundy, Clos Vougeot will be among the great.

Alphabetical List of
PRINCIPAL OWNERS IN THE
CLOS VOUGEOT

		ouvrées
Adrien	grower at Dijon	8
André, P.	shipper at Aloxe-Corton	26
Arnoux, Charles	grower at Vosne-Romanée	10
Capitan	grower at Ladoix-Serrigny	4
Champy Père & Fils	shipper at Beaune	52
Clair-Daü	grower at Marsannay	10
Drouhin, J.	shipper at Beaune	15
Drouhin-Laroze	grower at Gevrey-Chambertin	16
Engel, René	grower at Vosne-Romanée	32
Faiveley, J.	shipper at Nuits-St.-Georges	21
Fortier, F.	grower at Vosne-Romanée	4
Gouroux-Frères	grower at Flagey-Échézeaux	22
Grivelet-Cusset	shipper at Nuits-St.-Georges	15
Grivot, G.	grower at Vosne-Romanée	45
Gros, Louis	grower at Vosne-Romanée	56
Guichard-Potheret	shipper at Chalon s/Saône	5
L'Héritier-Guyot	shipper at Dijon	24
Jaboulet-Vercherre	shipper at Pommard	15
Jaffelin	shipper at Beaune	15
Laymarie	shipper at Éghezée (Belgium)	6
Lejay-Lagoutte	shipper at Dijon	40

		ouvrées
Missey, P.	shipper at Dijon	50
Mongeard-Mugneret	grower at Flagey-Échézeaux	6
Widow Mongeard	grower at Vougeot	10
Morin, J.	shipper at Nuits-St.-Georges	144
Mugneret, E.	grower at Vosne-Romanée	8
Mugnier	grower at Chambolle-Musigny	10
Widow Noëllat	grower at Vosne-Romanée	60
Ponnelle, P.	shipper at Beaune	4
Roumier	grower at Chambolle-Musigny	8

The *ouvrée* is an old Burgundian measure still widely used in the Côte d'Or. There are 25 ouvrées to a hectare, and a hectare is 2.4 acres, which means that there are about 10 ouvrées in an acre.

Just outside the walls, near the entrance of the castle, is the vineyard of La Vigne-Blanche, known as Clos Blanc de Vougeot. It produces white wine, made from the Chardonnay grape. The vineyard is very small, less than five acres in all, and most of it is owned by L'Héritier-Guyot, who is also a maker of cassis. The wine is very dry and flavoursome, and while it is not so outstanding as the red, it can be compared to the lesser wines of Corton, down in the Côte de Beaune.

FLAGEY-ECHÉZEAUX

The vineyard road slants down the hill from the vineyards of Chambolle, and along behind the rear wall of Clos Vougeot. The wall bends off to the left, but the road cuts straight, and to the right is the vineyard of Grands-Échézeaux. The great vineyards are still to the right of *La Route des Grands Crus*. The town is across the main highway, down by the railway, important only because the vineyards have been included in its commune.

The wine from Grands-Échézeaux is little known, and it

has been said that it is because the name, which sounds like a drunk's exclamation, "esh-eh-zo," is so hard to pronounce. This is as foolish a reason as any, the wines being excellent values, intermediates like those from Morey. The wines are a bridge between the full and sturdy Vougeots and the lighter, more delicate wines of Vosne-Romanée, the commune just to the south. They have great balance and distinction and are outstandingly good for the most part, largely because no one has been tempted to tamper with a wine so little in demand.

The ten first *cuvées* are never sold under the name of the *climat*, or vineyard, but always as Échézeaux, without

FLAGEY-ÉCHÉZEAUX

OUTSTANDING VINEYARDS (*Têtes de Cuvées*)

	acres
Les GRANDS-ÉCHÉZEAUX	23.
Les ÉCHÉZEAUX	106.

FIRST VINEYARDS (*Premières Cuvées*)*

	acres
Les BEAUX-MONTS or BEAUMONTS	14.
Champs-Traversins	9.
Clos Saint-Denis	4.5
Les Cruots or Vignes-Blanches	8.
Les Loachausses	10.
En Orveau	25.
Les Poullaillières	12.5
Les Quartiers de Nuits	6.
Les Rouges-du-Bas	10.
Les Treux	12.5

Note: Names listed in capitals indicate vineyards whose wines are likely to be found exported.

* These wines may be also sold as Vosne-Romanée.

Grands as a prefix. They combine body and strength as do all the other Côte de Nuits wines, improve considerably with age, and are closer to the Vosne-Romanée wines than to those from Clos Vougeot.

The Domaine de la Romanée-Conti is one of the owners of Grands-Échézeaux; René Engel also owns a section, and others are Louis Gros, and men named Groffier, Jayer, and Mugneret. Engel is a writer on the wines of France, his studies, essays, and columns appearing in various French wine journals, and he is highly respected among the Burgundians who make the wines.

The intermediate wines are particularly popular with those wine-lovers who want outstanding wines at reasonable prices even though they can afford the more famous and more expensive Burgundies. These intermediaries of the Côte de Nuits are usually better wines than any of those from the Côte de Beaune, with the exception of the great Cortons. The Pommards and Volnays rarely reach the excellence of these Grands-Échézeaux and Moreys. These are wines for those impressed by what is in the bottle, not by the label on it.

VOSNE-ROMANÉE

The vineyard road crosses the boundary of Vosne-Romanée scarcely a hundred yards from the wall surrounding Clos Vougeot. This commune produces more great wines than any other, and the fewest small ones, and yet its best vineyards total less than 150 acres. The wines from these are the most expensive on earth, and wine-lovers revel in their greatness. Even their names are a source of delight, and P. Morton Shand, once said they were "the mingling of velvet and satin in a bottle."

The greatest of the great is Romanée-Conti, scarcely $4\frac{1}{2}$ acres in size, which was bought in 1868 by the ancestors of the present owners for 330,000 gold francs, a sum equal then to some £14,000. It is the most precious vineyard in the world. Mme de Pompadour, the mistress of Louis XV, once tried to buy it, but it went to the Prince of Conti, who had the King's ear as director of secret diplomacy.

Closely following with this magnificent vineyard are La Tâche, a vineyard only 3½ acres in size, and La Romanée, which is only 2 acres in all. The biggest of the greats is Le Richebourg, almost 20 acres, the largest owners being Louis Gros, the Domaine de la Romanée-Conti, and Charles Noël-lat. The production of Richebourg is too small for the demand, while bottles are so rare from the smaller vineyards that drinking the wine is always a great event.

The largest owner in Vosne-Romanée is the Domaine de la Romanée-Conti, which takes its name from the vineyard that is its prize. The Domaine also owns all of La Tâche, which is better known as a *climat* than the actual commune of Vosne-Romanée and never carries the parish name on the bottle. The Domaine owns parts of Grands-Échézeaux as well, in addition to its portion of Le Richebourg. La Romanée is owned by the shipping firm of Liger-Belair.

The Domaine de la Romanée-Conti is owned by M. de Vilaine, who lives near Vichy, and who was the first in Burgundy to begin bottling his own wines. His introduction of estate bottling is revolutionizing the wine industry of Burgundy. His wines have set the standards for all great Burgundies.

Shortly after the phylloxera struck, in the last decades of the nineteenth century, growers began grafting vines on American stocks. The Domaine refused to, and until 1946 the gnarled old roots produced wine from the pre-phylloxera vines. They were preserved through constant care, but the war made this difficult, the yield was becoming smaller each year, and the Domaine was forced to succumb to the modern practice of grafting. Previously other old-fashioned and proudly successful methods were clung to, such as making a mulch of the old vines. But disease in the cuttings used for mulch ended this practice also, and now the Domaine uses fertilizers and manures like the other growers. The tenacity of the Domaine in holding to old ways has kept the wine great, and the magnificent care lavished on the vineyards continues to produce some of the outstanding wines of the world.

The greatness of the wines would lead you to expect that the cellars of the Domaine would have marble columns and perhaps a choir chanting in one corner, but the buildings in Vosne are as modest as the wines are great. The house stands at the head of a walled court, two long *chais* forming the sides, with the immaculate cellars underneath. M. and Mme Clin live in the house, acting as *régisseurs*. And in the centre of the court there is usually a manure pile. Here the wine and its needs are all-important, and æsthetic considerations are incidental.

Behind the cellar where the new wine is kept are two back cellars, where in the racks are some of the greatest bottles in the world. Here you can see the tradition behind a great label. As the Domaine has always bottled all its wine, a wine-lover opens a Romanée-Conti with the respect and anticipation he has gained through years of tasting. Romanée-Contis, more than any other wine, often reach the ultimate in absolute perfection due to the combinations of bouquet, flavour, body delicacy, and intensity. The connoisseur knows that the wine will be great, and he is in a frame of mind to appreciate the fine old wine, prepared for its magnificence. This is why these two back cellars are thought of with such awe and delight, for the Domaine has all the great bottles of the splendid vintages that are left.

Because of these bottles, other growers have begun estate bottling of at least part of their production. Formerly much of it was sold in the barrel to restaurant-owners in Belgium or Switzerland, who made annual trips to the vineyards to replenish their cellars. Shippers bought much of it, and most of the bottles went to Belgium, which is the largest buyer of Burgundy in the world, followed closely by Switzerland. The only bottles of the great Romanées that got out to the rest of the world came from the cellars of the Domaine. Today part of the wines from Gros and Noëllat are being estate-bottled, thanks largely to the example set by the Domaine de la Romanée-Conti.

These great wines of Vosne-Romanée are, to many, the supreme examples of great Burgundy. Their balance is magnificent, no one characteristic standing out, but all being superb, and together forming a wine that has a perfection almost unequalled. All are big, sturdy, full-bodied, with a velvety richness and the characteristic of acquiring a splendid nose with age. Le Richebourg is perhaps the fullest. Romanée-Conti, La Romanée, and La Tâche being somewhat more delicate, in descending order. The only Burgundian equals of these are the two Chambertins, Le Musigny, Corton, and the best wines of Clos Vougeot.

But these are not all the great wines of Vosne-Romanée, for the first *cuvées* are outstanding. They are on a par with the Bonnes-Mares and Grands-Échézeaux, and often superior to many Clos Vougeots. The best of these are: Romanée-Saint-Vivant, Les Suchots, Les Beaumonts, Les Malconsorts, and La Grande-Rue. Here it is important to note that wines from Les Verroilles, an Outstanding Growth, are never sold under their own name, but always under the name of Richebourg, while the third *cuvées* are sold simply as Vosne-Romanée.

Perhaps the outstanding characteristics of the greatest wines of Vosne are their lingering bouquet and rich, full character, coupled with a certain delicateness. Some connoisseurs claim that the wines are sometimes too highly chaptalized, the sugar added making for an occasional aftertaste that errs in the direction of sweetness. But if this is a flaw, it is not detectable to most of us, lost in the greatness of what is there. The wines of Vosne are among the most glorious in the world, and a bottle is a symbol of the greatest magnificence in wine.

VOSNE-ROMANÉE

Outstanding Vineyards (*Têtes de Cuvées*)

	acres
ROMANÉE-CONTI	4.5
La ROMANÉE	2.
La TÂCHE	3.5
Les GAUDICHOTS	3.
Les RICHEBOURG	20.

First Vineyards (*Premières Cuvées*)

La ROMANÉE SAINT-VIVANT	24.
Les MALCONSORTS	15.
La GRANDE RUE	3.25
Les BEAUMONTS or BEAUX-MONTS	6.25
Les SUCHOTS	32.25
Aux Brûlées	10.
Aux Petits-Monts	7.
Aux Reignots	4.25

Second Vineyards (*Deuxièmes Cuvées*)

CLOS DES RÉAS	5.
AUX RÉAS	25.
La Colombière	11.
La Combe-Brûlée	4.
La Croix-Rameau	1.5

	acres
Cros-Parantoux	2.5
Les Damaudes	6.
Derrière-le-Four	2.5
Hauts-Beaux-Monts	10.
Hautes-Maizières	6.
Les Jacquines	9.
Aux Raviolles	15.

Note: Names listed in capitals indicate vineyards whose wines are likely to be found exported.

NUITS-SAINT-GEORGES
AND PRÉMEAUX

Nuits-Saint-Georges is the capital of the Côte de Nuits because it is the biggest town and produces more wine than any other. It lies on both sides of the highway and is the home of many shipping firms, whose contribution to the world has been Sparkling Burgundy and grape juice.

Sparkling Burgundy was created by shippers to help them compete with Champagne sales and fame. It is made of small wines that could not normally command a good price. These are seldom worth drinking and are poor values in markets where the duty is the same as that for Champagne.

Living in this den of shippers is Henri Gouges, a wine-grower who has spent his life combating fraud in Burgundy. He is one of those responsible for the success of the *Appellations d'Origine* laws, which have meant so much to the winegrowers of the Golden Slope. He leads a full life, being vice-president of the French National Committee of Fine Wine-producers, and a most important member of the Committee of Appellations, the group responsible for unearthing cases of wine fraud and seeing that they are prosecuted. Along with all this he has time to make some excellent wine.

The wines of Nuits are noted among the local wine-growers for firmness, meaning that they are full of texture, or "mordant," with so much body that you can actually take bites out of them. Dark in colour, as well as full in body, they mature slowly. Heavy in tannin, with age they acquire a remarkable consistency in body.

NUITS-SAINT-GEORGES

Outstanding Vineyards (*Têtes de Cuvées*)

	acres
Le SAINT-GEORGES	19.
Les BOUDOTS	16.
Les CAILLES	10.
Les PORRETS and CLOS DES PORRETS	17.5
Les PRULIERS	17.5
Les VAUCRAINS	15.
Les Cras	7.5
Les Murgers	12.5
Les Thorey and Clos de Thorey	15.

First Vineyards (*Premières Cuvées*)

Les Chabœufs	7.5
Les Chaignots	14.
Château Gris	6.
Les Perrières and Clos des Perrières	7.5
Les Poulettes	6.
Les Procès	5.
Les Richemonnes	6.
Les Roncières	5.
Rue de Chaux	7.5

Note: Names listed in capitals indicate vineyards whose wines are likely to be found exported.

NUITS-SAINT-GEORGES-PRÉMEAUX

	acres
CLOS DE LA MARÉCHALE	24.
LES DIDIERS-Saint-Georges	7.
CLOS DES FORÊTS-Saint-Georges	12.5
Les CORVÉES	20.
Les Corvées-Pagets	6.
Clos Saint-Marc	7.5
Clos des Argillières	12.5
CLOS ARLOT	19.5
Les Perdrix	8.

Note: Names listed in capitals indicate vineyards whose wines are likely to be found exported.

Just south of Nuits is the town of Prémeaux. Its vineyards have much the same characteristics as those of Nuits-Saint-Georges, the soil, the undersoil, and the sun being almost identical with that of the more famous commune. Because the wines are so similar, unlike those from other neighbouring communes along the Golden Slope, the *Appellation* laws specify that Prémeaux wines go to market bearing the name of Nuits-Saint-Georges. The best vineyards are Les Didiers, Les Clos des Forêts-Saint-Georges, Les Corvées, and the Clos de la Maréchale, its 24 acres making up the largest single vineyard in Burgundy belonging to one owner, the Domaine Mugnier. It was formerly called Clos des Fourches. Selections of the finest barrels are estate-bottled and sold under the name of the Domaine.

In addition to the above, the best vineyards around Nuits are: Les Saint-Georges, fullest in body; Les Vaucrains, noted for bouquet; Les Pruliers, which has both body and bouquet; and Les Cailles and Les Porrets, lighter and more delicate than the others. The commune name usually precedes that of the vineyard in Nuits-Saint-Georges.

Côte de Beaune:
Famous Reds and Montrachet

THE vineyards of the Côte de Beaune begin below the limestone quarry where the Côte de Nuits leaves off and continue on below Santenay, some fifteen miles in all. Most of the wines are red, getting steadily lighter in colour, smell, and taste until you reach Meursault. The name Meursault is derived from the Latin for mouse-jump, where red wines and white wines are produced in adjacent vineyards, only the jump of a mouse apart.

Beaune, the barrel city and wine capital of the Côte d'Or, with a population of some 10,000, gives its name to the slope stretching above and below it. It is an old walled town, full of shippers and their cellars, and the houses of the proprietors of many of the surrounding vineyards. Burgundians say that when the wine is in the vineyard, you must be a good lover, and when it's in the barrel, you must be a good father. Beaune, especially, is a town full of wine fathers, anxiously watching their barrels.

One of these fathers is Georges Yard, who owns part of Les Bressandes, a *Tête de Cuvée* of Corton, one of the best red wines of the Beaune Slope. Yard got into the art of wine-making because his father fell in love with Corton, moved down from Paris, and bought one of the vineyards that make it, perhaps to ensure a steady supply for himself. He left his

131

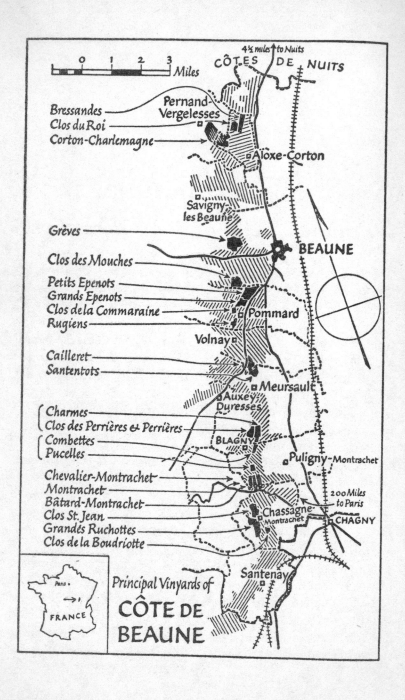

Principal Vinyards of
CÔTE DE BEAUNE

son the vineyard, and during the harvest Yard spends most of his time prowling among the vines, watching the grapes suspiciously.

In the old days the local lord set the day when the vineyards could be harvested, seeing to it that his own were finished first, there always being a shortage of pickers at harvest time. The monks, of course, outside the control of civil law, paid no attention to these edicts, and harvest time was one long glorious battle to get workers. It used to be fashionable for Parisians to go down to Burgundy for the harvest. The *vendange* is still a gay affair, the thirsty pickers drinking much new wine, for the sun is hot in the vineyards.

Today a board of wine-growers sets the dates for the picking of the grapes. Most wine-growers like to wait as long as possible after the permitted date, so that the grapes will contain as much sugar as possible. This is a risky time. Hail can destroy the whole crop, and even a high wind can knock the ripe grapes off the vines.

"Sometimes we're up all night," says Yard. "At the last possible moment I give the order, and the workers start combing the rows, bringing the bunches to the head of the rows in baskets, where men load them into bigger baskets, then dump them into lorries and haul them to the vats. Mine are downstairs."

Yard owns a house in the business section of Beaune, looking like a city house anywhere, wall to wall with the houses beside it. A garage door opens into a large room, two stories high, and on one side are the vats, two of them a dozen feet high, flanked by a large screw press, and the *égrapilloir*. Beneath are the cellars.

"A ripe grape has a bloom on the skin," Yard explains. "It looks like dust, and you can wipe it off with your finger. The bloom is made up of ferments containing yeasts. Nobody knows why they should cling to grapeskins, but they do, and one of them, *Saccharomyces ellipsoides*, helps change the sugar in the grape to alcohol. The stalk of the grape is full of tannin, and when the grapes don't have enough tannin themselves, some of the stalks are allowed to stay in the crushed grapes during the early fermentation. This usually takes four or five days here in Burgundy. After pressing, the juice is run into vats where it continues fermenting. This is usually over in a week and the wine is then drawn off into barrels. What's left in the press is called must. This is distilled, the result being called marc.''

Yard speaks of this pressing as a simple process. It is not. The sugar content of the grapes should produce at least $11\frac{1}{2}$ per cent of alcohol after ferment, and can produce as high as 15 or 16 per cent. The more alcohol the better, for this helps determine the keeping quality of the wine. Also, fermentation is a heating process which varies with the amount of alcohol, and the temperature must be carefully controlled. In the vats the liquid seethes and bubbles, sometimes quite violently.

"It is when the wine is in the *cuves* that we can get an idea of whether it's going to be any good or not. Before then, it's a matter of hopes and guesses. The liquid sinks to the bottom, and on the top is the must, a cap made of foam, and pulp and skins. When a wine is very active, chances are it will be good. When the must is lively, we say the wine is wearing its cap on the side of its head.

"Once the wine is in the barrel, its life begins. Quite literally. The wine is full of organisms, and these cells grow, changing the wine. Once it's in the casks, all we can do is guide it, and try to keep it from getting sick.''

In addition to the cells that help the wine to grow are many chemical actions that help to kill it. F. C. Lloyd, in his book *The Art and Technique of Wine*, lists five that have been clearly identified, and there are many others. *Acescence* fills the wine with specks of matter that change the alcohol into vinegar; *tourne* changes the wine to brown or purple, tiny bubbles appear on the surface, and the wine tastes as if it were watered; if the wine is low in alcohol or tannin, *graisse* destroys the unconverted sugar, and the wine tastes flat; *amertume* makes the wine bitter; *casse* makes it cloudy.

Yard shakes his head at all the dire evils that can affect the wine. "The big thing is the change to alcohol," he says. "During ferment, the grape sugar is transformed to carbonic acid and alcohol. In 1947 there was so much alcohol that the wines were too difficult to handle. The alcohol can chloroform the ferments, and too much paralyses them. Chances were you would get one very great barrel of wine, but two others would be terrible. I sold all my '47's to the shippers. There was no way of counting on the wine. You couldn't trust it."

He worries about his great red wines, and all during the five days or so of ferment they must be watched closely, checked every hour or so. This is easier for him than for most, because his apartment is on the top floor of the building, above the vats and the equipment.

It is a different matter for Claude and Pierre Ramonet, who live in Chassagne-Montrachet and own sections of the *Premiers Crus*, Ruchottes and Morgeot. Their father came to the Côte de Beaune in the nineteenth century and bought a small parcel of Ruchottes, and the two sons have gradually increased the holding through the years. The Ramonets make red and white wine, and their *cuves* are under various houses in the neighbourhood.

"We were up all night as long as the '47's were in the *cuves*," says Claude Ramonet. "Nobody about here has ever seen anything like it. The alcohol was 16 per cent, and some of it even a little more. We had to hold down the covers of the *cuves*, which were only half full. Usually we fill them to within a foot of the top, but the wine was so active we had to sit on it to keep it down."

135

It often happens, particularly as in 1947, that the wine contains so much sugar that it cannot all be changed to alcohol, the alcohol itself stopping the fermentation. This ruins the wine. Fermentation can be speeded up by heating, and one of the first processes in making wine is to get the *cuves* to the right temperature, for the wine has a second ferment once it is in the barrel. In the making of white wines, which differs from the making of red, the presence of excessive sugar in the wine, coupled with lack of acidity, causes it to turn brown when the air gets at it, and the wine becomes what is called maderized or oxydized.

"In making white wine, you leave the skins in contact with the juice if the grapes are white, but to make white wines from red grapes, as in Champagne, the juice does not remain in contact with the skins. By removing the skins you can make a white wine out of the same grapes you use to make red, although we use Pinot Chardonnay instead of Pinot Noir. To make *vin rosé*, you leave the skins of red grapes in the must for a time, then fish them out. *Rosé* wine is also made by blending red and white wine, but it's not the same thing."

For Ramonet and Yard, as well as many of the other wine-growers up and down both *côtes*, wine-making does not end until the wine is in the bottle. The wine changes and develops in the barrel, reaching what is called the point of fermentation three times a year. These coincide with the growth of the vine, occurring when new tendrils sprout, when the flower blossoms, and when the grapes are harvested. The seasons act on the barrelled wine in exactly the same ways they act on the grapes. This point of fermentation can be tasted in the wine, and it is at these times that adverse chemical reactions are most likely to take place.

Once bottled, the wine is known as *vin vieux*, "old wine," and it begins a life of its own, some air getting into the wine through the cork and enabling the wine bacteria to continue developing. Once the wine is in the bottle, the wine-growers can do nothing about it, and while they watch the wine as it ages, hoping for the best, they feel a certain remoteness toward it.

In Burgundy, wine is made neither for profit nor for entirely and purely altruistic purposes. Making wine is something inevitable and irresistible, and it is not merely because of the endless risks that wine-growers are realistic. The making of wine is absorbing, and the wine-growers know it.

ALOXE-CORTON AND
PERNAND-VERGELESSES

The finest red wine of the Côte de Beaune, comparable to some from the Côte de Nuits, comes from the vineyards around the little town of Aloxe (pronounced "Aloss"). It is reached by driving in from the highway, and from here the vineyard road meanders down to Beaune. Up the slope behind Aloxe is the little town of Pernand, whose claim to distinction is that it is the most primitive of all hamlets along the Côte d'Or. Its neighbours call it *cul terreux*.

The greatest vineyard of Aloxe is Le Corton, the principal owners of which are the excellent shipping firms of Louis Latour, thought by many to be the best shipper in Burgundy, and the Prince de Mérode, who also makes excellent wines. On a par with this vineyard is Les Bressandes, Yard being the principal owner. Almost as good as these two, and perhaps more famous, is Clos du Roi, the principal owners of which are Baron Thénard and the Prince de Mérode. The latter sells his wine exclusively to the very good shipping firm of Joseph Drouhin in Beaune. The Hospice de Beaune sells the wine from five parcels in Aloxe, the equivalent of 225 cases in 1949, under the names "Cuvée Dr. Peste," and "Charlotte Dumay," who gave the parcels to the hospice.

Voltaire loved the wines of Corton and attributed his longevity to them. Swept with enthusiasm, he wrote to the owner of Château Corton: "Your wine has become a necessity to me. I give a very good Beaujolais to my guests from Geneva, but in secret, I drink your Corton."

The Clos du Roi was planted by the last Duke of Burgundy, Charles the Fearless, in 1477. Originally a pond, the land was filled and planted with vines from ducal lands, and eventually became part of the royal domain of the kings of France, hence the name.

The red Cortons age faster than those of the Côte de Nuits, but are the slowest maturing of all the red wines of the Beaune Slope. Their outstanding characteristic is a beautiful balance, by far the best of all the Côte de Beaune reds, wines that have a delicacy combined with strength, which makes them a true transition wine between the sturdier wines to the north and the lighter wines to the south.

Charlemagne was an early owner of those vineyards that bear his name, which produce white wines. He gave his vineyards to the Abbot of Saulieu, and the subsequent dukes of Burgundy and kings of France followed the custom, bestowing their vineyards on other monasteries. In the 1500's, war, brigandage, and plague forced the local inhabitants to flee, and the Church could no longer tend the vines. A Beaune innkeeper named Charles leased the lands from the Church and for many years served the wines in his inn. By the seventeenth century the great holdings were divided up, and several of them eventually passed into the hands of the Hospice de Beaune.

The white wine from Corton-Charlemagne is one of the great Burgundies. Less known than Chablis and the Côte de

Beaune white wines, it can be classed with Montrachet in great years. Harder and perhaps more steely than the softer white Meursaults, it is a rare wine because production is small. The wines of Corton-Charlemagne, which must be made out of Chardonnay grapes, are big and golden in colour. Some connoisseurs assert that they can identify the perfume of cinnamon in the wine.

Like Gaul, the vineyard is divided into three parts, nearly half of the best section belonging to Louis Latour, who is proud of his possession and makes excellent wines from its grapes. Another excellent shipper is Louis Jadot. The rest is owned by some half-dozen superb growers, the largest of whom makes only 200 cases, while the smallest makes but 14, or one *feuillette*, which is half of a Burgundy *pièce*. This

ALOXE-CORTON

OUTSTANDING VINEYARDS (*Têtes de Cuvées*)

	acres
Les BRESSANDES	42.5
Le CORTON ·	28.
Le CLOS DU ROI	26.
CHARLEMAGNE	42.5
Les RENARDES	37.5
Les Chaumes	6.

The great white wine is CORTON-CHARLEMAGNE. Pinot Chardonnay, however, is planted in small parts of the following vineyards:

Le CORTON
Les Pougets

Note: Names listed in capitals indicate vineyards whose wines are likely to be found exported.

famous wine is slowly decreasing in quantity, largely because the vineyard is so difficult to tend. Its slope is as steep as many of those in Chablis, and it must be worked without the aid of teams. After every rain the soil must be hauled back up the slope on the backs of men. Old growers complain that their sons do not love the wine enough to do the work, and the great wine may soon disappear.

Formerly the lesser sections of Corton-Charlemagne could be planted in the cheaper and coarser Aligoté grapes. This, however, is no longer permitted.

On the label the great vineyard name of Corton precedes the names of the other fine vineyards, such as Corton-Bressandes and Corton-Charlemagne. The great wines take the name of the greatest vineyard and not the commune name.

The firm of Louis Latour sells a fine wine from the unclassified vineyard called Corton-Grancey, whose name has become a trade-mark. The outstanding wine of Pernand is the red wine from the vineyard of Îles des Vergelesses, whose character is similar to that of the red Cortons.

BEAUNE

The vineyard road, which runs down from Aloxe-Corton, leads straight into the town of Beaune, for it was in Beaune that most of the wines from the surrounding slopes were sold. Today much of it still is, by the firms of shippers and through the annual auction at the local charity hospital, the famous Hospice de Beaune.

Beaune is a wine town, proud and wealthy because of the fact. The city is tunnelled with wine cellars, and even the old walls have been turned into storage places for wine. For the tourist, it is a quaint little town full of buildings in a jumble of styles, with a pleasant square where there is a restaurant serving fair food, and several curio shops where you can buy miniature barrels and other souvenirs suggestive of wine. For the wine-buyer, Beaune is crowded with shippers, and it is hard to learn which are good, or even which are real firms, for the telephone directory lists several company names under one number. A good firm, as often as not, may have its name aped by a bad one as closely as is legal. Underneath all this, however, is the sincere and honest love for the great wines of Burgundy. In Beaune, one is always aware that wine is not a curiosity merely, nor a product for exploitation, but a glorious addition to good living. Burgundians love their wine, and Beaune is the capital.

The Hospice de Beaune, the heart of the city, is quite properly near the centre of the town, just off the square. The Hospice, which is crowded into the midst of other old buildings, presents a stern, four-storey façade to the street. An archway leads through the building into the main courtyard, and above the entrance is an ornate, ninety-foot steeple, projecting out over the sidewalk and unsupported by a tower. It has been there for a couple of hundred years and shows no signs of crashing, in spite of its lack of underpinning. The building is in medieval Flemish style, translated to Burgundy, and the steeple was the model for that of the Sainte-Chapelle in Paris.

In the immense and cobbled courtyard, steep, slanting roofs come down over the balconies, their coloured slates laid in patterns of yellow and green and black—the traditional Burgundian roof. It is here that the wine auctions are held, usually on the third Sunday in November. The bidding for each lot, or *queue*, lasts until a measured bit of candle has burned down to the mark. On the Saturday before the sale, bidders taste the wines from the barrels, which are kept in the cellars beneath a smaller inner courtyard. The prices paid are a barometer of what the vintage is worth, and of its quality, and buyers come from all over the world to attend the auction.

The tasting for the auction is usually the first chance outsiders have to analyse the vintage. Often the wine is still fermenting, making judgment difficult. There are always more buyers than barrels; hence the bidding is high, and although the Hospice owns vineyards only in the Côte de Beaune, the wines and prices are a basis for judging all those of the Côte d'Or.

Much of the wine goes to European restaurant-owners, for every good restaurateur likes to boast that he has wine of the Hospice. Shippers buy many of the barrels for much the same reason, for it is a mark of honour to have your name printed in the list of buyers published shortly after the auction. The wines are taken away by the buyers after the sale, and some suffer from inept handling, particularly after the barrels leave the country, an argument for estate bottling by the Hospice.

The Hospice was founded in the mid-fifteenth century, by the tax collector under Louis XI, Nicolas Rollin, of whom it was said that he could well afford to endow a

BEAUNE

Outstanding Vineyards (*Têtes de Cuvées*)

	acres
Les FÈVES	11.
Les GRÈVES	79.5
Les MARCONNETS	25.5
Les BRESSANDES	46.
Le CLOS-DES-MOUCHES	62.
Le Cras (or Crais)	12.5
Les Champimonts	41.5
Le Clos de la Mousse	8.5

FIRST VINEYARDS (*Premières Cuvées*)

A l'ÉCU	8.
Sur-les-GRÈVES	11.5
CLOS DU ROI	35.
En Genêt	12.5
Les Perrières	8.
Les Cent-Vignes	58.
Les Toussaints	16.
Le Bas-des-Teurons	18.
Les Teurons	39.
Aux Coucherias	56.5
Blanche-Fleur	23.
Les Chilènes	42.5
Les Epenottes	34.
Les Boucherottes	22.
Les Vignes-Franches	25.
Les Aigrots	56.5
Pertuisots	14.
Les Sizies	21.
Les Avaux	33.5
Chaume-Gaufriot	48.
Montée-Rouge	41.5
Les Montrevenots	20.
Les Theurons	19.

Note: Names listed in capitals indicate vineyards whose wines are likely to be found exported.

charitable institution to the poor because he had made so many of them. Its entire income derives from the sale of its wines, which have been auctioned annually for a century. The various vineyards under its control throughout the Côte de Beaune were given to the Hospice. Its scattered parcels total a little more than 125 acres, about the size of Clos Vougeot. The wine is always sold under the name of the donor and not under the name of the vineyard. The wines are not uniform, because they come from all over the Côte de Beaune, and while many are over-priced, there is some consolation in the fact that all the money goes to support the sick and the poor.

The vineyards of the commune of Beaune and of its satellite Savigny-les-Beaune are among the largest of the Côte d'Or. There are nearly 2,500 acres of classified vineyards, and more planted in Pinot Noir than in any other commune. The best wines come from several smaller vineyards owned by the Hospice.

Beaune wines are characterized by softness and lightness, pastels after the brilliant primary colours from the Côte de Nuits. The wines have less pronounced characteristics than those from the Nuits Slope. Among the best vineyards are: Les Fèves, which is noted for its finesse and delicate aroma; Les Grèves, which has more body and is therefore more velvety; and Clos des Mouches, also noted for body, and called "*très élégant*" by the local growers. Part of the vineyard of Clos des Mouches, which is near the commune boundary of Pommard, is planted in white grapes. A white wine is made from them by the excellent shipping firm of Joseph Drouhin.

Drouhin, an honest shipper with fine cellars that are old stone quarries built by the Romans, was a liaison officer attached to General MacArthur in the First World War. He was wounded in action and was awarded the Distinguished Service Cross. He is one of the directors of the Hospice de Beaune, and also controls the sale of that portion of Montrachet owned by the Marquis de Laguiche.

Beaune wines that are not sufficiently good to carry a vineyard name are sold simply as Beaune. For the better wines, the town name precedes the vineyard name, such as Beaune Clos-des-Mouches, or Beaune Bressandes. The last is a vineyard different from Bressandes in Aloxe-Corton. Some of the *cuvées* of Beaune-Grèves are sold as Beaune-Grèves de l'Enfant Jésus. The name comes from a favourite Burgundy expression for wines that are easy to drink:

"wines that go down as easily as a little Jesus in velvet breeches." It is used without any sense of sacrilege.

In these wines of the Côte de Beaune, *Têtes de Cuvées* are not so important, there being relatively slight differences between the best growths. Beaune wines should be less expensive than those from the Côte de Nuits and from Aloxe-Corton. The exceptions are the wines sold at auction by the Hospice, especially those from its prize *Cuvée*, named after the founder, Nicolas Rollin. This wine usually fetches the highest prices of all Burgundies, with perhaps the exception of Romanée-Conti.

All Côte de Beaune wines mature early, and few of them are considered *vins de garde*, wines to be laid away in the cellar. The wines of the commune of Beaune from the 1953 vintage, for instance, are now definitely ready to drink.

Names of the
PRINCIPAL CUVÉES OF THE
HOSPICES DE BEAUNE

The year-to-year variability in the quantity of the wines produced from the 125 acres of the Hospice de Beaune is demonstrated in the official figures issued by the committee in charge of the auction sales at the Hospice.

Most of the wines are sold under the name of the donor. The Holdings of the Hospice are somewhat scattered all over the Côte de Beaune.

The best wines are sold in barrel when less than two months old, and the lesser wines are distilled into eau-de-vie de Marc de Bourgogne. In 1949 the Hospice sold 175 *pièces*** of red wine, and 23 *pièces* of white wine, besides 11

* A *pièce* contains approximately 288 bottles, or 24 to 25 cases of 12 bottles each.

145

RED WINES

No. of *pièces* PRODUCED AND SOLD		COMMUNE OR TOWNSHIP	*Cuvées*
1949	1950		
14	30	*Beaune*	Guigone de Salins
14	29	*Beaune*	Clos des Avaux
14	20	*Beaune*	Nicolas Rollin
6	19	*Beaune*	Hugues et Louis Bétault
11	29	*Beaune*	Dames Hospitalières
2	5	*Beaune*	Pierre Virely
7	16	*Beaune*	Estienne
8	24	*Beaune*	Brunet
8	17	*Beaune*	Rousseau-Deslandes
7	24	*Pommard*	Dames de la Charité
8	18	*Pommard*	Billardet
9	14	*Savigny-les-Beaune and Vergelesses*	Fouquerand
5	16	*Savigny-les-Beaune and Vergelesses*	Forneret
5	19	*Savigny-les-Beaune*	Arthur Girard
9	33	*Aloxe-Corton*	Charlotte Dumay
9	23	*Aloxe-Corton*	Dr. Peste
3	5	*Volnay (Santenots)*	Gauvain
7	9	*Volnay (Santenots)*	Jehan de Massol
8	25	*Volnay*	Géneral Muteau
14	24	*Volnay*	Blondeau
4	9	*Auxey-Duresses*	Boillot
3	8	*Monthelie*	Jacques Lebelin

hectolitres, or roughly 300 gallons, of eau-de-vie de Marc. In 1950 the Hospice sold 416 *pièces* of red wine, 78 *pièces* of white wine, and in additon 8 hectolitres, amounting to some 215 gallons of eau-de-vie de Marc. This indicates how widely quantity of sale can vary.

WHITE WINES

No. of *pièces* PRODUCED AND SOLD		COMMUNE OR	
1949	1950	TOWNSHIP	*Cuvées*
3	15	*Meursault*	Loppin
4	15	*Meursault*	Jehan Humblot
4	16	*Meursault*	Baudot
5	14	*Meursault*	Goureau
6	11	*Meursault-Charmes*	Albert Grivault
1	7	*Meursault-Charmes*	de Bahèzre de Lanlay

POMMARD

South of Beaune the Golden Slope begins to rise somewhat, crooking to the west, so that the vineyards have a more southerly exposure. The slope of the land is less abrupt here, and the highway branches off to Pommard, running beside the walled vineyards whose wines bear the name of the handsome village.

Through a pass in the hills behind Pommard flow the headwaters of the Dheune River, to be channelled between

147

thick stone walls as the stream flows through the town. Its canal runs along beside the main street. The water gurgles against the stones, sliding swiftly under the squat, arched bridges, overhung with tall trees. Pommard is a town full of sunlight, greenery, mossy stone, and the sound of flowing water.

One of the handsomest buildings in Burgundy is the Château de la Commaraine, built in the twelfth century. It is a simple rectangular mass, with two square pyramids of tower at each end, low roofs of outbuildings extending on either side. The vineyard starts at the back door, looking like an immense lawn in summer, deep and green. Its owner is M. Jaboulet-Vercherre, one of Burgundy's most hospitable hosts, a good shipper who also owns a large section of L'Hermitage, the famous Rhône Valley vineyard.

The Pommard vineyards begin less than half a mile from Beaune, and like those of its sister commune, are among the largest in Burgundy. The wines are sturdier than those from Beaune and are apt to keep better. They are lighter in body and texture than those from the Côte de Nuits, unless chaptalized, the addition of sugar giving more body and slightly higher alcoholic content. Some Burgundy shippers over-chaptalize their Pommards, a regrettable practice that does away with the delicate characteristics of the wine. As in Beaune and Nuits-Saint-Georges, the town name always precedes the vineyard name on a wine label.

POMMARD

Outstanding Vineyards (*Têtes de Cuvées*)

	acres
Les ÉPENOTS	26.
Les RUGIENS-BAS	15.
Le Clos Blanc	11.

POMMARD

FIRST VINEYARDS (*Premières Cuvées*)

La PLATIÈRE	14.5
Les PÉZEROLLES	16.
Les PETITS-ÉPENOTS	51.
Les RUGIENS-HAUTS	19.
CLOS DE LA COMMARAINE	10.
La Chanière	25.
Les Arvelets	21.
Charmots	14.5
Les Charmots	9.
Les Argillières	9.
Les Sausilles	9.5
Le Clos Micot	7.
Les Combes-Dessus	7.
Les Fremiers	12.5
Les Bertins	9.
Les Poutures	11.
Les Croix-Noires	11.
Les Chaponières	8.
Les JAROLLIÈRES	8.
Les Chanlins-Bas	18.
Village de Pommard	65.

Note: Names listed in capitals indicate vineyards whose wines are likely to be found exported.

Pommard is probably the best-known of all Burgundies, not only because its name is easy to remember, but because the big vineyards produce a great deal of wine. The wines from Les Épenots are soft and round, with a good bouquet; those from Les Rugiens are considered the firmest of all Pommards; those from Les Argillières are the lightest.

The wines of Pommard are the most abused so far as frauds go, probably because they are more famous than most. Pommard gained its great fame in the seventeenth century, when it was spread by thousands of French Protestants who left the region to find religious freedom. But its great fame led to fraud, especially where wine is exported in barrels, and where a barrel of ordinary wine can become Pommard overnight.

VOLNAY AND MONTHÉLIE

Volnay is less than a mile below Pommard, the vineyard road cutting straight through Les Rugiens-Bas and Jaroillières and into the commune. Higher up on the slope, from Volnay rooftops you can see the vineyards stretching north to Beaune and south to Meursault, an almost unbroken stretch of green. Farther up behind the town, from the terrace belonging to the Marquis d'Angerville, one of the principal owners, you can see across the whole Burgundian valley and sometimes as far as the snow-capped Juras.

The land is somewhat rolling here, some vineyards being more exposed than others, so that certain sections are now and then endangered by frost, while others are undamaged. Because of the frosts, and also as insurance against hail,

VOLNAY

OUTSTANDING VINEYARDS (*Têtes de Cuvées*)

	acres
Les CAILLERETS	36.
Les CHAMPANS	28.
Les FREMIETS	16.
SANTENOTS	20.
Les Angles	9.

VOLNAY

FIRST VINEYARDS (*Premières Cuvées*)

En CHEVRET	15.
CLOS DES DUCS	6.
La Gigotte	9.
Grands-Champs	17.5
Brouillards	17.
Les Mitans	10.
En l'Ormeau	11.
Pointes-d'Angles	3.
Pitures-Dessus	9.
Chanlin	10.
Carelles-Dessous	5.
En Ronceret	5.
Les Aussy	7.5
Les Lurets	21.
Robardelle	10.5
Carelle-sous-la-Chapelle	9.5
Clos des Chênes	41.
Taille-Pieds	18.
En Versueil	2.
Village-de-Volnay	32.5
La Barre	3.
Pousse-d'Or	5.

Note: Names listed in capitals indicate vineyards whose wines are likely to be found exported.

which strikes in scattered areas, the vineyards are much parcelled. Attempts have been made to use smudge pots and to disperse storm clouds with cannon, but these have been only slightly successful. Volnay takes its name from the ancient goddess of hidden springs, and today's wine-growers are as likely to appeal to her as to smudge pots.

Volnay wines are extremely pleasant, round and light, yet

with a fine bouquet. Their bouquet is the most pronounced of all the wines of the Côte de Beaune, excepting the Cortons. They are lighter in colour than the wines of Beaune and Pommard, perhaps the most agreeable wines of the Beaune Slope. Because of their perfume, that first fresh whiff you notice after opening the bottle, and because of their flowery bouquet, the more lasting aroma, they could be called the Musignys of the Côte de Beaune. Volnays mature rapidly, but an old Volnay from a good grower is a wine of fine balance, flavour, and bouquet.

Volnay's best vineyard is Les Caillerets, and there is an old French saying that the wine-grower who does not have vines in Caillerets does not have Volnay. Another saying about Volnay comes originally from old Latin: " You can't be gay without drinking Volnay." It sounds better in French: " *On ne peut être gai sans boire du Volnay.*"

The vineyards date from the Gallo-Roman period, and relics are often found in them. In the old days, from the thirteenth to the seventeenth century, Volnay and Pommard made a grey-pink wine called *vin de paille,* one of the most famous of the ancient wines. The grapes were laid on straw mats to dry before being pressed. In those days more white Chardonnay was planted than Pinot Noir, giving the wine its colour and its name, called "pheasant's eye," *œil de faisan.*

Just south of Volnay, off to the right, and up a lane, is the tiny village of Monthélie. Its wines can occasionally be found, and because they are much less known than Volnay, they are much cheaper. They are lesser wines, failing to reach to high quality of the fine Volnays.

Still farther south is the village of Auxey-Duresses, whose wines can also be found now and then. Both red and white wines are made, and the red Cuvée Boillot is auctioned off by the Hospice de Beaune. The wines are on a par with those of Monthélie.

152

MEURSAULT

Below Volnay, *La Route des Grands Crus* begins to pass through the vineyards of Meursault, the hills rising fairly steeply above the sloping land. The town itself is old, a strong garrison having been quartered there during the Roman occupation, and some of the vineyards were planted then. Meursault is a wealthy town, and the streets leading out from its Grand Place pass solid stone houses.

In the square is the inn called Le Chevreuil, one of the few to be found in the small Burgundy towns where some of the lesser local wines can be drunk with such specialities as hot *terrine de lapin* and *escargots*. The Château de Meursault is just outside of the town in a spacious park, owned by the Comte de Moucheron, a proprietor of several vineyards and also a shipper.

The best wines of Meursault are white, and the Hospice de Beaune owns several vineyards of them, auctioned as the following *cuvées*: Bahèzre de Lanlay, Jehan Humblot, Loppin, Goureau, Baudot, and Albert Grivault. Meursault has its own hospice, founded in the twelfth century, its gate on the main highway just below the town.

A great bottle of Meursault is a symbol of great hardship as well as great joy, for the vineyards are hard to tend. A custom still exists, called *La Paulée*, a rest taken by the vineyard workers in the middle of the day, the name, perhaps derived from the Greek *paula*, which means "rest." A newer custom was begun in 1922 by Comte Lafon, one of the patriarchs of the town, a great lover of Burgundies, and an extensive vineyard owner in Meursault as well as in Montrachet and Volnay. He began giving a yearly dinner for some three hundred growers and shippers following the sale of the wines of the Hospice de Beaune. Each person brought

153

his own wines, and the Comte gave a barrel of his best Meursault as a prize for the best book written that year on Burgundy wines. He died during the war, and a token award is still made, but it is no longer a barrel of Meursault.

MEURSAULT

WHITE WINES

OUTSTANDING VINEYARDS (*Têtes de Cuvées*)

	acres
CLOS DES PERRIÈRES and Les PERRIÈRES	42.5

FIRST VINEYARDS (*Premières Cuvées*)

LES GENEVRIÈRES (Dessus & Dessous)	42.5
Les CHARMES	39.
SANTENOTS	Varies *
Sous-BLAGNY	5.5
Les Bouchères	10.5
Le Porusot-Dessus	17.
La Pièce-sou-le-Bois	28.
En Dos-d'Ane	7.5
La Jennelotte	12.

The best known SECOND GROWTH is:

La GOUTTE D'OR	14.

Note: Names listed in capitals indicate vineyards whose wines are likely to be found exported.

* Most of the good red wines are permitted to be sold as Volnay. Some Santenots is planted in white-wine vines, the small area varying in size.

In Burgundy the three greatest feasts following the sales at the Hospices de Beaune, of which *La Paulée* is one, are called *Les Trois Glorieuses*. One is held in the cellars of the Hospices, another in the vat rooms of the Clos de Vougeot.

The white wines of Meursault are among the greatest of white Burgundies, somewhat softer, slightly less powerful, and perhaps less distinctive than the Corton-Charlemagnes or Montrachets. The wines are dry, although somewhat less so than steely Chablis, and are delicate and perfumed, with a colour that is like straw. The lesser wines have a tendency to maderize.

The best vineyard today is Les Perrières, the principal owners of the 43 acres being Mme Grivault, Comtesse Lafon, and men named Ampeau and Matrot. Its finest section is the Clos des Perrières, owned by Mme Grivault.

The red wines are full, with plenty of bouquet, and the best-known vineyards are Les Santenots (sold as Volnays), Les Cras, and Les Pelures, part of this last producing some white wines. The red wines are good, but not in a class with the excellent whites.

PULIGNY AND ITS
MONTRACHET

Just below Meursault lies the village of Puligny. The vineyard road swings into the square and then out past some of the greatest vineyards in the world, those which produce what has been called "divine Montrachet."

The great vineyards, up behind the town, are walled in along the road. Square stone arches every dozen yards or so lead into the various parcels. On the right is the great Montrachet, with Chevalier up the slope behind it, and beside this is the vineyard that used to be called Les Demoiselles.

Across the road are Bâtard-Montrachet and Bienvenue-Bâtard-Montrachet, and there were so many jokes about the Chevalier and the Demoiselles that the name of the latter was changed to Cailleret some years ago, a word that means to curdle or clot. The intimation is said to be that the jokes were so bad that the wine was turned to vinegar.

The Montrachets are the greatest of all white Burgundies, and one of the greatest white wines in the world. The greatest is Montrachet itself, whose vineyards produce less than one thousand cases in a good year—nowhere near enough to meet world demand. As a result, much fraudulent Montrachet is sold, and nowhere is it more important to know the names of the owners.

It is more difficult to make white wine than red, and some owners hire experts to tend the vineyards. These men receive half the yield as their share for doing the work. This system is called *mie-fruit*, and though the expert's name may not appear on the vineyard deeds, it will appear on the label of the bottle as a stamp of authenticity. For such great wines, only estate bottlings should be bought.

The largest holdings are as follows: the Marquis de Laguiche, Baron Thénard, Bouchard Père & Fils, Mme Boillereault de Chauvigné, Calvet, Comte de Moucheron, Fleurot-Larose, and Lafon. Bavard is *mie-fruit* with Mme Boillereault de Chauvigné, Monnot is *mie-fruit* with Comtesse Lafon. An excellent producer up to 1948 named Roizot owns a portion, which is now rented to a shipper at a price higher than the sale of the wines could ever bring.

It is a great honour to own part of the vineyard which produces the prototype of all great white Burgundies. Ownership is a sign of wine nobility. Baron Thénard, whose cellars are in Givry, down in the Chalonnais, is chairman of the board of St. Gobain, France's greatest glass trust, which makes most of her wine bottles. He is the owner of Dijon's largest paper, and yet he asserts that he is proudest of his small slice of Montrachet, that it is his most prized possession.

The little town is handicapped by a lack of cellars, for an underground stream prevents digging them. These are necessary for coolness, which helps keep the pale green colour of the wine. The lack of deep cellars makes wine-making difficult, a further reason for selection, for without the protecting coolness, the wine may have a tendency to maderization.

Part of the small quantity of wine made each year from the vineyard of Montrachet has been off the market for the

PULIGNY-MONTRACHET

OUTSTANDING VINEYARDS (*Têtes de Cuvée*)

	acres
MONTRACHET (in part)	10.

FIRST VINEYARDS (*Premières Cuvées*)

Le CHEVALIER-MONTRACHET (in totality)	15.5
Le BÂTARD-MONTRACHET (in part; see village of Chassagne)	24.
BIENVENUE-BATARD-MONTRACHET	6.
Les COMBETTES	17.
BLAGNY BLANC	11.
CHAMP-CANET (a part is classified as *2ième Cuvée*)	11.5
PUCELLES	16.5
Les Chalumeaux	17.5

Note: Names listed in capitals indicate vineyards whose wines are likely to be found exported.

157

past decade. It is kept as a memorial to the memory of
Comte Lafon, who died during the war. Each year M. Monnot meticulously makes the wine, only 24 cases in 1949,
and when it is safely past its first fermentation, he delivers
half to the Comtesse Lafon, a small barrel called a *feuillette*,
which is placed in her cellars. Instead of being bottled the
following year, the wines are permitted to remain in the
barrel. The '44's are still in barrel, brown and maderized.
The great '45's are past their prime and spoilt, as are the
'46's and the '47's and '48's. And yet the Comtesse refuses to
sell. Monnot makes the most beautiful wine on earth, and
Mme Lafon lets half of it maderize in memory of her hus-
band.

Chevalier-Montrachet is the best vineyard after Montrachet itself, a third of which is over the line in the commune of Chassagne. Bâtard-Montrachet ranks next. The
other vineyards produce superb white wines, but they are
not to be compared with the great Montrachet. This tiny
bit of soil, whose stone wall gives it the look of a cemetery,
produces what many believe to be the greatest white wine
on earth.

CHASSAGNE-MONTRACHET
AND SANTENAY

The vineyard road cuts across the main Paris-Riviera highway a few yards from Montrachet and immediately enters
the backward little cluster of stone buildings called Chassagne, which has also pegged the famous wine to its name.
Although only a third of Montrachet is in the commune, the
inhabitants of the town are proud of what they have, and the
two local owners of small parcels are looked up to with
respect.

Most of the vineyards are to the south of the town, and are under-classified by the *Appellation d'Origine* laws. The classification is now being reviewed. The best vineyard producing white wines is Les Ruchottes, whose principal owner is Claude Ramonet, an impeccable wine-maker. Fifteen growers own portions of Bâtard-Montrachet, and while that vineyard is considered better than Les Ruchottes, Ramonet's wines often equal and sometimes excel some of those from Bâtard-Montrachet.

The wines of Chassagne have an unmistakable flavour. They are dry, without hardness, and have a little floweriness, though without any sweet aftertaste. The wines possess a certain expansiveness, with no hard core. Those from Morgeot are similar and live longer.

CHASSAGNE-MONTRACHET

WHITE WINES

OUTSTANDING VINEYARDS (*Têtes de Cuvée*)

	acres
MONTRACHET (in part; see village of Puligny)	9.

FIRST VINEYARDS (*Premières Cuvées*)

Le BÂTARD-MONTRACHET (in part; see village of Puligny)	32.5
Les RUCHOTTES	7.5
MORGEOT	9.75
CAILLERET	15.
Criots-Bâtard Montrachet	4.

CHASSAGNE-MONTRACHET

RED WINES

Outstanding Vineyards (*Têtes de Cuvée*)

	acres
Le CLOS SAINT-JEAN	36.
CLOS DE LA BOUDRIOTTE	5.
Les BOUDRIOTTES	40.
Le Clos Pitois	

First Vineyards (*Premières Cuvées*)

	acres
La Maltroie	23.
Les Brussanes, Le Grand Clos, Le Petit Clos	45.
Champgain	71.5
Les Chaumées	2.5

Note: Names listed in capitals indicate vineyards whose wines are likely to be found exported.

The red wines of Chassagne are little known and, because of this, are excellent values. They are soft and well balanced, reaching perfection in about five years, though they can be drunk when younger. They are a transition wine between those of the Côte d'Or and the lighter Burgundies from the Côtes of Chalonnais, Mâconnais, and Beaujolais. The Clos de la Boudriotte has more tannin than any of the others, with a resulting fuller body, the French saying that the wine is more *corsé*. Clos Saint-Jean is somewhat lighter than Clos de la Boudriotte.

Below Chassagne is the last wine town of the Côte d'Or, Santenay. Santenay produces no great wines, all of them being red and light. Again, it is possible to recognize in the wine, the transition from the Côte d'Or Burgundies to those of the Côte Chalonnaise. They are rarely sold under their vineyard names.

List of

PROPRIETORS OF THE
MONTRACHET VINEYARD

In the autumn of 1950 a local wine-grower, in order to demonstrate the unbelievably small quantity of genuine Montrachet, volunteered the following estimates of the amount of *pièces* or barrels produced. Taking into account the age of the vines, very young or very old vines having a small yield, his total estimate for the 1949 vintage did not exceed 900 cases. At least ten per cent of this figure is kept by the growers for their own personal consumption. An additional 200 to 300 cases are sold to friends. Hence the maximum of authentic Montrachet available for sale throughout the world barely exceeds 500 cases.

	AREA	*Pièces* *
Marquis de Laguiche	48. *ouvrées*	6.
Baron Thénard	40.	8.
Bouchard Père & Fils	24.	4.5
Mme Boillereault de Chauvigné and her wine-grower, Joseph Bavard	18.	4.5
M. Duvergey, manager of Calvet & Cie., shippers in Beaune	15.	4.
Count de Moucheron, shipper in Meursault	8.	3.
Fleurot-Larose, shipper in Santenay	7.	1.
Comtesse Lafon and her wine-grower, Julien Monnot	7.	1.
M. Roizot, who in 1949 leased his vineyard to Thévenin, shipper in Puligny-Montrachet	7.	1.

* A *pièce* contains approximately 24 cases of 12 bottles each.

	AREA	Pièces
Dr. Blanchet and his wine-grower, P. Mathey	6. ouvrées	1.
M. Amiot and Mlle Girard, two small growers		1 each

The *ouvrée* is an old Burgundian measure still widely used in the Côte d'Or. There are 23 *ouvrées* to a hectare, and a hectare is 2.4 acres, which means that there are about 10 *ouvrées* in an acre.

PRINCIPAL OWNERS OF THE CHEVALIER-MONTRACHET

	Acres	Pièces
Bouchard Père et Fils	2.5	8.
Messrs Jadot and Latour (brothers-in-law, joint ownership)	*Ouvrées* 10.	2.
Chartron	16.	14.
Domaine Leflaive	3.	5.
Déleger	6.	2.
Poupon, (including M. Millon, wine-grower)	4.	.5
Joseph Bavard	4.	.5
Lochardet	3.	.5

At the present time the local production of Chevalier-Montrachet is less than 500 cases of authentic wines.

The Bâtard-Montrachet vineyard is partly in the township of Puligny and partly in the adjoining township of Chassagne.

The principal owners on the Puligny side are: Messrs Leflaive, Poirier, Henri Coquet, Bavard, Clerc, Meunier, and E. Monnot.

The principal owners in the Chassagne part of the vineyard are: Messrs Coffinet and Gagnard, Julien Monnot, Morey, Lequen, and Jouard.

162

The Wines of
Southern Burgundy:
Chalonnais, Maconnais,
and Beaujolais

THE Côte d'Or ends at Chagny, where the main Paris-Riviera Route No. 6 swings down from the hills to meet the Golden Slope highway coming down from Dijon. From Chagny to Lyons is ninety miles, and from the scattered vineyards off to the right of the road come most of the Burgundies seen on French wine lists. Divided into three *côtes*, the vineyards also make up most of the Burgundy exports to Switzerland, the second-largest importer of Burgundies. Swiss imports are large because Chagny is only some six hours from Geneva by car. The two restaurants in the little town are well known to the wine-loving Swiss, who like their good food and their carafe Burgundies.

After leaving Chagny, you barely have time to catch your breath before you skirt the Côte Chalonnaise, which takes its name from the small city perched glumly on the banks of the Saône, a dozen miles to the southeast. The land is flat, the vineyards sparse and small, and over to the west is what is left of Cluny, once the great monastic centre where medieval monks tended vines, and migrated all through

Burgundy to found new monasteries and vineyards. The ancient vineyard road that runs straight south from Chagny instead of swinging east to Chalon, passes through the four best-known communes: Rully, Mercurey, Givry, and Montagny. The commune names have become the *Appellations Contrôlées* recognized by the *Appellation d'Origine* laws, for the Chalon Slope.

The change in soil marks a change in the wine, but the Chalon wines still bear a resemblance to those of the Côte de Beaune, perhaps because the Pinot Noir is the grape used in the vineyards. The best wines of the Chalon Slope are the reds of Mercurey, lighter than Beaunes, though sometimes almost as rich, the sort of wine that is often called "unpretentious and good."

The wine of Givry is a little lighter than that of its neighbour Mercurey, fresh, clean, and pleasant, the best vineyards being Clos Saint-Pierre, Clos Saint-Paul, and Cellier aux Moines. The owner of the last is Baron Thénard, whose cellars are under the little town. The houses in the town are in the Louis XIV style, the open market is a domed roof supported by stone columns, and the streets are noisy with the sound of water splashing from ornate fountains. The great cellars are much more ancient, however: huge stone rooms with twenty- and thirty-foot ceilings, with gravel on the floor under the barrels, and wide stairs and archways that seem a better setting for sword fights than for fine wines.

The commune of Rully produces a small red wine, some of which is made into sparkling wine. Montagny produces a white wine, the most apt description of which is "pleasant."

On down the valley of the Saône is Mâcon, a pleasant town rising up from the river banks to the high hill. Four miles above the town is the Château Saint-Jean, now converted into a de-luxe hotel, a large handsome building set in the middle of an immense park. In Mâcon, there is an excellent restaurant in the Hôtel de France et d'Angleterre, on the quay, whose specialities are *écrevisses à la Nage, quenelles de brochet, jambon en croûte*, and *poulet à la crème*. The chef used to be M. Burtin, who cooked for the Kaiser before the First World War.

It is from the Mâcon Slope that one of the best white Burgundies comes, in a rolling valley half a dozen miles west of Mâcon. It is the first truly southern valley in Burgundy, where people speak more slowly and move more quietly, and the men wear berets creased into a peak to shield their eyes from the glaring sun. Five neighbouring communes have the right to call their wines by the famous name Pouilly-Fuissé.

The best comes from Fuissé, which tacks Pouilly to its name. The town is reached by turning south off the west-running highway and swinging down a back road and across a railway crossing, which is called Patte d'Oie. Three or four country lanes come together looking like a goosefoot, hence the name. The road winds through a fold in the hills into the boomerang-shaped valley, with Solutré in the crook, and the neighbouring Fuissé in the farther tip. Behind is a bulging crag that looks like a miniature Gibraltar, and one has the feeling that the sea is just beyond the cratered valley's rim.

Here the white Pinot is allowed to grow much taller than elsewhere, almost chest-high in places, for the sun is warm enough to swell the grapes without the aid of heat reflected from the chalky earth. The harvest is the latest of all Burgundies, often two weeks after that in the Côte d'Or, the wines being allowed to contain much sugar. In all, there are some 1,100 acres planted in vine.

The white wine from Solutré is more feminine than the other Pouillys. The best vineyards are Les Chailloux, Les Boutières, Les Chanrue, Les Prâs, Les Peloux, and Les Rinces. In Fuissé the wine is stronger and more masculine, the best vineyards being Château Fuissé, Le Clas, Menetrières, Versarmières, Les Vignes-Blanches, Les Châtenets, Les Perrières and Les Brûlets. The road winds up the hill that puts the curve in the valley, across to the communes of Vergisson and Chaintré. Vineyards of both have the right to Pouilly-Fuissé, and a good wine often came from the commune of Vinzelles, but it is now less well made than before the war.

The vineyard laws permit the use of some Aligoté and Merlan vines in the vineyards, but when the wine contains pressings from these grapes, the label on the bottle must say so. The same is true in Burgundy, where Aligoté is sometimes planted. Putting the grape name on the label is rare in France, Sancerre, in the Loire Valley, and Alsace being the only other places where it is necessary or customary. In France the law controls what grapes may be used in the vineyards, so variety names are unnecessary in most places.

The pale-golden wine of Pouilly-Fuissé, with its slight greenish tinge, can be drunk young. Because of its strength and vigour it can keep quite well, but keeping does not pay, for after five years the wine no longer develops much.

When chilled, it is wonderful with sea food and white meats, and is particularly delightful with what the French call *charcuterie*. That all-embracing term generally means prepared pork meats such as sausages, *pâtés*, and the other spicy meats that can be lumped under the term *delicatessen*. The country is famous for its hot sausages and the variety of its *charcuterie*, as well as game such as hare, venison, and pheasant or woodcock, stuffed with truffles. A strong cheese is made in the region.

In Chalon-sur-Saône begins the famous food and fabulous eating for which Burgundy was always famed. The country inns and little towns serve good food to travellers, which cannot be said of many of those in the Côte d'Or. Just to the south is Charolles, from whose deep green pastures comes the famous Charollais beef. From Chaintré you can look east across the Saône to the plains of Bresse, the home of chicken and birthplace of Brillat-Savarin. Mâcon is famous for its fish, the perch and pike from the river, frogs from Bresse ponds, snails from the vineyard hills. And to wash it down is the wonderful Pouilly-Fuissé. The Mâcon Slope also makes a small red wine, but in Mâcon the wines that are drunk are Pouilly-Fuissé and Beaujolais.

The district of Beaujolais begins just south of the Pouilly vineyards, and on the maps the vineyards sometimes seem to intermingle. In these northern valleys of the district many have the right to call their wine either Mâconnais or Beaujolais, but in the valleys farther south are the classified growths of Beaujolais. Each successive valley is watered by a stream or two, the slopes facing generally southeast, soaking in the sun from the time of the first tendril to the cutting of the last bunch of grapes.

Beaujolais is made exclusively from the Gamay grape, which reaches heights here because the Burgundian soil becomes granitic, rather than calcareous and chalky. Everywhere else the Gamay is a despised vine, but here it becomes one of the noble plants.

Beaujolais is one of the most widely drunk red wines in the world, one reason being that it is excellent when young. It is the great carafe wine of France, sold in barrels, and drawn off in bottles for drinking. Many Paris cafés specialize in young Beaujolais, which is called *vin bourru*, with a rolling Burgundian *r*; probably indicating the contented sound you make after drinking some.

The northernmost important commune in Beaujolais is Juliénas. Its wines are fresh and fruity, the prize of gastronomic Lyons, where it is the carafe wine supreme, drunk when scarcely a year old. It is a red wine that can be drunk very young, from six months to two years. Its neighbouring commune is Saint-Amour, whose wine is very similar in character to Juliénas though somewhat lighter.

The best-known of all Beaujolais wines is that from the commune of Moulin-à-Vent. Chiroubles is now the best-known Beaujolais in France, Moulin-à-Vent is the best Beaujolais exported, somewhat heavier than any other. It is second largest among the districts. The vineyard soil is thin and pinkish, and on a hill above the main valley is the windmill that gives its name to the wine. Without vanes now, it is classed as a national monument, a symbol of Beaujolais. The best vineyards are Les Carquelins, Le Moulin-à-Vent, Les Chants-de-Cour, and Les Burdelines. All together, the commune has some 1,700 acres in vines.

The district of Chénas is just above Moulin-à-Vent, and wine from the southern part of the district, where the famous windmill is located, often goes to market as Moulin-à-Vent. Below the district of the windmill is Fleurie, whose wine is more fruity than the others, and is particularly a Beaujolais, best when slightly chilled. Of all the outstanding Beaujolais that will stand shipping, Fleurie is the most characteristic and thus the most typical Beaujolais available in the United States. The other good communes of Beaujolais are Morgon, and Brouilly. Morgon wines last longer than the other Beaujolais.

The wines of Beaujolais flow to Lyons as inevitably as the Rhône and Saône, and a parable on the wall of almost every café and restaurant throughout southern Burgundy reads thus: "Three rivers bathe Lyons; the Rhône, the Saône, and the Beaujolais." No doubt it is true. The Lyonnais claim that one of the modern wonders of the world is the fact that the city lets some Beaujolais get away from it, to the rest of France and even overseas.

All the wines of southern Burgundy from the three *côtes* —Chalonnais, Mâconnais, and Beaujolais—should be drunk young The wines bearing district and commune names in addition to the *côte* name are always better, a wine from Les Carquelins being better than a Moulin-à-Vent, which would be, in turn, a better wine than one called simply Beaujolais. In France wines called simply Beaujolais may be perfectly wonderful, but they would not be a good value bought in bottle, and certainly not anywhere outside France where the same duty would have to paid for this ordinary wine as for a truly great one. These wines of southern Burgundy should always be lower in price than those from the Côte d'Or. In France very young Beaujolais wines drunk from carafes taste better when slightly chilled.

Vintages mean less in southern Burgundy than in the Côte d'Or. The good ones in the past decade are 1947, 1948, 1950, 1952 and especially 1953. None of the wines show much improvement after five years.

These wines of southern Burgundy are different from the great Côte d'Or wines in another way; you swallow them, you don't sip them. The reason is simple. That's the way people seem to like to drink them. It is almost impossible to take swallows of the Chambertins, or Musignys, or even Cortons, and it is difficult to take large swallows of the lighter Beaunes. But when you get to southern Burgundy, all that changes. When drinking, one has a desire to take big draughts of the wine, in much the way one drinks beer or cider. One reason may be that cold drinks can be drunk faster than hot ones. But it is more than that. The wine itself is light and refreshing and makes you want to have a lot in your mouth at once. And this is particularly noticeable when you are eating food. The Côte de Nuits produces sip wines, the *côtes* of southern Burgundy produce swallow wines. By the time you get down to Provence, the wines are guzzle wines. It is not a question of temperament, but of geography.

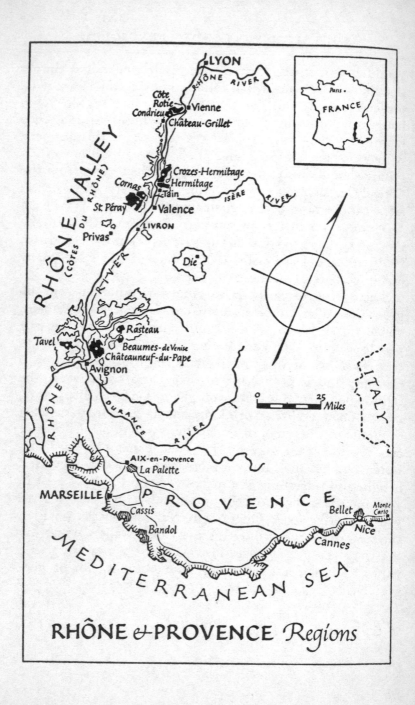

LYON

RHÔNE RIVER

FRANCE

Paris

Côte
Rotie
Condrieu
Vienne
Château-Grillet

RHÔNE VALLEY

(CÔTES DU RHÔNE)

Crozes-Hermitage
Hermitage
Cornas
Tain
St. Péray
Valence

ISÈRE RIVER

Privas

LIVRON

Die

RIVER

Rasteau
Tavel
Beaumes-de Venise
Châteauneuf-du-Pape
Avignon

RHÔNE

DURANCE RIVER

0   25 Miles

ITALY

AIX-en-Provence
La Palette

MARSEILLE

P R O V E N C E

Cassis

Bandol

Bellet

Monte Carlo

Nice

Cannes

M E D I T E R R A N E A N   S E A

RHÔNE & PROVENCE Regions

The Rhône Valley
and Its Sturdy Wines

LYONS, that sprawling metropolis of central France, surrounded by hills and divided into sections by the two rivers that flow through it, with the greatest tradition of cooking of any city in the world, stands at the head of the Rhône Valley. To the east is the country of Bresse chicken and Brillat-Savarin; to the west is the Massif Central and Périgord, from which come truffles and *foie gras*; from the north come the wines of Burgundy, and from the south come the riches of the Rhône Valley: fruits, fish, and the full-bodied wines. Lyons is the mouth of the horn of plenty.

From the kitchens of its great restaurants, Chez la Mère Fillioux, Mère Brazier, Morateur, and Mère Guy, come *poulet en vessie* (chicken cooked in a pig's bladder to retain all its juices, also referred to as *en demi-deuil*, or half-mourning), *quenelles Nantua*, and its famous *charcuteries*.

The first great vineyards begin across the river from Vienne, an old Roman town thirty miles south of Lyons. Here is the great restaurant of Fernand Point, near an old Roman obelisk called La Pyramide, which gives its name to what is often called the greatest restaurant in France, the Restaurant de La Pyramide. Many of Point's wines come from the vineyards across the river—reds from the Côte Rôtie, whites from Condrieu.

171

The Roasted Slope is a steep hillside less than two miles long and averaging about a hundred yards from top to bottom. Terraced every few feet with old stone walls that hold the precious earth in tiny pockets, some of the vineyards are no bigger than a living room. The slope faces southeast, and while the seasons here are two weeks ahead of those in Burgundy, the grapes broiling on the vines all through the summer and early autumn, the *vendange* or harvest is at the same time.

The principal Côte Rôtie vine is the Syrah. Like the Gamay, it was brought back from the Near East by the Crusaders, according to legend. The grapes are grown from a single length of vine held by a tall stake, the vine arching over to be tied to a second bracing stake. When the vines are bare, the stakes bristle along the steep slope, looking like stacked rifles.

The best slopes are those just below the town of Ampuis and are divided into two sections, the *Blonde* and the *Brune*. The story goes that one of the early lords had two daughters, he left them the vineyards and these took on the personalities of the girls, the Côte Blonde, being young and gay at first but petering out with age, the Côte Brun being quiet and reserved in youth, but turning into a grand old lady. The wine-growers tell you that is the reason why the reds from the Brunette Slope are more *corsé*, holding their strength longer, having a heavy body and strong character, while those from the Blonde Slope, just to the south, are lighter and softer and much more *tendre*, a word that means much the same when used in connection with wine as with women.

Some of the vineyard names of the two slopes are occasionally found on bottles, but the wine is usually sold as Côte Rôtie. The best vineyards are La Brocarde, Les Chavaroches, Les Clos and La Claperonne, Fontgent, Grande Plantée and La Garelle, Grosse Roche and La Balaiyat, La Landonne, Le Mollar, Le Moulin, Les Moutonnes Le Pavillon Rouge, La Pommière, Tharamon de Gron, and La Turque. The best owners of the some 130 acres are Bonnefond, Cachet, Chapoutier, Dervieux, Pouzet, and J. Vidal-Fleury, who owns the most, plus some hundred others who own small parcels.

The red wines of the Côte Rôtie do much of their ageing in the cask, some longer than five years. This practice sets the pattern for the reds of the Rhône Valley, for it takes time for the wines to cast off their heavy deposit, still longer to clear. The wines gain enormously with age, developing slowly, often taking a dozen years to round out, and then holding for an amazingly long time. If well kept, many last for thirty or forty years, and if some old bottles from the end of the last century happen to turn up now and then, they are usually marvels. Many think that the rich, deep-red wine, full and generous, is the best of the Rhônes. Unlike other wines, the Côte Rôtie reds have a strong taste of truffles, or of raspberries, a taste easily distinguishable and not a mere suggestion, as flavours often are in other wines.

The laws controlling place-names which went into effect in the autumn of 1940, specify that eighty per cent of the vines must be Syrah, and though the laws limit the amount of production per acre, the vineyards never reach the maximum figure because of the terracing. The entire production of Côte Rôtie wine averages less than the equivalent of twelve thousand cases. The production looks greater when you walk through the caves and sheds where the barrels are kept, but you can easily spot the older vintages and their small yield by the thick mould on the old barrels. The few new ones are almost untouched, standing out dark against the mould-white walls and floors, the whiteness looking like snow.

Condrieu is the neighbouring district, just downstream on the bend of the river. There the production of wine is much smaller than on the Côte Rôtie. The vines start at the town and run south, some two dozen growers owning the 17 acres planted in the Viognier grape. The white wine is full of perfume and has a strong distinctive taste imparted by the local soil, a characteristic called *goût de terroir*. Most of the wine is drunk in Vienne and Lyons.

The best white wine of the Rhône Valley comes from the vineyard just south of Condrieu, called Château Grillet. Its 4 acres, owned by a single proprietor, Henri Gachet, produce less than a hundred cases a year. They also are planted in Viognier. The wine is considered the outstanding *vins du pays*, or local wine, of France. Superlatively dry and well-balanced white wines, not so soft as Meursaults, they are as great as those from Pouilly-Fuissé, with a slightly drier and more austere "finish," or aftertaste. Finish is the lasting end-taste of a wine, such as dryness, floweriness, sweetness, or softness.

Few foreigners have a chance of tasting these good wines of France, for it is the habit to import only the great names. Local pride in some Rhône wines, however, have made their names known, and today many of them are being exported. Among the most famous are those from the vineyards near Tain, some fifty miles south of Lyons.

Above Tain is the steep slope called L'Hermitage, supposed to be one of the oldest vineyards in France, and taking its name from a legendary hermit. One story goes that he was hiding from some invading Romans on top of the hill. When he got hungry, wolves and foxes brought him food. The food made him thirsty, so God sent down a group of wine-growers from heaven, which is where all good wine-growers go. The wine-growers planted vines, which grew grapes and ripened in a single night, and the hermit drank the glorious wine all his life, praising God with each swallow.

You couldn't pick a pleasanter spot in which to be a hermit, high up above the Rhône on the south-facing hill. The grapes are the Syrah, a planting made compulsory in the third century by the Emperor Probus. Even though it is the southernmost of the great French wine districts the vines may suffer from *coulure*, a malformation of the budding grapes caused by excessive rain or storms during the time of flowering.

In Hermitage and the other vineyards of the Rhône valley sections are called *quartiers*, perhaps because they are so small. Both red and white wines are produced, and both are rough when young. With age, however, and when exceptional and carefully selected, the reds rank with a great claret or Burgundy. Harsh and bitter when young, after five years in the cask, where they throw a heavy sediment, the red wines can become soft and velvety. When old, the red Hermitages are enormously rich in aroma and aftertaste, with a fine perfume, and a marvellous bouquet, only slightly less than the Côte Rôties, and a colour all their own. Instead of having the complete red spectrum, the wines have a brownish tinge, which the French call *pelure d'oignon*, or onion skin. They are essentially a big wine, and George Saintsbury has called them the manliest of French wines.

The full white wines are among the longest-lived of all dry whites, and many of them are good after twenty years. The whites will eventually maderize, however, and taste best when somewhere between six and fifteen years old. They have a marked tendency to be hard when young and are one of the few dry white wines that cannot be drunk then, taking three or four years to soften. The wines are excellent with highly seasoned foods such as curry.

The white wines come from vineyards in the centre of the Hermitage Slope, most of which are planted in Marsanne vines, with some five per cent planted in the Rousanne variety. Less than thirty thousand cases of white wine are produced each year. One of the most famous is that called Chante-Alouette. This is the name of a vineyard, but the name has also been used as a trade name by the firm of Chapoutier, and the wine is usually a blend of those from the better vineyards. The best vineyards are Beaumes, Maison-Blanche, Chante-Alouette, Les Recoules, and La Chapelle.

Twice as much red as white Hermitage is produced by the sixty-odd vineyard-owners. It is a common practice for an owner to have vines in several different *quartiers* and blend the wines from the various sections. It is also permitted under the laws to plant other varieties than the Syrah in small quantity, and these varieties add special qualities to the wine. The best red-wine vineyards are Les Bessards, Le Méal, Les Murêts, L'Hermite, L'Homme, Gros-des-Vignes, La Chapelle, Varogne, La Croix, Les Diognères, Les Greffieux, Les Signaux, and La Pierelle.

L'Hermitage is just below that group of vineyards which produce wine sold under the name of Crozes-Hermitage, but the wines of Crozes cannot be compared with those which are entitled to the simple name, Hermitage. As in the Côte Rôtie, the vine-growers are publicity-conscious, and the stone walls that divide the terraced vineyards are whitewashed with many of their names: Chapoutier, Paul Jaboulet *Ainé*, and Jaboulet-Vercherre. One of the best and largest growers is Jaboulet-Vercherre, who is also a shipper. His older vintages of this excellent and velvety masculine wine are splendid examples of Hermitage's greatness. Their great tradition is being carried on by Jaboulet's son, who is beginning to take over the business.

Just south of Tain, on the right bank of the Rhône just opposite Valence, are the two small districts of Cornas and Saint-Péray. The vineyards were given to the monks some time before the beginning of the tenth century, on condition that the brothers should give an annual luncheon to their colleagues, the main dish to be a big fish caught in the river. Cornas produces a red wine, while Saint-Péray produces white, some of which is made into a sparkling wine. Occasionally, the Saint-Péray wine-growers wait for the noble rot, carefully picking the grapes one by one and placing them on large plates. The wines are small and rarely distinguished.

For some reason, the fame of Hermitage has been overshadowed in the past decade or two by the red wines from a district far to the south, Châteauneuf-du-Pape. You reach the district by driving south along the Rhône, through Valence, where the great Restaurant Pic serves its glorious food, on down through Montélimar, famous for its nougats, where the restaurant of the Relais de l'Empereur has been taken over by the former chef of the Savoy Hotel, London, and almost to Avignon. Avignon, which was the seat of the Papacy for nearly a century, is 140 miles down the Rhône from Lyons. Some 10 miles away the popes built a summer residence, deep in the midst of vineyards, and while the vineyards still produce a great red wine, all that is left of Châteauneuf-du-Pape are a few crumbling walls. The town boasts two restaurants, both excellent, La Mère Germaine and La Mule du Pape, and one of the most famous wines of France. The road swings round the crenelated remains of the castle and through the town, past a small triangle called the Place, which has a handsome old fountain, moss-covered and shaped something like a chocolate fudge sundae. Every evening and at week-ends the square is full of local vineyard workers talking politics, the favourite activity of southern France, indoors or out.

The wines of Châteauneuf-du-Pape were the first to pass regulations concerning place-names and qualities for labelling and marketing their wines, setting the pattern for the *Appellation d'Origine* laws that today control the production of all France's great wines. The prime mover of these early laws was Baron Le Roy de Boiseaumarié, a wine-grower and a great sportsman, who is today president of the National

Wine Office, the French special chamber of commerce for wines, as well as president of the National Institute of the Appellations d'Origine and owner of the Château Fortia vineyard.

The vines are planted farther apart at Châteauneuf than in any other of the fine-wine districts of France, often with five or six feet between the rows, the vines spreading out bushily from a single root. You cannot see the soil for the flat round stones that cover the vineyard, stones as big as your fist, and the grapes ripen baked in the southern sunshine and the boiling heat reflected from the stones. A dozen varieties of wine go into the making of Châteauneuf, which accounts for such great differences in the wine.

Production varies immensely, for if the sun is not hot enough, the grapes stay small. A million gallons of red wine were made in 1947, and some 4000 gallons of white. In 1948, 315,000 gallons of red wine were made, and only 950 gallons of white; in 1949, 460,000 gallons of red, and 2,800 gallons of white. Most of the wine is sold in barrels to French restaurateurs. The white wine is a good small wine, merely a novelty.

The red wines of Châteauneuf must have an alcoholic strength of 12.5 per cent, the highest minimum for any of the wines of France. Because they are a blend of so many varieties of grape, a fact that gives them body and outstanding flavour, the grapes must be sorted by hand; Châteauneuf is the only southern red wine where this is necessary. Lighter than the Côte Rôtie reds, softer and faster-maturing than both Côte Rôties and Hermitages, the red Châteauneufs can be drunk when scarcely three years old. Strong in alcohol, they are cheaper than the other two famous reds of the Côtes du Rhône. The best-known vineyards are Château Fortia, Château de la Nerthe, Château Fine-Roche, Rayas-Cabrières, Vaudieu, and La Gardine, but there are many other good vineyards. The best growers and shippers are

Baron le Roy, Brotte-Armenier, Brunel, Chapoutier, Jouf-fron, Ponson, and Tacussel.

Châteauneuf-du-Pape and the nearby district of Tavel make up the southern wine districts of the Côtes du Rhône. Tavel produces one of the best *rosé* wines of France for export, and it is the most famous, for its high alcoholic content preserves it during travel.

Tavel is walled in by cliffs, small hills of sandy limestone baking in the sun, and, above the vineyards, knolls covered with olive trees and brush. The square is reminiscent of Louis XIV architecture; and there is a daily game of *boule* in the dust, the players crouching over the balls in their wide berets, smoking pipes and joking in the thick accent of Provence.

Tavel is mainly made from Grenache grapes, and the pink wine has a ruby colour as a result, with none of that orange tint so characteristic of many poor *rosés*. One of the best producers is the local co-operative, and another is Château d'Aqueria.

Tavel tastes best when drunk chilled, and goes with any food that can be eaten with wine, red or white. Because of its universality and light, refreshing taste, it is a superb luncheon wine.

Vintages along the Côtes du Rhône are not so important as in those districts farther north, though there are many mediocre years, if few downright bad ones. The 1933's and '34's are excellent, particularly the long-lived Hermitage reds, which are well matured and are great wines, but hard to find today. The '37 is a glorious wine, robust and long-lived, which will last for decades. The '42 vintage was not so good as those in other districts, the vineyards needing chemicals that were unobtainable. 1943 was classed as a very good year. 1945 reds were full and heavy, rated excellent, the whites gaining in fullness what they lacked in delicacy. 1946 was much better than average, the whites outclassing the reds. 1947 was a great year, the wines full and round, maturing rapidly. 1948 produced a small yield of average quality, while '49 produced good wines on the light side. The '50's were good, '52's and '53's excellent, and 1954 was better than in most other districts.

Wines bearing district names and vineyard names are always better than those merely called Côtes du Rhône. The wines from the Rhône Valley have always been somewhat under-rated, perhaps because the country is so full of tall tales, most of which revolve about the mistral, that fabulous wind which begins somewhere in the neighbourhood of Lyons and blows all the way down to Marseilles, always for an odd number of days. The stories, the history, and the food always seem to go down easier when swallowed with the local wines.

The wine districts are sparse along the Rhône Valley, but in between are other fabulous things from old France. Aix-en-Provence has perhaps the most beautiful street of any town on earth; the Roman ruins of Arles, Orange, and the other great outposts of the ancient conquerors are here; and everywhere is the scent and savour of southern France, and its warm-blooded people. Nowhere is their spirit reflected more brightly than in the wines they make.

Provence
and the Sunny Wines of the Riviera

AIX-EN-PROVENCE, that ancient capital of the ancient province, is a watering-place, the scene of one of France's most wonderful music festivals, a university town, and the birthplace of Cézanne. It sits astride the Paris-Riviera highway. The southern road leads to Marseilles and bouillabaisse, the marvellous and unctuous fish stew simmered best at the Strasbourg and also Campo. Here live Marius and Olive, those two basic comic characters whose prototypes can be seen sipping their *pastis* along the Cannebière. The road that swings east over the high plateau takes you to Saint-Raphaël, the first town of the Côte d'Azur, that Golden Horn of sand and rocky sea coast called the Riviera.

The towns, the beaches, the perfume of Grasse, and the famous people who holiday along the coast may be better known than the wines, but are no more wonderful. Vineyards are planted all across the twenty-mile-wide coastal strip in the valleys from Marseilles and on over to Monte Carlo and the Italian border. Yet only four districts are recognized by the *Appellations d'Origine* laws: La Palette, Bellet, Bandol, and Cassis.

La Palette is a district some twenty miles east of Aix toward Saint-Raphaël, the only fine-wine district not along the coastal strip. As in other districts, both red and white wine are made a well as the *rosé*, which is made from a wide variety of grapes, principally the Grenache and the Ugni Blanc, but none of the Burgundy varieties are grown. The best vineyard of La Palette is Château Simone.

The wines of La Palette and the others of Provence are rarely drunk outside of France, 60 per cent slaking the thirst of those on the Riviera, another 35 per cent being served in other parts of France, and only some 5 per cent being exported. Half the wine made, by far the best, is *rosé*, a sturdy, heady wine that travels well because of its high content of alcohol. The red wines are rough, much like the Italian wines, and they were famous in the days of Cæsar, who issued them to his legions when they headed home. The white wines are dry and strong—one grower says they are like tarpaulin with lace around it—but production is so small that they are never shipped, their virtues in no way comparing with those of the other fine white wines of France.

Bellet is the only recognized district on the Riviera itself, a group of vineyards up in the mountains behind Nice. Nearly all of the *rosé* it produces is drunk in the fabulous hotels and restaurants between Cannes and the border; at Eden Roc, where celebrities bathe; at La Réserve in Beaulieu, one of the most luxurious seaside hotels on earth, where no better food in the world can be had when you're wearing bathing garb; at the Château de Madrid, high above the Grande Corniche between Nice and Monte Carlo; at the Casino in Monte Carlo, or the fabulous old Hôtel de Paris. Perhaps the finest restaurant on the Riviera is the Bonne Auberge on the road near Antibes, which is the only great restaurant of France that has a woman chef, and where the pride of the establishment is wine from the owner's own vineyard. The *rosé* comes to the table as accompaniment to that most delicate of all fish, the loup, the pride of the Mediterranean.

The other two wine districts lie along the coast road between Saint-Raphaël and Marseilles. Bandol vineyards pro-

duce a *rosé* second only to that of Cassis, and its white wine
is also of fine quality. Just off the coast from Bandol is the
tiny island of Porquerolles, which boasts a single hotel, a
magnificent beach, and one of the least-known wines of
France, a *rosé* that is rarely obtainable anywhere else, kept
on the island to be an accompaniment to the excellent food
served in the quiet hotel.

The wines served along the coast do not come only
from the recognized districts. Other wines are placed in a
special category called "Superior Quality," and these are
produced by domaines such as Château de Selle, and Château
de Saint-Martin, two of the best-known. Their pink wines
are famous locally, and some of them are exported, but they
are made without any legal controls over grape varieties,
soil, or vinification.

The finest *rosé* of the Riviera, and the one most popular in
Marseilles as an accompaniment to the rock fish of the
Mediterranean and the simmering bouillabaisse, comes from
Cassis, the tiny seaport from which Marseilles gets most of
its fish. Of all the varying shades of *rosé* wines from Provence, those from Cassis are the most beautiful—truly pink
and dry, with no orange tint. James Beard, the American
cook and author, was one of the first outside France to discover the wonder of this perfect summer wine, one that
should be drunk slightly chilled, and with a flavour delicate
enough to complement the most delicate of the rock fish,
as well as distinct enough to hold its own against the more
highly seasoned Mediterranean dishes.

The harbour of Cassis is shaped like a fishhook, with the
main buildings of the town along its shank and around the
curve. The road in front of them doubles as a quay, the fishing boats tied up along its length, the nets stretched out on
the cobbles to dry. The waterfront buildings, three storeys
high and painted in pastels—pink, lemon, bone-white, or
faded blue—house the antique-shops, the fish markets, the

G 183

stores and restaurants, where the talk is mostly of fish, wine, women, and weather, depending on which is the most trouble at that particular moment.

In summer the tourists arrive, in the restaurants demanding to be served the fresh-caught fish and the white or rosy wines made in the valley. These wines are usually served too cold, which ruins their flavour. The waiters are much more casual about the wine than in other vineyard districts of France, perhaps counting on the hot sun to warm it up quickly to a more proper temperature.

Behind the town on the slopes of this fabulous valley are the vineyards and the houses of the growers, looking as if they were about to slip down on the houses near the water —an Alpine village gone Mediterranean. One of the growers is a retired English colonel, who came to Cassis in 1921, bought a house for himself and companion, and proceeded to enjoy life industriously. To do this, he started raising chickens.

"Even chickens are happy in Cassis, although it gets terribly cold in winter, in spite of what people say," says the colonel. "But the chickens didn't make me happy. Beastly devils had to be fed on Sunday. We'd planted grapes right away, and when the vineyard next door came up for sale, we got rid of the squawking devils and went in for wine. Get three or four free days a week that way."

The colonel, who first impresses you as an enormous man, perhaps seven feet tall, with a great nose, immense mouth, massive forehead, and enormous ears, but who is actually a man a little under average height and with normal-size features, claims he knows nothing about winegrowing and even less about the studied technicalities of wine-making, in spite of the fact that all the local people insist he makes the best wine in the valley. "When we started out, I bought a book, second-hand. We figured that just about everything else in the world had changed, or would soon, except the making of wine. The book was published in 1803, and I follow its orders like a good subaltern. We're slaves to that damn book. The wine of Cassis is good, sometimes it's wonderful, and we make a natural wine. No need to muck it all up with dosing and doctoring and cutting. Might ruin the wine."

The colonel likes to keep the alcohol content of his wine down. "There's no reason for wine being as strong as whisky. It will last longer and travel farther, but I don't want to wait ten years to drink it. And it travels far enough. A fellow wrote me from India to send him a cask. I wrote him a letter telling him I'd send it, but wasn't sure how it would stand that hot trip. Tarred up the ends of the barrel and sent it off, and a few months later he wrote me to send another barrel. I don't like to ship it that way, though. Safer in bottles. We've got some we made before the war, keep it out of curiosity. It tastes fine."

The colonel doesn't go out of his way to ship his wine abroad. "I can sell all my wine right here. And it's a damned nuisance making out all those forms, and fussing with the labels and the shipping. Nobody knows about Cassis wines, anyway, and I don't know how anybody can sell it abroad. Then there's all that business of proof that has to go on the bottle. Once I got a book and read about it, under-proof and over-proof. I memorized it all pat. But I forgot it the next day."

There is, of course, a story of how the good wines came to Cassis.

Once upon a day, God was up in heaven, taking a vacation after creating the world. Gabriel came over to Him to report that people were complaining, down on earth. "What's the matter down below?" God asked, and Gabriel began polishing the mouthpiece of his trumpet with his thumb. "Well, they're complaining that everything is too flat and smooth down there. Oh, they like it, mind You, they think

185

it's a wonderful world, but they're just a bit bored with it all." God scowled and looked hard at Gabriel's trumpet for a long moment, and then He smiled. "I've put so much time and effort into the world, it seems a shame to end it all. Listen, Gabriel, take a big sack of hills and crags, and boulders and alps, and sprinkle them around. But do it neatly, mind. I don't want the world all messed up, even if the mortals do."

So Gabriel loaded up a big sack and went down to spread some roughness about. It took him all day, and by evening he was pretty tired, and he still had a lot of mountains left. There was nothing to do but carry the left-overs back up the highway that leads to Paradise. Now, as everybody knows, the earthly gate of the Highway that leads to Paradise is at Cassis, and as Gabriel started up, he gave the big sack on his shoulder a hitch. The sack had been in for some pretty rough wear during the day, and that last extra hitch was too much for it. The bottom tore open and all the left-over hills tumbled down on Cassis.

Gabriel went up the Highway that leads to Paradise and reported his day's activity to God. But he didn't tell Him about the torn sack.

The next day God heard the sound of weeping coming up from the earth below, and, listening closely, He could hear the bawling of children, and the dry, hard sobbing of bitter men. He jumped up straightway and went down to find out for Himself.

As He came through the earthly gate of the Highway that leads to Paradise, which, as everybody knows is right at Cassis, a terrible sight met His eyes. A bent and twisted man was hacking at the hard, steep earth with a wooden hoe, sobbing bitterly; and seated on a rock beside the road was a humped and crooked woman, holding a skinny baby to her shrivelled breast. They, too, were crying as if their hearts were cracked.

186

"What's this?" God bellowed, and the noise made the baby wail even harder. "Are you the fine creatures I put on this fine earth? What's happened to you? Why are you so crooked and lean, and why are you grubbing at that poor earth while your wife and baby sob?"

The man looked up at God and rubbed the back of a dirty hand across his nose. "Look at this earth," said the man. "Every day I work it, trying to raise a few poor olive trees and tend these miserable grapevines. But the trees bear no fruit, and all we get from the vines is thin, sour wine."

God looked at the thin vine the man had been hoeing and then at the huddled woman and the bony child. He was deeply touched, and a tear rolled down His cheek and fell on the withered vine.

And suddenly, as God's tear splashed on it, the vine began to grow, strong, green leaves to sprout along its length, and bunches of golden grapes to form under the leaves. And as the vine grew, its strength spread to the other vines, and in an instant the entire slope was covered with a fruitful vineyard. In another moment the entire valley was a mass of emerald vine leaves and ruby grapes. And that is the origin of the glorious wine of Cassis, which, as everyone knows, is at the gate of the Highway that leads to Paradise.

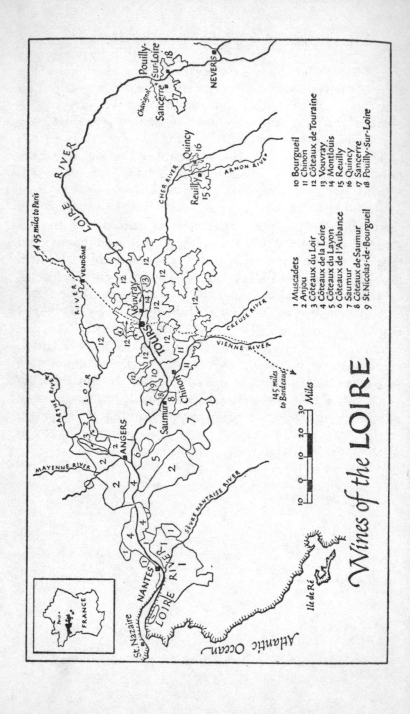

Wines of the LOIRE

1 Muscadets
2 Anjou
3 Côteaux du Loir
4 Côteaux de la Loire
5 Côteaux du Layon
6 Côteaux de l'Aubance
7 Saumur
8 Côteaux de Saumur
9 St. Nicolas-de-Bourgueil
10 Bourgueil
11 Chinon
12 Côteaux de Touraine
13 Vouvray
14 Montlouis
15 Reuilly
16 Quincy
17 Sancerre
18 Pouilly-Sur-Loire

95 miles to Paris

145 miles to Bordeaux

Miles
10 0 10 20 30

Atlantic Ocean

Ile de Ré

St. Nazaire

NANTES

LOIRE RIVER

SÈVRE NANTAISE RIVER

MAYENNE RIVER

ANGERS

SARTHE RIVER

LOIR

RIVER of VENDÔME

TOURS

Vouvray

CREUSE RIVER

VIENNE RIVER

Chinon

Saumur

CHER RIVER

Reuilly

Quincy

ARNON RIVER

Chavignol

Sancerre

Pouilly-Sur-Loire

NEVERS

LOIRE RIVER

FRANCE

Paris

The Charming Wines of
The Loire

THE source of the Loire, the longest of all French Rivers,
is in the mountains of the Massif Central, far below
Lyons, but its famous vineyards do not begin until the stream
winds north past Nevers. The districts of Pouilly-sur-Loire
and Sancerre lie on opposite sides of the river north of the
town; over to the west near Bourges are Quincy and Reuilly
and after the great bend in the river begins, along the
placid banks and uplands of the valley of the Loire,
stretch the other districts that produce the most charming
minor wines of France: Vouvray, Chinon, Bourgueil,
Saumur, Layon, Anjou, and Muscadet.

The vale of the Loire is the oldest civilized part of France,
the retreat of kings; and the residence of royalty in this
garden of France perhaps accounts for the fact that its people
speak the purest French of all. The gentle countryside and
the famous châteaux have earned for the region the title of
the Smile of France, and the wines are as pleasant as the
countryside. Bourges, that old cathedral town which domi-
nates the land in the bend of the Loire, was the capital of the
Duchy of Berry, and it is the fountainhead of the early
kingly history of France, perhaps because Jacques Cœur
came from there, the man who became treasurer for Charles
VII and supplied the King with enough money to begin

189

uniting France into one kingdom. The chances are that he also supplied the King with domestic help, for Berry still supplies most of the nursemaids and servants who staff the mansions of France, and "Berrichonne" is synonymous with servant. The country is full of the old Romanesque churches and their painted frescoes, which attract as many to the Loire Valley as its châteaux and its wines. The Loire peasant is as gentle as the country he tends, easy-going and cheerful, a farmer interested in the wonders of the land as well as in what it produces, and that sets him apart from his Burgundian counterparts, concerned with more earthy matters. "*Vieille France*" is what the French call the vale of the Loire, and if Paris is the heart of France, the Loire is its soul.

The first wines that reflect the delights of this country come from the district producing Pouilly-Fumé, often confused with the Pouilly-Fuissé wines of the Côte Mâconnaise in Burgundy. The white wines of the two Pouillys are strikingly similar; they are of the same quality, coming from similar soil, the result of the same methods of vine-tending and wine-making. Yet there is a pronounced difference in taste, for the wines of Pouilly-Fumé are made from the Sauvignon vine used for Bordeaux white wines.

The grape is called "white smoke" in Pouilly-Fumé, for a reason lost in the darker smoke of the Middle Ages. Some say it is because of the look of its white blossoms in flower; others point to the white bloom on the grapes at harvest time for an explanation. At any rate, the wines have a flavour of cheese or truffles, a characteristic taste that is a reflection of the *goût de terroir*, that distinctive tang of the wines reflecting the soil from a certain locality, that the German growers call *Schmeck*.

It is odd that such a distinctive dry white wine should come from the grape that produces sweet wines in Bordeaux. It is little known in France, even though it was Marie

190

Antoinette's favourite and was admired by Napoleon. Little of it is produced, and it tastes best when young. The best-known wine comes from the vineyards of Château du Nozet, which was built in the nineties as a reproduction of an older Renaissance château by the grandmother of the present owner, the Baron de Ladoucette. Among other good vineyards are Boisjibaude, Bouchot, Soumard, and Girarmes. The control laws for the district went into effect in 1937, when a distinction was made between Pouilly-Fumé and the wine called Pouilly-sur-Loire, which is made from a lesser grape variety called Chasselas. The light, fresh wine of Pouilly-Fumé has a unique and fruity flavour of clean delicacy, in which one can almost taste the essence of spring.

Like Pouilly-Fumé, the 2,500-acre Sancerre district across the river produces a fine white wine. Because it is short-lived, the clean, dry wine should be drunk young. From the Château de Sancerre, on top of the hill behind the town is one of the most beautiful panoramas in France, a long sweep of its longest river. It is perhaps here that the wine tastes best.

The district of Chavignol adjoins. As in Sancerre, there are some twenty-five vineyard-owners, and part of the production is *rosé* wines, delicious when one to three years old, but so low in alcoholic content that they do not always travel well.

Thirty miles west of Sancerre is Bourges, near which are the two small districts of Quincy and Reuilly, both producers of white wines. These are also rarely exported because of low alcoholic content. Their characteristics are much like those of their bigger neighbours.

The centre of the wines of the Loire is Tours, 150 miles south of Paris in the heart of the château country—not wine châteaux like those in Bordeaux, but beautiful castles that were the homes of kings. The Touraine is reached by driving south through Chartres, the most famous cathedral town in France, dominated by magnificent Gothic spires. Near Tours are the great châteaux, Amboise, Chenonceaux, and Chambord. The first is situated on top of a hill, and beneath its crenelated walls is a delightful open-air restaurant on the river bank, the Hôtel de Choiseul, where such local specialities as *terrine de lapin* and blood sausage are featured, along with local wines. Tours is on the south bank of the Loire, and above and below the city are scores of châteaux. The most famous vineyard district is just upstream, across the river.

The vineyards of Vouvray lie on the high slopes above the river and eight communes produce the wine, although some of their names rarely appear on the bottle; Rochecorbon, Vouvray, Vernou, Sainte-Radegonde, Chançay, Reugny, Parçay-Meslay, and Noizay. Much of this wine is served in the local restaurant of Pont de Cisse (which also specializes in that local pork *pâté, rillettes*), whose terrace looks across to the vine-covered slopes.

The casks of wine from these vineyards are stored in deep caves cut into the hill rising above the river. But the caves were not dug for storing wine. People have lived in them from prehistoric times, and still do; as you drive along the river bank to Vouvray, you can see houses the back halves of which are caves, and some of them are merely façades, the rooms being dug back into the hillside.

Among the handsomest of the caves turned over to wine are those of Marc Brédif. Brédif's house has four sides, the caves opening at a proper distance behind it. They are high, vaulted caverns; and deep in the back, some three hundred feet beneath the hill top, is a circular tasting-room, with an old round grindstone set up in the middle for a table. In the chalky walls niches have been cut to hold bottles of the various vintages, the oldest dating back to the 1870's.

The white wines of Vouvray are soft and dry, with a

slight taste toward sweetness, which may become complete, depending on the vintage and the lateness of the time of picking. The soil also affects the sweetness, some vineyards producing wines much less dry than others. Unlike the Sauternes, most of the Vouvrays produced from the Chenin grapes are short-lived, characterized by a youthful, fruity freshness. The most expensive Vouvrays are old and sweet, but few of these are exported, for most people prefer their Vouvrays young and dry. There are exceptions, however, for occasionally a vintage can live half a century.

One such was that of 1893, when there was an enormous harvest and wild rejoicing in Vouvray. Halfway through harvest the growers ran out of barrels. Here was a glorious vintage, the greatest in the memory of living men, and no place to put it. The juice was stored in pitchers and crocks; even bottles were filled; and people coming to the press rooms with containers had them filled free. Vases and pots crowded every room, not overflowing with flowers, but with the sweet fermenting wine. At the harvest festivals old men jigged, grandmothers flirted with the boys, and joy and love were everywhere.

In the spring of 1895 everybody was still raving about the harvest two years earlier, and at harvest time the growers found that the same thing was happening all over again, but even bigger and better. It was unbelievable. This time there was an even greater shortage of containers, and people were still so enthralled with the 1893 vintage that the growers had trouble to convince outsiders that the harvest was worth raving about.

Both these wines are in their prime today, more than half a century after the harvest. But of the thousands of bottles made, there are probably less than a hundred left. Such an old wine is unusual among the great wines of Burgundy and Bordeaux, and fond old wine-drinkers spend many happy hours talking about them, but it is incredible when a district that produces good small wines comes up with such a great vintage.

Like all the Loire Valley wines, those from Vouvray are supposed to be short-lived. They are bottled the spring after the harvest, reach their prime after five years, and are thought of as being nice little wines that taste good with a light lunch. For years they were considered too delicate and light in alcohol to be shipped, and were passed off by connoisseurs as local wines, *vins du pays*, pleasant enough to drink when passing through the château country. They were good enough to wash down *andouillettes*, the local sausage made of tripe and lights, and tasted fine with *rillettes*, a *pâté* that comes in little pots and is spread on bread. But once or twice a decade the Loire Valley districts produce wines that are more than a something to drink with local specialities. When a great year comes along, the most scorned of vineyards may produce a fine wine. As the growers insist on telling you, it is impossible to make any hard and fast rules about vineyards or vintages. Each district is a family, and the poorest can have great children.

Few of the wines are sold with vineyard names on the labels, so buying should be from reputable growers and shippers, the latter of whom own many of the vineyards. One of the best growers is Mouzay-Mignot, who is president of the Vouvray syndicate of growers; some good shippers are the Château de Montcontour, once classified as a historic monument, destroyed by the Germans during the Second World War, and now rebuilt, Ackerman-Laurence, and Monmousseau. There are some two thousand vineyard-owners of Vouvray producing between half and three-quarters of a million gallons of wine each year. Their alcoholic content is between 11 and 15 per cent. Wine-growers often wait for the *pourriture noble* to make sweet wines. The wines turn golden when old, with a full, sweet, flowery flavour that still retains much of its fruitiness.

Vouvray vintages set the pattern for all those of the Loire, 1921 being the greatest of the century, while '28 and '29 were also outstanding, as were '33, '34, and '37. Those of 1943 were also good, while '44 was merely average. Production in 1945 was small, twenty-five per cent of normal, but the wines were excellent—big, full, and sweet. The vintage of 1946 was good; 1947 was a great year, definitely on the sweet side.

As in most districts that produce sweet wines, the greater the year, the sweeter the wine. Better than average is the consensus on 1948, while '49 was very good, with a marked tendency for dryness. As in most other districts in France, the '52's and '53's vie for first honours.

Across the river from Vouvray is Montlouis, whose white wine was so little known that it once went to market under the name of its bigger brother, Vouvray. Much of it is sold directly to local or Parisian restaurants in either barrel or bottle. As in Vouvray, the vineyards are planted in what is called the Pineau of the Loire or in Chenin, a larger grape of the Gros Pinot variety of Burgundy's great vine.

Wines from both are evenly balanced, ranging from slightly dry to somewhat sweet. This last characteristic the French call *mœlleux*, and Rabelais spoke of the "wine of taffetas" because of its velvety and silky, somewhat foamy texture in the mouth.

Some wines are particularly heavy in sugar. Bottled before all this sugar has been transformed into alcohol, they develop carbonic acid gas, becoming somewhat sparkling without any added doses. The French call this characteristic *pétillant*. Much of the Vouvray is made into a fully sparkling wine called *mousseux*, a dose of dissolved cane sugar being added to the wine when it is bottled, and the second fermentation changing the sugar to carbonic acid gas and making the wine bubbly. From these vineyards come the sparkling wines given away as prizes on the wheels of chance that are so much a part of every French fair or carnival.

North of Vouvray is a small district that produces pink and white wines called Jasnières, but these are rarely shipped, even to Paris. Its white wine rarely has that creamy quality called *mœlleux*, and often takes a half-dozen years to develop.

Downstream from Tours and Vouvray are the red and pink wine districts of the Touraine slopes. Bourgueil and Saint-Nicolas-de-Bourgueil are on the northern bank of the Loire. Chinon is opposite, in the wedge of land formed by the Loire and a tributary called the Vienne, reached by driving past Azay-le-Rideau, that loveliest of all Loire châteaux, which was built as a sixteenth-century Versailles by the treasurer of Francis I and was confiscated by the King on its completion.

The high plateau of chalky soil that makes up the vineyards of Bourgueil is planted in what is locally called the Breton vine, actually the Cabernet Franc of Bordeaux, and so Chinon is, too. Both wines are much alike. The smaller the wine, the less distinctive are its characteristics, and even neighbouring districts may be remarkably similar.

Rabelais, who drank more wine during his lifetime than some would consider seemly, and whose Pantagruel and Gargantua do the same, was born near Chinon, lived there for years, tended a vineyard, and was a monk, in name if not in spirit. The town is sandwiched in between the river bank and a great bluff on which crumble the ramparts of the enormous castle whose massive walls were stormed by Joan of Arc, and its stones pilfered by Richelieu to build his own castle nearby. Parts of the town have not changed much since the days of Rabelais. It is easy to imagine him reeling homeward up the steep cobbled streets after a heavy all-night bout with the local wine of Chinon, which he praised as lavishly and as often as he drank it. His spirit permeates the town, and his ghost is supposed to appear whenever there is some particularly heavy drinking. Even the old hotel overlooking the rooftops to the river is called Gargantua. The local promotion organization, the Chanteplure, has gone so far as to design a special glass for the local wine, with the Rabelaisian phrase: "Always drink, never die," etched on the side.

In the old days, when all French wines were drunk mostly where they were made and the great wines were not so good as they are today, Chinon and Bourgueil lived up to their reputation. Their wines are better now than then, but so are the great wines, and in spite of Rabelais, whose sentiments are echoed by Balzac, who came from Tours, these red wines are rarely shipped.

On down the Loire lies the old town of Saumur, dominated by an ancient and rambling castle that is now a horse museum, the most famous in the world because the great cavalry school and mounted troops of the French Army are stationed there. Of the six districts of the Anjou Slope, Saumur stands first, not only because its sweet white wines make a good sparkling wine, but because the riverside bluffs are tunnelled with vast, high caves, perfect for ageing.

The sparkling wines of the Loire differ from those of Champagne, keeping the taste of the wine, where Champagne actually is transformed into a sparkling something unique. Saumur, particularly, is overpriced if it costs as much as Champagne, and it suffers from the fact that it is usually taxed as much as Champagne. Heavier and fuller than the sparkling wine of Vouvray, it is made of two-thirds white Chenin and one-third Cabernet. The big shipping firms in Saumur that make the sparkling wine had bad luck in 1949, when late rains rotted the grapes, turning the harvest into a small sour wine.

Just down the river from Saumur begin the wine districts

of the Anjou. There are over fourteen thousand wine producers in the Anjou. They make both pink and white wines. Many of the pink wines are not true *rosés*; they are pale and tinted faulty wines, with an orange cast instead of a true pink, yet they have a clean, fresh taste, and, like all the wines of the Loire, can be enjoyed drunk in quantities.

These average only 10 or 11 per cent of alcohol and, like all Loire Valley wines, lose their characteristic charm and lightness when the percentage of alcohol is higher, the wine becoming harder and its fresh bouquet disappearing. As wines need at least 11 per cent of alcohol to be shipped safely, that degree protecting them from the rough handling and temperature changes, these pink Anjous are usually better when drunk on the spot.

The two best and most famous of the Anjou districts are the Coteaux du Layon, thirty miles of vineyards scattered along the banks of the small Layon River, south of the Loire, and the Coteaux de la Loire, on the north banks of the river. The wines from the slopes of Layon are extremely high in alcohol, and the best vineyards are picked only after *pourriture noble* has set in. The best vineyards of the Layon slopes produce sweeter, more full-bodied wines, which last longer than those from the best vineyards of the slopes of the Loire.

The best wine from the Coteaux du Layon is the sweet white wine from a vineyard called the Quart de Chaume, one of the vineyards near the town of Chaume in the commune of Rochefort. Quart de Chaume wine is the sweetest of the Anjou whites, much like a sweet Vouvray, more flowery than Sauternes. It has a lightness and bouquet that make it unique, in spite of the fact that in most years its alcoholic content is between 13 and 16 per cent. Originally all the Chaume vineyards were owned by one man, rented out to workers in return for a quarter share of each vintage.

The lord reserved the right to choose which section of the vineyard his quarter should come from, and it came to be called Quart de Chaume, and was, of course, the best in Anjou. Now the vineyard is owned by three proprietors: Lallane, Courtillé-Roynet, and Marcel Breyer, who also owns one of the choicest sections called Château de Belle-Rive of Quart de Chaume, and the neighbouring vineyards of Château de Plaisance and Château de Suronde, of Chaume.

North of the Coteaux du Layon is the Coteaux de l'Aubance, a small district that produces noteworthy *rosés*. It also produces some white wine, much drier than those from the slopes of Layon. Farther down the river are the vineyards of Coteaux de la Loire, mostly on the north bank, where the best surround the little town of Savennières. The wines are drier than those from Layon, very high in alcohol, and very slow in maturing. The best vineyards are the Château de Savennières, La Coulée de Serrant, Château d'Epiré, La Roche-aux-Moines, Clos du Papillon, and Château de la Bizolière.

Upstream is the Coteaux du Loir, a district on the small tributary of the great river, whose wines are white and sweet, red and indifferent, *rosé* and charming.

The vineyards of Muscadet lie far down the river, near the city of Nantes. They are the only classified vineyards in Brittany. All of the wine is white, and little of it is ever shipped out of the district, though some can be found in a few French restaurants. Pleasant and dry, the wines are most appealing with oysters and sea food. Prior to the control laws, they were openly blended with Chablis, to stretch the supply of that scarce and famous wine.

That most of the pleasant Loire wines are not much exported is not so great a loss as it might seem. Nearly every tourist drinks some while sightseeing through the château country, between bouts of listening to the guides tell the fabled tales of the kings and queens who fell in love with the garden of France. And if amour and intrigue become tiring, there is always the legend of Joan of Arc to delight you between swallows, or the lusty stories of Rabelais and Balzac—stories as varied as the wines.

The White Wine of
Alsace

ALSACE, the martyred province of France, and with Champagne the only one whose wines are not yet fully controlled by *Appellation d'Origine* laws, stretches its vineyards and orchards along the left bank of the north-flowing Rhine, separated from Lorraine and the rest of France by the Vosges Mountains. Most of its vineyards and towns were battlegrounds during the last war, and the destruction was enormous.

You would never suspect it, going east from Paris across the Île de France and skirting the Champagne country, then through Lorraine and up into the mountains. War damage has almost disappeared, and tourist interest focuses on the wonderful *quiche Lorraine* and preserves served in Bar-le-Duc at the Hôtel Metz, or on the watering-place of Vittel, where much of France's bottled waters come from, or on Münster, to the south, the cheese from which is famous the world over. As you drive up through the peaks and crags of the mountains, the country is peacefully Alpine, and when you break through into the valley where the town of Orbey perches, you are ready for the fabulous *foie gras* and trout, the ham and sausage, the mounds of ice cream and whipped cream, that are the specialities of the Hôtel Beausite. But when you come through the pass into the foothills, you can see some of the price that France has paid.

The best-known wine towns are Ammerschwihr, Kaysersberg, Kientzheim, Mittelwihr, Riquewihr, Ribeauvillé, and Bergheim, all north of Colmar, although the vineyards begin farther south. Mittelwihr was completely destroyed in the drive across the Rhine; only a few walls were left standing. Along one of them, called the Wall of Martyred Flowers, the Alsations planted red, white, and blue flowers during the occupation, in defiance of the German order that the French national colours should not be displayed. In Bennwihr there used to be 184 houses; four were left standing. The ruins of the Château of Koenigsberg stand on the heights, the ancient stones looking down on the newer havoc.

The towns are rebuilt, workers taking the stones from the piles of rubble to build new houses, but it is a changed Alsace now with only patches of the old. Once the Germans were routed, the first task was to replant the vineyards, and the first buildings were large modern co-operative cellars, so that the wine-growers of each town could again make their wines. It has been a giant's task.

Strasbourg, the capital of Alsace, and famous for its *choucroute*, its brownstone cathedral with the handsome stone ladies above the portals and the immense and ugly clock on the inside, lies 275 miles due east of Paris, in the middle of the Alsatian plain, on the banks of the Rhine. The plain was once a vast lake, now shrunk to the meandering Rhine, and coming across the towering Vosges, crowned with forests and old castles, you can look down and across the wide plain, rich with orchards and fields of hops and wheat, to the Black Forest of Germany.

Twenty-odd miles south of Strasbourg is Sélestat, and still farther up the Rhine is Colmar, whose museum contains the weird and famous Grünewald altarpiece. All three towns have an ancient quarter ribboned with canals and crammed with old half-timbered buildings, surrounded with the ugly rash of modern suburb and factory develop-

ments. The towns divide the winegrowing district of Alsace
in two, the best being that called the Haut-Rhin, between
Colmar and Sélestat; that called Bas-Rhin stretches north
along the foothills and slopes between Sélestat and Strasbourg.

The wine villages lie back from the Rhine, on the slopes
and rises of the Vosges foothills, surrounded by their vineyards. Some of them survived the most recent war, as well
as a thousand years of earlier ravages, and the half-dozen
that are left are as magical as ever. Perhaps the loveliest
wine town of France, next to Saint-Émilion in Bordeaux, is
Riquewihr. Fifteenth- and sixteenth-century houses and
courtyards lie within the encircling city walls. There is an
old inn where the flowery wines are served in green-
stemmed glasses, the colour of the stem adding to the green
gold of the wine. And above the stone arches leading into the
old *cours* are long flower-boxes full of blooms, and trained
against the sandy walls are vines and fruit trees, leafy green
along the old streets. Wrought-iron painted signs hang above
the shops, oxcarts rumble over the cobbles, and the water
from the town fountains splashes from the mouths of mythi-
cal beasts, to burble down the open gutters. Kaysersberg is
almost as lovely with a stream running through the town.
Houses are built right over it, the water slipping darkly
under the arched stone channels. Here and there on the
rooftops is a platform made out of a barrel top, a stork's
nest perched on top, to bring good luck. Alsace is a land
worth seeing.

To taste the wine from the neighbouring vineyards you
go down into the cellars under the houses, full of great casks,
some of them taller than a man and twice as long. Many of
the cellars date from the fourteenth century, and some of
the barrels date from the eighteenth. The heavy braces
across the ends are carved with harvest scenes or garlands.
The new wine is put into old barrels in Alsace, where it rests

from October to March before being bottled, being racked once in the first month of the year. Old barrels are especially prized, particularly one in which an exceptional vintage has aged, for the wood soaks up some of the wine, and a great old barrel will lend its greatness to the new wine. To taste a wine, the wine-grower twists a wooden spigot in the end of the barrel, squirting the wine into a straight-sided glass not much bigger than a three-ounce glass. And in Alsace it is the custom never to spit out the wine being tasted, as you do everywhere else in France.

The Germans ruled Alsace from 1870 until 1918, claiming the province as spoils of the Franco-Prussian War, and when the province returned to France, the winegrowers had a problem. Under German control Alsace vineyards were planted in poor-quality vines that gave a large yield, and in 1918 all the vineyards had to be replanted. To make it clear that poor grapes were no longer being grown, it became the custom to label Alsatian wines with the name of the grape on the bottle, and the custom has continued.

The best vine is the Riesling, that grape which produces all the great German wines; and the next-best is called Gewürz-Traminer, which is not quite so dry, a selection of Traminer vines that boast of a slightly more prominent bouquet than Riesling, and make the most highly perfumed white wine of France. The wine is dry, not containing much sugar, but its spicy perfume makes it taste somewhat sweet.

A belief has grown up that the Gewürz is much better than the Traminer, but the difference is slight. Some wine is grown from the Muscat grape, which gives the richest wine, and two Pinot varieties are planted. The better is called Tokay, a Grey Pinot that gets the name Tokay because it is supposed to have been brought in from Hungary. The other variety is the Pinot Blanc, planted in hope that it would produce wine as great as that grown from the same vines in

Burgundy. It has not done so, and the wine of Alsace is a comparatively small wine, though fresh and good; gourmets call it a luncheon wine. The French say it is a wine that lets itself be drunk, meaning that it is one you take big swallows of, not one you sip.

Far down the list comes Sylvaner, a vine that produces a smaller wine, and that has somehow become one of the best known. The Sylvaner is planted most extensively in the lesser vineyards of the Lower Rhine. *Edelzwicker* is a blend of wines made from the best grapes; a wine blended from noble and ordinary varieties is called *Zwicker*. *Vin gris*, famous in the world as the Alsatian *rosé*, does not exist in Alsace and must always be made fraudulently abroad. A true *rosé* of Alsace comes from only three or four much distinction.

The wines of Alsace are often compared to the great German wines of the Rheingau and the Moselle, but are not in the same class. The Riesling grape produces the best wine of both districts, but the similarity ends there, the soil and climate producing wines with very different characteristics. The Hocks of the Rheingau, which are supposed to take their name from the adjacent town of Hochheim, are white wines made from grapes picked late, often after the noble rot has begun. There are four classifications of these wines. Those called *Auslese* are wines made from select bunches of grapes. *Beeren Auslese* are wines made from the best grapes selected from these bunches. *Trockenbeeren Auslese* are wines made of selected overripe grapes which have been left on the vines until they have lost their excessive moisture. Each successive class is progressively sweeter and more unique. *Spatlese* is the word used to indicate late picking with no special selection of grapes.

In Alsace, however, there is none of this late picking. The German wine-growers use old barrels too, the wine-making is much the same, and yet in spite of all this the wines are entirely different. Alsatian wines suffer from the traditional comparison with the great German wines, just as does a picnic lunch when compared with a five-course dinner, but it's nice to have both.

The Alsatian vineyards bristle with tall stakes, higher than a man, to each of which a vine is tied, and the tendrils are looped down on each side of the stake, looking like loving-cup handles when in leaf. Each town is surrounded by its great blocks of flowing green, following the contour of the land. There is no official classification of all the vineyards as yet, although many say this will be the tendency as elsewhere in France and within a decade or so Alsace may have fallen into line. Until then, you can only buy wines from a particular commune, the name of the vineyard rarely getting on the bottle. As it is, the wine from any one type of grape is blended together by the owner, who usually has several different parcels.

Many different *eaux-de-vie* are made in Alsace, and right among the vineyards are great raspberry and strawberry patches, and orchards which yield the fruit that is distilled to make the strong colourless spirits. Some thirty pounds of raspberries are needed to make a bottle of *Eau-de-Vie de Framboise*, which makes it fabulously expensive and almost impossible to find. While genuine *Framboise* is dying out on account of its prohibitive cost, *Fraise*, made from strawberries, *Mirabelle*, from yellow plums, and *Kirsch*, from cherries, are still there to take its place. Even these are expensive, and the commercial brands are mixed with alcohol and synthetic flavours as often as not.

The wine merchants and shippers of Alsace are like those anywhere else in France, or worse, making it almost impossible to buy a genuine Alsatian wine from a good vineyard. The shippers overblend the wines, selling them so cheaply that the genuine Alsatian bottles seem highly overpriced. The honest grower who wants to bottle his own wine is faced with the dilemma of meeting the shippers' prices or charging higher prices for his wine. When the vineyards are eventually classified, this difficulty will lessen, and the tall bottles cooling in the high ice-buckets will then contain a wine that will take its place with the other fine wines of France.

Vintages, strangely enough, follow the Burgundian, not the German pattern. Recent years have been very good, and the '54's provide quite a surprise for the critics of this vintage. '53 was great and '52, as in all parts of France, was outstanding.

Alsatian wines taste best when drunk young, not over five years old, their freshness being one of their main attractions which they will lose with age. Like most dry white wines, those from Alsace also have a tendency to maderize.

The Lesser Wines from
Mountain and Plain

THERE are vineyards all over France. Even in Paris the vine grows, and each year an auction is held at which the wines grown in the vineyards of Montmartre are sold. Some people insist that the wine is not at all bad, and what it lacks in quality, it makes up in novelty. It is plain to see that when a Frenchman finds himself in a spot where he can plant a vine, he does so.

In the middle of the nineteenth century there were some five million acres under vine, and wine was France's principal source of income. Even today winegrowing is France's biggest business, although only half as many acres are planted. Last century saw the beginning of scientific research in wine, after many centuries of by-guess-and-by-God study of vines and wine-making. Wine exports were being hurt by the tendency of the wines to go bad during a sea voyage, and Louis Pasteur was requested to find out why. He went to the Arbois, his native province in the Jurals, to experiment, and while his studies made it possible for wine-growers to discover why wine acted as it did, his findings were more useful to dairymen. Pasteur found that wine could be made to age faster by running oxygen through it, causing it to become soft, losing that greenness of acidity which made a new wine taste unpleasant. To age wine through oxidation, it is stored in large vats, where it is cooled before being placed back in the barrels. Pasteur also found that heating wine kills the organisms that cause fermentation, thus permitting wine to live longer. But the process made wine lose its freshness. Even so, wines that are too light in alcohol or that might deteriorate quickly can often be saved by pasteurization.

For sterilizing, the wine is brought up to a temperature of 55° to 65° C. depending on the composition of the wine. For an acid and highly alcoholic wine, 55° C. is needed, 60° C. for a wine of average acidity and alcoholic content, and 65° C. for a wine having little acidity and little alcoholic content. The temperature should never rise above 70° C. Pasteurization is carried out in the complete absence of air.

Pasteur's findings about the cause of fermentation, the effect of oxygen, and the usefulness of heating for preserving poor wines were of help to vintners in making great wines greater because it enabled them to understand the processes wine went through.

Pasteur selected Arbois for his experiments because immense vineyards were planted there and the wines were light. The Côtes du Jura produced wines of every kind—red, white, pink, and yellow—from a strip of vineyards across the Burgundian plain from the Côte d'Or. The phylloxera wiped out more than half of the vineyards, and production is slowly decreasing today. Among the best wines are those of Arbois, white or pink. Many Frenchmen believe that the *rosé* d'Arbois is one of the best in France, on a par with Tavel, although expert opinion ranks it lower. Its white wines are particularly well liked in Bourg and the Bresse country, that marvellous farm area just to the south of the vineyard district. Below Arbois is Château Chalon, famous for its yellow wine, and the longest-lived of any in France. After fifty years the wine is deep golden, completely maderized. This is the only wine of France in which maderization is a desired characteristic. Another wine is called *vin de*

209

paille, not merely because it is the colour of straw, but because the grapes are laid on straw mats after picking and allowed to dry in the sun for a time to make them richer. Some of these wines are splendid after more than sixty years. Southwest of Château Chalon is the best white wine of Côtes du Jura, from the tiny district of L'Étoile, which also produces *vin jaune, vin de paille*, and sparkling wines.

The Jurals give way to the mountains of the province of Savoy to the south, and from their slopes come white wines from a district called Crépy, on the French shores of Lake Geneva, and another wine from a district near the head-waters of the Rhône, called Seyssel. From farther to the south comes the light wine called Clairette de Die from the district of the same name. These wines, rarely shipped outside the district where they are made, are typical *vins du pays*.

Inland from the wine districts of Bordeaux, and east of the city itself, are the minor districts of Bergerac and Monbazillac. Bergerac is properly more famous for Cyrano, who came from there, than for its heady red and white wines. Between Bergerac and Saint-Émilion are the district of Mont.avel and Sainte-Foy-de-Bordeaux, * whose wines resemble mediocre Saint-Émilions. Near by is the Côte de Duras, whose red and white wines are even smaller than their reputation or production. The best wines from this area are the sweet wines of Monbazillac, drunk as dessert wines in many French homes. The wines have a big body, and while they are often called "poor man's Sauternes," the quality of some of them is fair and makes them worth sampling.

The wines of the Pyrenees come from three districts in the foothills. Jurançon wine was put to the lips of newborn Henri IV immediately after his birth in 1553, and this may explain why he called it his favourite wine. The whites, left four years in barrel, are a deep golden colour when drunk,

* A district of the Bordeaux region.

and would probably be better if bottled younger. The wine has a perfume all its own, often described in flowery terms for it is sweet, spicy, and unique. Farther east and north is Gaillac, from which come the sweetish white wines frequently made sparkling, and also some dry white wines that are better ignored. The best thing in the district is the Toulouse-Lautrec Museum in Albi. Near by are the small vineyards of Blanquette de Limoux, where the sparkle is also exploited, many of the wines being slightly crackling. The wines are small, and are an argument for insisting on Champagnes.

On the Mediterranean border between France and Spain, and stretching along the coast, are a series of districts that produce some acceptable wines with little distinction, rarely exported. Banyuls produces a sweet wine known as *vin de liqueur* in French, of little interest in countries where Sherry and Port can be had. Banyuls is a sweet natural wine, often drunk by those French who like sweet apéritifs before eating, and as a dessert wine. Similar and also of slight distinction are the wines from the nearby districts of Maury, Rivesaltes, Côtes d'Agly, Côtes de Roussillon, and the district of Muscat de Frontignan. These wines often taste like Spanish wines, heavy and slightly sweet, although not fortified, reminiscent of poor Sherries, while others are close to the Chianti wines of Italy, and often as good.

Some of the coarsest wines of France come from the Midi and that great plain of Languedoc which stretches from Arles, near the Rhône, over toward the Spanish border. These are the common wines of France, sold by alcoholic percentage because they have little else to recommend them. When old, the dark-red wines look brown on the side of your glass, and these wines are often called *pelure d'oignon.*

These plantations were vastly extended at the time of the phylloxera, as were the vineyards in North Africa, particularly those of Algeria, and when the great vineyards of

France were rebuilt and began producing, sale of their lesser wines suffered from the competition of the cheap Midi and Algerian growths. This competition is one of the reasons why the great districts worked so hard to clear up fraud, and attempts were made to improve even the smaller wines of the great regions.

At the same time, these cheap wines came to be used as blend wines to stretch out the more famous regionals, a practice that does credit to nobody. Tank lorries and tank cars roll north daily to the shipping firms of France, and by the magic of malpractice the cheap wine from Algeria and the Midi are transformed into wines with famous names.

Half the wines of France come from the Languedoc, from the four departments of Gard, Hérault, Aude, and Pyrénées-Orientales. The best are from Corbières, just north of Perpignan, and Minervois, just inland from the coast behind the bulk-wine centre of Béziers. Good red wines also come from Saint-Georges; and from near Montpellier, which boasts of the Wine University of France, comes Costières de Gard. All these have their names controlled by law. The only white wines from the area having an *Appellation Controlée* are Clairette de Languedoc and Clairette de Bellegarde.

The wines of the beautiful island of Corsica are heady, especially the *rosés* made in the northern part of the island between the Cap Corse and Île-Rousse. The only superior wine exported to the French mainland is Patrimonio. This strong pink wine, high in alcoholic content, is found on many a wine list in the small restaurants of Nice, and along the Riviera where bouillabaisse, strong in saffron and pungent with its "*poissons des roches*," requires the virile characteristics of the Corsican wine. But if Corsica has little right to international fame as a wine-producing country, it rests on its laurels as the birthplace of Napoleon Bonaparte and

for contributing the word *maquis* to the language, the name
for its uncrossable sagebrush and symbol of the French resistance movement. Corsican wines were much more popular
at the beginning of the century and found a market in metro-
politan France prior to the large plantings of Provence wines.

France proper imports more wine than any other country,
and most of it comes from her North African departments
of Oran, Algiers, and Constantine. Together these departments, which are part of France, form Algeria, the largest
and most abundant producer of table wines on earth. Wine
is also imported from Morocco, to the west of Algeria, and
from Tunisia, to the east, France's two North African
protectorates.

French North Africa is largely Mohammedan, and Islam
prohibits drinking. The people of today might have been
happier if the Christianized Berbers, who took over from the
Romans during the fifth century, had not been thrown from
power, first by invading Arabs and then by the Turks.
Descendants of all three groups in the eighteenth century
became the Barbary pirates. This scourge of the Mediterranean was laid low by U.S.A. and the French, who completed
colonizing the area by 1850. Shortly thereafter the French
extended the ancient vineyards originally planted by the
Phœnicians in the ninth century. When the phylloxera struck
the vineyards of France proper, in the second half of the
nineteenth century, these vineyards were greatly extended.
Today the large vineyards of Algeria total more than 750,000
acres, owned by some 5,000 growers. These produce over
300,000,000 gallons (15,000,000 hectolitres) each year, a
seventh of all that is produced in European France.

Algerian winegrowing really became important in the
early decades of this century, when modern methods and
large-scale production were introduced. Chain-line production brings the wine to vat rooms, where it is stored in
glass-lined vats as large as houses. The vineyards are about

the size of those in California, Australia, Argentina, and South Africa, planted in the same lesser varieties of grapes. Carignan, Alicante Bouschet, Aramon, Mourestel, and Mourvèdre are the principal red varieties, all heavily planted in California, while Clairette and Ugni Blanc are mostly used for whites. Anybody who has tasted French wines has tasted those from Algeria, for these were used as a base for many of the shippers' wines sold as Burgundy and Bordeaux.

Attempts have been made to standardize the wines, but have failed, for many of them are distinct. Plains wines come from the areas of Mitidja and Issers surrounding the city of Algiers, Mostaganem around the port of Philippeville, and Bône in the department of Constantine. The wines are heavy, coarse, and undistinguished and are used primarily for blending. Hillside wines come from the areas between Cherchell and Ténès, from near Oran, near Philippeville, and from Sidi-bel-Abbès, famous as the headquarters of the French Foreign Legion. The wines from the mountain vineyards run from 12 to 15 per cent in alcoholic content, and often can be a delightful surprise. The districts of Miliana, Médéa, Aïn-Bessem, and Bouira produce small quantities of very creditable white and *rosé* wines. In Oran the vineyards of Tlemcen, near the Moroccan border, and those near the town of Mascara, after which the eye-paint is named, produce some of the better table wines.

Some of these wines can be very good, even though plantations of fine grape varieties are rare, and good wines suffer from the bad reputation of the general run of Algerian wine. Probably the best comes from the Domaine de la Trappe de Staoüeli and the Domaine de l'Harrach, near Algiers; but other good ones come from the Domaine de la Lorraine, near Bône, Domaine de Guebar, Domaine du Comte d'Hestel, near Constantine, and the Domaine Saint-Pierre, near Oran.

Champagne

Most Famous Wine of All

CHAMPAGNE made its place in the Gay Nineties, when the salesmen from French firms spent thousands every month to convince people that it was impossible to have a good time without a bottle of the sparkling wine.

Although some people feel that Champagne should be reserved for launching ships, most feel a pleasant surge of excitement as the wire muzzle is twisted off the cork and it is slowly pried loose, the expectant pause giving way to happy chatter as the cork pops, the wisp of smoke curls up, and the sparkling wine foams into the tall glasses. Many frown on the practice of allowing the cork to pop, but others believe that the pop is half the fun, and the Champagne-makers are more tolerant about this than the connoisseurs, merely suggesting that the cork should come out into your palm and not go flying off across the room. They are also pleased if the Champagne is properly cold, so that it won't foam all over everything, and if it is served in tulip-shaped glasses, not the shallow sherbet type, which dissipates all the carefully manufactured bubbles and destroys the flavour of the wine.

Everyone who loves Champagne is shocked by the current ridiculous fad for swizzle sticks, those abominations which allow the uncomprehending to twirl all the bubbles out of

H

the sparkling wine. Some even go as far as to have their own special swizzles made out of platinum and gold, always handy for instant use in the fashionable bars and night clubs of Paris and Rome, London and New York. With a few twirls of the swizzle, years of special care and labour can be destroyed in seconds.

The makers of the gay, sparkling wine of Champagne have their capital in Reims, the old cathedral town one hundred miles east and slightly north of Paris. Although Reims is out of the vineyard district, in the middle of a wide and rolling plain, the city is blessed with deep catacombs and old stone quarries, and when the Champagne-makers were in need of a storage place for their bottles, the chalk tunnels of Reims were just the thing. Some of them are a hundred feet underground, and in times of war practically the entire population has gone underground to live. One firm has over fifteen miles of tunnels.

The actual centre of the old province of Champagne, and the centre of the vineyards that produce the wine, is Épernay, a town of 12,000 people, seventeen miles south of Reims, on the southern bank of the Marne, that calm and winding river that joins the Seine near Paris. Across the river are the vineyards of the Marne Valley, the best of which are on the slopes above the town of Ay (pronounced *AH-ee*), one of the oddest place-names in France. Ay has cellars directly under the vineyards, and it was once said that the grapes did not have to be picked; the workers merely squeezed them, and the juice ran straight down into the *caves*.

Épernay boasts of a stately avenue, naturally enough, called Champagne, which begins at a modernistic column erected in honour of the Resistance Movement, and continues along the slope parallel to the river. Across the flats on the other side you can see the beautiful vineyards, and up the southern slope, behind the rows of impressive buildings that house the Champagne firms, are vent holes of various shapes and sizes, the air shafts leading down into the cellars, which burrow back into the hill.

Over the hill below Épernay, and running south, is a string of towns separated by vineyards, a long, curving ridge that looks like a vast amphitheatre. It is the Côte des Blancs, some fifteen miles long. The principal towns are Cramant, Avize, and Mesnil, all looking as if they were about to slip down to the valley floor. Many of the big firms have press houses in each town throughout the Champagne districts, *vendangeoirs*, to which the vineyard-owners bring their grapes at harvest time and where the baskets of white grapes are inspected by a member of the firm. Each firm accepts grapes at different hours of the day, and when a load is rejected by one, the owner hustles on to another press house in hopes of making his sale there. The single vineyard road is jammed with carts in harvest time.

All the vineyards of the Côte des Blancs are appropriately planted in the white Pinot and the Chardonnay. Some hundred years ago all the vineyards were classified on the basis of 100, all those between Cramant and Mesnil being rated over 90 per cent. These are the *têtes de cuvées* of the White Slope. Before harvest a representative committee of the growers meets and sets a price. At the same time a committee of the Champagne firms decides on a price they are willing to pay, always lower. The two groups meet, warily, and talk about the price. If they can't agree, as is not unusual, the prefect in Reims is called in to arbitrate, and if his figure is not agreeable to both groups, as happens rarely, that year's grapes are not sold. Since the late 1930's, vineyards have not produced enough to meet the demand, and firms buy under a quota system, which is a constant cause for complaint. Many of the firms own vineyards, each identified by a stone marker that looks like a headstone, to ensure themselves of a portion of each harvest, at least. When the

217

price is fixed, there is no haggling. Each owner sells his grapes at a figure reached by multiplying the agreed price by the percentage rating of his vineyard.

Such foresight is necessary in Champagne, for the grapes must be gathered and pressed quickly. Except for some of the vineyards of the Moselle, those in Champagne are the farthest north, so the harvest is set as late as possible to increase the sugar content; but this is dangerous, because the frosts come early in Champagne. The vineyards are full of smudge pots, and by each stands a jerry-can full of kerosene, left-overs from the war, some painted the olive drab of American field equipment, others the dull blue of the German. In 1950, however, the harvest was begun in mid-September because of an early attack of rot.

Once the prefect sets the date for the beginning of the harvest, pickers stream into the vineyards, carefully rejecting grapes and bunches that are under-ripe, and their loads are hustled into the press houses and quickly squeezed. The presses are large, some dozen feet across, and so made that the heavy press block can be swung over a second press pan, the juice running into vats on the floor beneath the presses, so that, once begun, the pressing never has to stop. The juice is then rushed off to the vat rooms of the Champagne firms, where it is allowed to ferment.

Some of the wine of the Côte de Blancs is made into a Champagne called Blanc de Blancs, white Champagne from the white Pinot only, whose light colour makes it easily distinguishable from the golden wines made from black grapes. Blanc de Blancs is not often sold under firm names, but under the village or commune name, called Blanc de Blancs of Cramant, or Avize, or Mesnil. It is known as *Champagne de Cru*, and is most liked by those who prefer exceedingly light wines. Some wine from the white grapes is made into Crémant (not to be confused with the town of Cramant), a white wine, made of red and white grapes, which is only partly sparkling. But most of the white wine made from the white grapes of the Côte de Blancs is blended with the white wine made from the red grapes planted north of the Marne, to make those Champagnes which are most familiar.

Each firm has its own secret blend of the various wines, which it is constantly modifying because of differences in the wine from year to year, changes in the taste of different countries and attempts to improve its blend. Blending is difficult, for each firm tries to make its Champagne taste the same from year to year. The new wine is raw, hiding its potential qualities, and the tasters must know what it is going to taste like once matured. What makes this harder is that the sugar content varies from year to year, so before fermentation cane sugar dissolved in wine is added, in order that when the fermentation changes it into alcohol, all the wine will have the same alcoholic content, usually 12 per cent by volume.

All the white grapes come from south of Épernay, out of the vineyards of the White Slope, but all the black grapes come from the vineyards to the north of the Marne, those along the river and those from the slopes of the mountain that rises out of the plain between Épernay and Reims, which is called the Montagne de Reims. These vineyards stretch in the shape of a question mark round the wooded mountain. Those of Mailly and Verzenay face north across the plain to Reims, five miles away, where the cathedral rises out of the distance. These are *hors classe* vineyards, rated at 100 per cent. Next to them on the curving slope, facing northeast, are the first category vineyards of the commune of Verzy. Facing southeast are the 100 per cent vineyards of Ambonnay and Bouzy, also in the district called Montagne de Reims. Facing south along the Marne Valley, to make the shank of the question mark, are the 100 per cent vineyards of Ay, flanked by those of the first category in the communes of Mareuil and Dizy.

All these vineyards are planted in Pinot Noir, or a variety, the same that is used to make the great wines of Burgundy. But in Champagne the wine is small and acid because of the soil, an outcropping of the same Kimeridgian clay you find in Chablis. There the warmer sun matures the grapes better but in Champagne sugar must often be added. Here bare chalk outcroppings break up the stretches of vineyard, and even the plantations look white when ploughed, the soil often being only a couple of inches deep. The vines are trained high, with double or triple rows of wire stretched along the root tops, and three or four long vine tendrils stretched along the wire, looking like a woman's hair pulled back from her forehead.

When the black grapes are pressed, they are run through as quickly as possible to avoid prolonged contact with the skins, which might impart their colour to the juice. For pink champagne, the juice is left with the skins a little longer.

Some firms make special blends of wines coming from only the 100 per cent vineyards, but most of the Champagnes are blends of several different grades. In Mailly a co-operative was formed during the depression, when the firms refused to buy the harvest, which began making a Champagne from the black grapes of the member growers. They have had tough going, starting with no capital, and building their own *vendangeoir* during the off season. After regular working hours the members dug the caves in the soft chalk underneath, progressing during the winter at the rate of a yard a day. Today the co-operative has nearly sixty members, and produces a vintage Champagne, both pink and white, the favourite wine at the George V and Plaza Athénée hotels in Paris. Such a sparkling wine from only one commune is rare in the black Pinot districts.

Most houses produce vintage Champagne, all the wine the product of one particular harvest, but most also produce cheaper non-vintage Champagne, a blend of two or more years. This is perfectly logical for a manufactured wine, the addition of wine from good years improving the quality of those from bad vintages.

Although Champagne is what it is because of the soil and climate that produce the wine, the manufacturing process is important, too. Everybody denies that it was Dom Pérignon who devised the process, but because nobody knows who it actually was, the blind old monk still gets the credit, from tradition. All over Champagne you can see his statue, reproductions of the original in the court of Moët & Chandon in Épernay, standing in his monk's robe, holding up a goblet, with a couple of bottles at his feet, and a beatific expression on his Roman face. He was the first to think of putting a piece of cork bark in the neck of a bottle instead of a wad of cloth, and as he was a cellar-master, he probably noticed that wine had a second fermentation the spring following the vintage, even if he didn't think of adding some sugar to increase it.

In any event, a dose of sugar is what makes all the bubbles, called a bead by Champagne-makers, who will tell you that the smaller the bead, the better the Champagne. After the wine has been hauled to the vat rooms, it is poured into glass-lined tanks the size of a small room, where the wine is allowed to ferment for three or four weeks.

The different wines ferment separately, each in its own vat, until some time in December or January, when all the doors and windows of the vat room are thrown open and the cold air stops any last vestiges of fermentation. The wine is then drawn off its lees. This operation, called racking, is usually performed three times. Each time, the wine is cleared, or fined, with fishtails or the whites of eggs, which helps rid the wine of suspended impurities. After the first racking the new wines are blended, and after the third any wines from other vintages that are considered needed to make the proper blend are added. By March the wine is bottled, with a dose of cane sugar dissolved in wine added to each bottle. Then the bottles are sealed with a temporary cork held down by a steel-wire clamp and stored in the cellars, neck nestling into neck.

With spring, the miracle of Champagne begins. The sealed bottles of wine are dozens of feet underground, stored at a low constant temperature, one that never varies. But when the sap begins to rise in the trees, somehow the bacteria begin to work in the wine. A second fermentation begins. The sugar is turned into alcohol, the process forming carbonic acid gas, building up a pressure in the bottle that is often more than a hundred pounds to the square inch. In the old days, before the cellar-masters knew how much sugar to add, and before bottles were uniform, one would sometimes explode, often starting another bottle, until the echoing pops sounded like firecrackers; but this happens rarely today.

The bottles rest flat for four years, during which time the fermentation forms a deposit in the wine. When fermentation has finally ceased, the side of the bottle opposite the deposit is painted with a blob of whitewash, and a line of whitewash is smeared on the punt, that thumb-deep depression in the base of each bottle. The bottles are carefully placed in slanting racks, neck down. These racks, called *pupitres*, are tables with oval holes in them big enough for the bottle necks and shoulders. For four months a worker labours to get the sediment down in the neck of the bottle, wiggling it one day, turning it a bit the next, and gradually tipping the bottle more upright. Gradually the deposit moves down, and when its tail is against the cork, the bottles are stacked, standing on their heads, the cork of one resting in the punt of the bottle beneath it.

They stay that way until the firm gets an order for shipment. Then they are placed neck-down in a heavy, partitioned wicker basket holding six, and lugged to that part of the cellar where the disgorging, or sediment removal, takes place. A worker holds the bottle upside down against a gauntlet on his left arm, with corked mouth in his hand. Standing in front of a barrel with a hole cut in its side, he works the cork loose with a pair of pliers. It flies into the barrel with a bang, the man twists the bottle upright, runs his left thumb round the neck, smells it, tastes his thumb, and before the wine begins to foam, slaps the bottle in a circular rack, the mouth against a rubber nipple, the punt against a breast-shaped pad.

The trick is to have the sediment shoot out with the cork, and the bottle is so held that the air space pops up through the Champagne, blowing out the sediment before it has a chance to fall down into the sparkling wine. Some firms freeze the necks of the bottles, so there is no risk of losing any of the wine. Other firms do not, because they think freezing hurts the wine.

Next to the disgorger is another worker, who takes the bottle from the circular rack and sets it in a similar one in front of him. This machine has a superstructure of silver-plated knobs and tubes, and a couple of bottles hanging on it, upside down. One contains a bottle of the same Champagne that is being handled, from which to fill up any bottles that have lost too much in the disgorging. The other bottle contains cane sugar dissolved in wine. A dose of this is added to the wine, depending on which type of Champagne is wanted: *Brut*, *Extra Dry*, or *Sec*.

In the old days before the turn of the century, people liked sweeter Champagne than they do today. Champagne was then a dessert wine more than anything else, but it has become less sweet through the years because people's tastes have tended toward dryness. Occasionally Champagnes are made without the addition of sugar but not many people care for them. The favourite of the Champagne firms is *Brut*, to which up to $1\frac{1}{2}$ per cent of sugar by volume is added. Up to 3 per cent is added to make Extra Dry, up to 4 per cent for Dry, which amounts to about a teaspoonful of syrup per bottle. *Demi-sec* Champagne contains up to 8 per cent, and sweet or *Doux* up to 10. The amount of sugar added varies with different firms, some making a *Brut* containing only the minimum ¾ per cent and they change their formula from time to time.

Brut costs more than the others, because the smaller dose of sugar does not disguise the taste of the wine under a smothering sweetness. Good Champagnes have little sugar added, their natural sugar content being enough to form the bubbles. But sugar is often added to the cheaper Champagnes to hide the shortcomings of the wine.

The dosing is gauged automatically. The bottle is then handed on to the corker, whose machine squeezes the thick cork, which is made in sections. By means of a weighted metal plunger, the cork is forced down into the mouth of the bottle. This is another ticklish operation, for the bottle then goes to the fourth man of the disgorging team, whose machine puts the metal cap on the cork and tightens the wire muzzle round the top of the cork and the bottle lip. The banging on of the metal cap forces the cork in farther, and if the cork goes in too far, the wire muzzle won't hold properly, the cork will work loose, all the bubbles will fizz away, and the wine will go flat.

The bottle then goes to the packing-room, where it is labelled and wrapped. All in all, a bottle of champagne goes through eighty-four hands from cellar to shipping crate, and the workers must be highly skilled. In addition to his wages, a worker gets a bottle of ordinary wine a day so that he won't be tempted to tipple the Champagne, and as further encouragement to abstinence he also gets two or three bottles of Champagne a month, which he often sells.

Champagne costs so much not only because it has to be handled so often, but because it has to be kept in bottles so long. In addition, press houses in the vineyard districts are needed to process the grapes. Some firms have as many as a dozen such *vendangeoirs*, and each one costs something like £5,000 a year to run. But the main reasons Champagne costs so much are the heavy taxes levelled against it, extra taxes because it is sparkling.

The vineyards of Champagne are probably the most sub-divided in the world, as insurance against hail, the theory being that a storm will hit one section and miss another, and if the grower has sections in different areas, the chances are he will not lose all his grapes. The result, of course, is that expensive farm equipment is impractical, for a grower would spend too much time moving it from parcel to parcel and would not have enough time for working. And as labour costs rise, so will the price of Champagne.

In 1950, Champagne firms sold over 33,000,000 bottles of the sparkling wine, half of this in France, large portions to French colonies and 3,000,000 bottles to England. The United States imported less than 2,600,000 bottles.

Champagne amounts to 40 per cent of all wines exported from France and is its greatest wine export. Ninety-nine per cent of the exports are made by the Champagne houses and only one per cent is exported by growers.

Champagne vintages are less important than vintages in other wine districts, for Champagne is a blended and manu-factured wine, but there are a few that are outstanding: 1934, 1937, and some 1938, 1941, 1942, 1943, 1945, 1947, 1948, and 1949.

Like all white wines, sparkling or not, Champagne should be drunk fairly young, say within ten to fifteen years after the harvest. This, in spite of the fact that some connoisseurs like to talk about bottles decades old. Like all white wines, Champagne has a tendency to maderize with age, turning brown and musty. Because of the gas pressure in the bottles, Champagne is also more likely to become corky.

The Brandies of France
Cognac and Armagnac

BRANDIES are perhaps the most wonderful spirits ever devised by the genius of man. The wonder of their excellence is known the world over. A fine old brandy has become a symbol of the richness of civilized living, and its powers of resuscitation have been lauded for centuries. The drinking of a glass of fine brandy is one of life's great luxuries. Time makes brandy, man can only help.

Tasters buy brandy by smell, and more than half the pleasure of a great brandy comes from its heady aroma. The most sensible glass is one of good size, with a small amount of brandy in the bottom. While many people insist on large balloon glasses, others prefer the long and comparatively slender tulip shapes. Both are excellent, for they permit of swirling the brandy in the glass, which brings the liquid into contact with the air, while their shapes form an enclosing chimney so that none of the fine bouquet is lost. Such glasses are pretentious, however, when the brandy is young and mediocre, and many people who serve fine wines follow them with insignificant brandies. A great wine deserves to be followed by an old brandy.

Brandy is an *eau-de-vie*, the water of life, the French term for all distilled spirits which in northern Europe are called *aqua vitæ*. By European nomenclature, even whiskies are classed as *eaux-de-vie*, or spirits.

In France, the term brandy is usually limited to distillations of wine, mainly Armagnac and Cognac, although undistinguished brandies come from other districts, and to distillations of the residue of stems and pulp remaining in the vats after the pressing, which is called *marc*. Marcs are made in most of the wine districts of France, but the best come from Champagne, Burgundy, and the Rhône Valley. The finest bear the names of the vineyards from which they come, are produced in very small quantities, and rarely reach the market. When well aged, they have a distinctive, grapey, earthy, leathery taste. A fine *Marc de Champagne* is light, with much finesse. Burgundy marcs are fuller and heavier. Most of them are sold simply as *Marc de Bourgogne* although better ones carry the name of vineyard or domain, such as *Marc de la Romanée-Conti, Marc de Musigny, Marc de Chambertin, Marc de Nuits-Saint-Georges*, and *Marc du Marquis d'Angerville*. The most expensive is the *Marc des Hospices de Beaune*, sold at the annual auction sale. The most notable of those from the Rhône Valley is the *Marc de l'Hermitage*.

Many brandies are called *alcools blancs* because of their white colour. *Quetsch* is distilled from purple plums, *Mirabelle* from tiny yellow plums, *Framboise* from raspberries, *Fraise* from strawberries, and *Kirsch* from the stones of small cherries. They are colourless because they are not aged in wood, but in crockery, and are slow in maturing. All are exceedingly dry, and some of the best can be found by searching out the small producers and peasant growers who make them—a practice followed by good French restaurateurs.

In Normandy, cider is distilled to make *Calvados*, the finest apple brandy in the world. The name is taken from the department of Calvados, and the best comes from the Vallée d'Auge, its greatest cider-making district. When old, Calvados can be a magnificent brandy, but fine ones can rarely be found outside the cellars of Normandy. A distillation is made from the residue of apple pressings when making cider, and this is usually called *eau-de-vie de marc de cidre*.

In Normandy, dinners are so enormous that something called the *trou normand* has become a custom. This is a pause between courses, when the diners take a short rest, fortifying themselves for following courses by a glass of Calvados.

All these brandies bear only a family resemblance to liqueurs, which are distilled from various concoctions of herbs and berries, sometimes with a brandy base. There are hundreds of liqueurs, and in the nineteenth century new ones were created whenever some great event was worthy of being commemorated. Among the best are Chartreuse Verte, which contains more than one hundred separate ingredients, Chartreuse Jaune, which is made of fewer ingredients and is less powerful, and the world-famous Benedictine. Others are Crème de Menthe; the Cherry liqueurs, of which the best come from Denmark; and the triple secs, such as Cointreau and Orange Curaçao, these being the most commonly drunk liqueurs in France. Many are still made by monks, who began the making of liqueurs in the first place. But liqueurs are not brandy.

The distilling of wine began centuries ago, because the resulting product could be transported easily and made bad water safe and palatable. It was the only hard drink then known to man, and up to the last century brandies had complete control of the spirits market. As a result of the inroad made by whiskies, brandy-makers have tried to reduce brandy to the levels of whiskies thus sacrificing its position as the greatest of all distillates in the effort to regain economic supremacy. Brandy still remains unique, however.

The name probably comes from the Germanic word *brannt, Branntwein* meaning burned wine; but as one would expect, the greatest brandy comes from France.

Ships from the north used to put in along that part of the French coast just above the Gironde estuary, mostly at the port of La Rochelle, to pick up cargoes from the salt deposits. It was not long before the local inhabitants reckoned that they might sell the traders wine as well. What was good business for Bordeaux, down to the south, would be good business for folk who lived along the Charente River.

Unlike many good ideas, it worked too well, and by the seventeenth century too much wine was being produced. Although Villeneuve talked of the water of life as early as the fourteenth century, it was a knight named Croix-Maron who is supposed to have popularized the idea of distilling the wine, the product being easier to ship, taking up only one-tenth of the hold space, and being harmed not at all by the sea journey. He was also pleased to discover that it tasted magnificent, which prompted him to announce without a trace of modesty: "In cooking my wines, I have discovered their soul."

He was right, for by the time Napoleon arrived on the scene, nearly two hundred years later, almost every brandy made anywhere in the world had come to be called Cognac, after the town of that name on the Charente River. Spanish brandies came to be called *coñac* in imitation, and the name persists today, although the only resemblance is that both are distilled from wine. The same name is also applied to brandies from South America. Until the 1930's, when reciprocal treaties forbade the practice, brandy made in the United States was also called Cognac, with no attempt to convert the spelling.

Cognac was properly incensed at this imitation, for it was the wine from which the brandy was distilled that set Cognac apart, making it uniquely great. The small white wine of the vineyards along the Charente were hard and acid, but all the unpleasantness disappeared in the cooking. What is more,

229

the casks were made from specially seasoned oak from the nearby province of Limousin. The best oak comes from the edge of a forest, it is said, and certain sections are supposed to be better than others, being classed in separate growths or *crus*. The tannin picked up from the wood during ageing gives another special distinction to the brandy, to say nothing of the precious secrets of the distilling itself, or the fine art of blending the brandy from different vineyards.

Napoleon re-established the supremacy of real Cognac over its spurious competitors by drinking Cognac brandy exclusively and carting it all over Europe on his campaigns. During the nineties the only fashionable brandy was the one called Napoleon's "Return-from-Russia" Cognac, and one of the favourite gambits of wine wags is to state that the main task of Napoleon's armies was to lug Cognac about so that it could bear his name.

Many firms still call their best Cognacs Napoleon Brandy. They claim that it has become a tradition in the industry, but it is more accurate to say that such a firm calls one of its grades Napoleon Brandy in the hope that unknowing buyers will really believe the Cognac is from the same stock from which the Little Corporal was supplied. There is no real Napoleon Brandy on sale anywhere today, and even if there were, it would not be so good as an old Cognac bottled yesterday. The name is false and purposely misleading. Cognac does not age in bottle, and for that matter, neither does any other *eau-de-vie* or liqueur, though a few believe they can detect a slight mellowing in a long-bottled *alcool blanc*. The high alcoholic content preserves it in exactly the same state as at the moment it was bottled.

The brandy of Cognac comes from a district now limited by law. No other brandy in France is entitled to be called Cognac, the name of the chief town in the centre of the vineyards. Many of the big firms are located there, while most of the others have their offices and plants in Jarnac, a small town ten miles farther up the Charente toward Angoulême. Before World War II the Charente was used to transport the Cognac to the port of La Rochelle for shipment, and the rows of horse-drawn barges was one of the sights of the region. Today most of the transport is by lorries.

During the winter after the harvest, the vineyard-owners get a permit to distill their wines, and they sell the raw colourless brandy to the shipping firms, which store it, barrel piled on barrel, in warehouses; and there it rests, waiting while time turns it into great Cognac. All the buildings near Cognac firms are stained black, as if the buildings had once been on fire and the sooty smoke had leaked out through the cracks. The stain is made by evaporating alcohol fumes, which, according to local intelligence, cause the growth of a microscopic fungus when the fumes hit the air.

The vineyards of the Cognac district are divided into six classes: those called Grande Champagne, to the south of the town of Cognac; Petite Champagne, south of that, with the town of Jarnac in its centre; the Borderies, to the west and all three surrounded by those vineyards called Fins Bois. These, in turn, are surrounded by Bons Bois, while over on the coast and on the two islands just off shore are vineyards classed as Bois Ordinaires. Originally the word *Champagne* meant chalky soil, the districts being at that time land surrounded by woods. The Bois were later cleared and planted with vineyards. Brandies from the districts are aged separately, then blended by the shippers.

This is not a wicked practice, however, as it would be if wines were blended, for the brandy from each district lacks certain qualities, according to brandy experts. The brandy from Grande Champagne, for instance, ages very slowly, and is heavier, more pungent and finer than that from Petite Champagne, which ages quite rapidly. Most firms sell a Cognac called Fine Champagne, a blend of the two, but it is expensive, not only because it has to be aged so long, but because it takes some ten bottles of wine to make one of brandy. To put brandy within the reach of everyone, the Champagnes are blended with Borderies, a soft, fat, supple full-bodied, quickly ageing brandy, and with Fins Bois, which lacks finesse, and Bons Bois, which has a taste imparted by the earth, this *goût de terroir* destroying what finesse it has. Each of these brandies ages successively faster, and ordinary brandies are made of a large proportion of the distillate from Bois Ordinaires vineyards.

All these vineyards used to be planted in Folle Blanche, which is being replaced, about two-thirds of the plantations now being in Saint-Émilion vine, a variety of Ugni Blanc. This vine produces more, and flowers later, and is therefore not so likely to be frozen. The name of the vine has nothing to do with the Bordeaux district of the same name.

The vineyards were almost completely wiped out when the phylloxera struck in the late 1870's. That misery was added to by the fact that the grafted American stocks were subject to another disease, characteristic of the extremely chalky soil of Cognac, called green sickness. As a result, the number of acres in vines dropped from nearly three-quarters of a million to less than one-fifth, which is what is in vine today.

The wine is distilled twice. It is first brought to a boil and yields a spirit of some 25 per cent alcohol, or about 50 proof. Then it is distilled again, the first and last of the steam, the head and tail, being discarded, and only the middle distillate, called the heart, is kept. The heart ends up at between 60 and 70 per cent proof of alcohol, 120 to 140 proof, and raw enough to corrode the hide off a mule.

Some say that the secret of a great Cognac is the temperature at which distillation takes place, which may account for the present-day use of old-fashioned pot stills. New-fangled stills and distillation methods are constantly being

introduced in the district, but few are successful, the centuries-old methods and equipment still proving the best.

The new Cognac is next poured into barrels of the
Limousin oak, where it remains anywhere from six to fifty
years. The brandy loses about 2 per cent of its alcohol each
year through evaporation, more at the beginning and less
toward the end of the ageing period. After half a century
the proof is down to 80 or 90, which has proved to be the
best strength at which to drink it, for then the brandy is at
a peak of perfect balance, and longer ageing would only
weaken it still more, with no increase in flavour or body or
aroma.

At one time it was thought that the alcoholic content
steadily declined, and then after thirty years or so suddenly
increased again. Where the increase came from remained in
the realm of mystery, and while this change is physically
impossible, a few of the old brandy-makers still believe in
the miracle. In any event, once bottled, a brandy ceases to
improve with age, kept from change by its high alcoholic
content. A fifty-year-old brandy bottled yesterday is on a
par with a fifty-year-old brandy bottled a century ago, and
is probably better if the brandies were of the same quality
to begin with.

Most Cognacs are a blend of different years, as well as of
different districts, the label indicating the age of the oldest
brandy, not that of the most in quantity, unless more specifi-
cally identified. Some firms now and then bottle vintage
Cognac, all of it coming from a particular year, but this is
rare.

Although all other *eaux-de-vie* come to market clear and
colourless, it has become the habit to prefer a brandy that is
brown. In really old brandies this colour comes from the
tannin in the barrel wood, but in the less expensive grades
burned sugar is added, the caramel colouring the Cognac to
the wanted shade. To improve the smooth flavour of their

cheap Cognacs, some unscrupulous firms add vanilla flavouring, which is relatively hard to detect. A good brandy should taste dry and smooth, with little or no aftertaste, and because vanilla flavouring lingers in the mouth, it can be detected in this way, even if you cannot smell it. This doctoring might not be thought so wicked if it was mentioned on the bottle, or if cheap brandies were not thus disguised to sell as fine Cognacs. Fortunately, there are enough honest firms to make it possible to get good brandy at fair prices.

There are all sorts of letters and galaxies of stars on Cognac bottles, each firm having its own system. The use of the star was introduced after the phylloxera, when it was decided that good vintages ought to have a star. The second good year after the phylloxera was to have two stars, and so on. But the star markings soon became cumbersome.

Three Star usually means the cheapest brandy of a firm's line, at least three years old, and often six, diluted with distilled water to bring it down to about 42 per cent or 84 proof. Nearly all brandies are diluted to this strength, and while you can find brandies that have reached this witching point merely through age and evaporation, such half-century-old brandies are fabulously expensive. Brandies between seven and twelve years old are usually called VO or VE, "very old" or "very extra"; VSO, VSOP, and VVSOP are older than ten years, the last meaning "very very superior old pale." There are some remarkable VSOP's, which are scarce and hard to find. They may be from thirty to sixty years old. It is odd that old brandies should be called "pale," when darkness has become a criterion of distinction.

These signs and their meanings change, with whim and regulations. The best way to buy brandy is by price, but *only* if it is a bottle put out by a good firm, when price expresses its value, and provided it is sold by a reliable merchant.

The young brandies taste fine when mixed with soda or

made into cocktails or toddies, but such mixing is sacrilege to older brandies. It takes years to get the smooth, wonderful flavour into an old brandy, and mixing or diluting destroys it. Young brandies are a let-down after a fine meal, and older ones can be bought for only slightly more. In the 1930's an old brandy cost at least twice as much as the young ones, but in the '50's they cost less than a quarter more, and are today one of the best values in things to drink. You don't save money by buying good brandy, but you get more for it.

Brandy evaporates rapidly because of its alcohol and ethers, and as it is drunk rarely and in small amounts, small bottles are good value—just the opposite of wine. It is still the fashion to use large display bottles, but the last half never tastes so good as the first.

Gravity is an important element in the making of Cognac. That is why most of the big firms are built on hillsides. The barrels are trundled into an upper floor of the blending plant after being brought from the *chais* where they have been ageing, and then dumped into great vats which hold over 6,000 gallons. Pipe lines lead from these vats to others, in which the blending takes place, the Cognac passing through thick wool filters which look like the top of a bass drum. Wooden paddles whisk the various Cognacs together to make for thorough mixing, and here and there are wooden man-hole covers so that the blenders can watch the flowing. The blended brandies are run into man-high vats on the floor below, and these are tapped when needed, pipes carrying the blends down another floor to the bottling-room, where machines rinse the bottles with brandy, and men place them on an endless chain, where other machines fill, cap, and label them. This bottling-room is supervised by a man in a glass-enclosed booth that looks like the control room of a battleship, where with a system of spigots he can control which vats are being tapped. Small firms do this all by hand.

Blending is an art, for each part of the world seems to have special preferences in colour and flavour. The English climate, for instance, imparts a musty taste to brandies, and the blender must see that bottles for England have that particular mustiness the English associate with good brandy. Since each barrel tastes slightly different, it is difficult to make a brandy type that will taste the same all the time, and it is the blender's job to make the taste as consistent as possible. From time to time, firms change their formulas, always trying to make new blends more popular, which is why bottles of any particular brand may taste different from shipment to shipment.

If it were not for its brandy, the great flat stretch of sun-broiled land with Cognac in its centre would be known only as the birthplace of Francis I and from the fact that good melons are grown there. Cognac is a quiet, stolid town, its streets and buildings bleached grey by the scorching sun, and even its large park still and dusty in the hot summer. But the heat is what makes the wine from which Cognac is made, and everybody agrees it is worth the discomfort. And as is usual, there's the classic Cognac story, probably apocryphal, a little worn by now, but still told to everyone who comes to the hot little city on the winding Charente. It seems that a party of bishops were having dinner in Rome, and one of them was asked where he came from. "I am the Bishop of Angoulême," he informed the company. The announcement was greeted with silence and blank stares. "I am also the Bishop of Cognac," he stated, and at once there was a chorus of gasps, and the other bishops exclaimed in chorus: "Ah, the splendid See of Cognac!"

It is good to know that Cognac tastes better than any of the stories about it.

ARMAGNAC

Armagnac comes from the land of d'Artagnan, a fabled region once rich and famous, where witches can still be found to bring you luck or curse your enemies, where barn dances are the favourite winter sport, and the mourners sit down and eat a dish of beans together after a funeral. The cold wind howls down from the Pyrenees in winter, and the rolling lands broil brown under the searing southern sun in summer. This is the land of the Gascons.

The city of Auch is on the eastern edge of the Armagnac district, a hilltop town of some 16,000, crowned by a cathedral that was started in the fourteenth century and finally completed by Louis XIV. It boasts an almost unknown marvel of France, a magnificent choir seat decorated with hundreds of tiny carved wooden figures, each a minor masterpiece. The artist was a pupil of Michelangelo, and the wood he worked had been left to harden and blacken in water for a hundred years.

Many of the townspeople and those from the countryside have Spanish names and faces; they are descendants of Goths and Visigoths, returned from raids into Spain, who liked the wide spaces of Gascony so much that they settled there. Since Gascony was the birthplace of Henri IV, many of the local people are Protestants and many of their farms are marked by cypress trees so that there will be no doubt of their faith. But even the Protestants have kept to the old custom of church seating: women in front, men behind. It's a strange land.

The brandy of Armagnac is as distinctive as the people who make it and the land from which it comes. Strong and heady, a fine Armagnac boasts a full-bodied pungency when well matured and properly cared for, which gives it a powerful character of its own. Most of it goes to market in a bottle as distinctive as its taste, round and flat, with a long neck, called a *basquaise* after the neighbouring region where it originated. But the way Armagnac is made bears only a family resemblance to the process of making Cognac, for all the Armagnac firms are small, and there are no great blending plants.

Following the harvest, portable stills travel about the countryside to the different growers. The apparatus looks like a small old-fashioned locomotive, and growers insist that one still can be better than another. Distillation is a single continuous process, carried on very slowly, the new wine becoming raw brandy which comes out at about 52 per cent or 104 proof. The brandy is then poured into barrels made from local oak, the oak of Armagnac imparting more tannin to the ageing brandy than other oaks. Local growers feel that a good third of the Armagnac character comes from the oak in which it ages.

The best vineyards of the district are in a region named Bas-Armagnac, called Lower Armagnac because the country is less hilly then the rest. The very centre of this district is named Grand Bas, the special vineyards being somewhat sandier and for that reason producing a more delicate brandy. The vineyards of Ténarèze make up the second district, and those in Haut-Armagnac form the third. All produce wines of the slope, the vines planted in tall *Y's*, their tendrils strung on wires.

The growers set their prices, and meet buyers, at the Café de France, in Eauze, a tiny and charming village in the centre of the vineyard districts. There, over glasses of the hard, local wine, they discuss their Armagnacs, arguing about vintages, exchanging tricks of the trade, discussing markets. Now and then, to prove a point, a grower will pull from his pocket a small sample bottle of his brandy, biting out the cork with his teeth.

Brandy is rarely drunk when being bought and sold, and

much of it is rarely tasted. A few drops are poured into the palm and perhaps touched with the tongue, but usually the hands are rubbed together, then cupped in front of the nose. The brandy character can best be detected by the sense of smell. One grower claims that his father spent his entire life buying Armagnac and never tasted a drop.

After a few sniffs of the warmed and evaporating Armagnac on his palms, an old grower will have enough clues to be able to make good guesses as to the age of the brandy and the vineyards from which the original wine came, and perhaps even the particular lot from which the brandy was distilled. Buyers travelling about to growers in various districts are apt to depend more on their taste, however, for they must be able to detect in young Armagnacs those qualities that will make it distinctive after a quarter-century of ageing.

Because it is the land of the most famous of the Three Musketeers, most firms have their Réserve d'Artagnan, much the way Cognac firms resort to sticking Napoleon's name on a bottle. Perhaps the only person who really has the right to use the famous name is a direct descendant of that roistering gallant. He is the Marquis de Montesquiou, a moustached young man who bears a marked resemblance to his ancient ancestor.

The Marquis is the owner of Château de Marsan, a great turreted castle near Auch, parts of which date from the tenth century. The panelled rooms and great halls are filled with portraits of a thousand years of famous ancestors. The Marquis, who is also the fifth Duc de Fezensac, which is a nearby commune full of vineyards whose wine becomes Armagnac, works the château and its estate as a model farm and experimental station. He is apt to tell you that local legend says Armagnac is an aphrodisiac and was d'Artagnan's favourite drink.

The Marquis is one of the men primarily responsible for

re-establishing the greatness of the name of Armagnac, for
in this ancient land of French tradition little of the tradition
attaches to the creation of fine Armagnac. In the days of
Queen Victoria, Armagnac was thought to be too lusty a
brandy, too powerful in aroma to be allowed in the drawing-
room. Until *Appellation d'Origine* laws were passed, in fact,
Armagnac was shipped north to be blended with Cognac.
Today tastes are sturdier and fine Armagnacs can again be
drunk outside the region of its birth and under its own name.

Yet all Armagnac is not fine, and perhaps the principal
reason is the lack of tradition among Armagnac shippers.
Most shippers carry their business in their hats, and their
concern is selling gallons of the local brandy, with little
interest in maintaining a world-wide reputation for great
quality. There is a great difference between fine and cheap
Cognacs, but there is a still greater difference between
Armagnacs, and many of them are simply bad. In France,
when anybody wants a cheap brandy, he buys Armagnac,
and few people in France realize that there are great Armagnacs as well. The Marquis feels that it is part of his heritage
to make the most of the soil on which his family has lived
for so many generations, and to see that fine Armagnac is
available outside the walls of his château. Some of the honest
firms, such as Samalens and Cavé, work in co-operation with
the Marquis to establish a tradition as great as that of Cognac,
whose finest brandies can be obtained anywhere in the world,
whether in Saigon or Saskatchewan. Armagnacs sell at
the same price levels as Cognacs, yet it may be a hundred
years before Armagnac brandies will have made their
reputation and established a tradition of excellence.

Age is not the only criterion when it comes to Armagnac,
for peasant growers are scattered through districts whose
vineyard product varies from fair to excellent, and blending
can result in good or bad brandies. Armagnac, especially,
is distinguished by a *goût de terroir* that reflects the quality

of the soil in the taste of the brandy. Oak barrels and the skill used in distillation can all be reflected in the final result. Care during ageing can also make an enormous difference. Many shippers show little concern with these details but are anxious merely to buy the brandies from the peasants at the lowest possible price and sell them to gullible markets at the highest.

The strenuous efforts of the Marquis de Montesquiou and other honest merchants are beginning to bear fruit however, for the quality of some of the great Armagnacs is being maintained. At the Château de Marsan it is customary to be served a dinner which features the traditional Gascony dish, *poule au pot*, a young chicken simmered for hours with vegetables and dumplings, followed by a fine old Armagnac. And in every bedroom it is the custom, as old as the brandy itself, to place a small decanter of Armagnac. It is considered an insult if any is left in the morning. The Marquis sees to it that brandy of the same quality goes into all bottles bearing his name. That has always been the tradition. It merely became necessary for someone to believe in it. The Marquis de Montesquiou, Duc de Fezensac, descendant of d'Artagnan, does so.

Appendix

SERVING AND DRINKING
WINES

Wine Rules

Drinking Wine is one of life's great pleasures. Through the centuries certain ideas about wine-drinking have been formulated, as guides to help you to get the most from a bottle. Personal preferences are more important than any rules. The rules themselves are little more than tested preferences. Certain wines taste better than others with specific dishes.

If rules inhibit your enjoyment of wines, there should be no rules. As you learn about wines by tasting them with your own palate, you will invent your own guides. No rules about wine fall into the realm of etiquette; they merely indicate the most pleasing combinations of food and drink and help you to avoid unpleasant ones. What tastes right to your palate is likely to please another's.

French Wine-drinking

Wine and food go together, one bringing out the virtues of the other. The two complement each other. This basic fact is at the bottom of the Frenchman's surprise at the way other people eat and drink. A Frenchman will sip a sweet and syrupy concoction before eating and think nothing of it, drink cheap and acid wine with his food, and top it off with an equally sickening and powerful liqueur. How you insult your stomach seems to depend on where you were brought up.

A dinner consists of a number of courses so that there will be time to have two or three different wines. Soup is served, for it acts as an alkalizer; the vegetables are served separately, for few taste good with wines. A cheese course is added because cheese brings out the taste of wine better than anything else. And

243

the whole meal is planned so that each course is better than the one before. The wines are also served in an ascending order of excellence.

Two wines are served, and a variety of courses, so that you will have a basis of comparison. One wine, the wine you like best, can give much satisfaction. But if more than one wine is served, it is possible to play that delightful gastronomic game fondly called the music of the wine. When the first wine is drunk with the first course, you leave a little of it in your glass. When the second wine comes along, you drink it with the second course and taste the first wine against it, and so on.

Cocktails

Many wine-lovers are heartily opposed to cocktails. There's no doubt that a strong cocktail, with a pronounced flavour, paralyses your taste buds, and usually everything else as well, which is the reason why a glass of chilled dry Sherry or a dry Champagne often replaces the cocktail before a dinner where wines are being served. Sweet drinks, such as Manhattans, tend to make it difficult to taste the wines. When drinking wines, most pleasure is derived if drinks made only from grapes are served.

Food and Wine

The only rules are that dry white wines taste best before red wines, and that great wines taste best when they follow lesser ones of a similar type. There are many classic marriages of food and wine, the fruits of centuries of trial and error. A fine Montrachet or Haut-Brion Blanc might taste well with a chicken sandwich, but would taste glorious with poached sole or a perfectly roasted chicken. A smaller wine would better complement the sandwich, such as a Chablis or Vouvray. A Châteauneuf-du-Pape would add marvellously to the deliciousness of a grilled steak; a Chambertin would be wonderful with a prime roast beef. The great gamut of French wines offers a wealth of choice for any dish. The detailed sections of this book covering the districts will offer suggestions that you can adopt to make your own combinations for wining and dining.

Smoking

The French are much less strict about the ritual and regimen of serving wine than wine-lovers of England and America. Many wine-growers smoke while drinking wines, but never with meals.

Sweets and Sours with Wines

Sour foods and tart dishes can spoil the taste of wines, as do highly spiced foods. Sweet dishes and fruits completely deaden the taste for dry wine. Sweet wines exist for accompanying sweet foods, and there is a wide gamut of them to accompany fruits and custards. Champagnes and Vouvrays taste particularly wonderful with fruits, and the golden Sauternes and Barsacs can be perfect companions for other desserts.

BUYING WINES

Value

Many good wines are low in price—but the value of a wine is always measured on how much you get for your money. A fake bottle of Burgundy at 15s. is expensive, a genuine bottle of Richebourg at £1 is good value. A reliable shipper's Monopole, or regional wine, may be priced the same as a classified Bordeaux growth, but the first is a bad buy. For a few shillings less it might be a good one.

Restaurants

Some people distrust restaurant wines, and with reason. Not only are prices marked up enormously, anywhere from three to four hundred per cent, but the wines are bought cheaply from doubtful shippers, bear fancy labels, and are frequently of poor vintage. The theory is that customers will not know the difference. There are many fine restaurants, however, that are exceptions. This is not limited to foreign restaurants, for a fine wine card is also a rarity in France. Few restaurants and hotels make any effort to carry or sell good wines. Their wine cards are a jumble of Sherries and Champagnes, Bordeaux and California wines, with no attempt to classify them into groups.

Vintage Charts

In England and America much wine-drinking is done from vintage charts. Wines from a district such as Burgundy or Bordeaux vary enormously in a single year, and a good vintage from one commune can be a bad one in the next.

It is perhaps easiest to think of vintage charts as a table of generalities, full of exceptions. In Burgundy, for instance, 1947 was the vintage of the century, and yet many growers made poor wine because their grapes were too high in sugar, which could not be converted properly to alcohol during fermentation, and poor wines resulted. 1945 is rightly called a great year for white Burgundies, and yet the Chablis vineyards were ruined by hail early in the year, and no wine was produced. In Burgundy, if you buy other than estate-bottled wines, the year on the label may not be the same as that of the wine in the bottle, for many shippers stretch good vintages with bad ones, or sell poor vintages as fine ones. There is no such difficulty, of course, when buying chateau-bottled Bordeaux, or wines from lesser or more southern districts where vintages are less important.

It is no wonder that shippers are tempted to put false vintage labels on bottles. Many wine-lovers are slaves to their charts, and if a year is not lauded in the tables, they will not consider the wine. Perfect examples are the 1946 and 1948 vintages, which were good in many districts, but 1946 and 1948 wines are hard to sell because they are rated low on most charts and thus have a poor reputation. A vintage chart can be a great help when buying wines, but it is a mistake to assume that the entire glorious gamut of wines can be reduced to a series of formulas on a tiny card. A chart is most helpful when its limitations are appreciated. (See Vintage Chart, pages 256-8.)

Halves and Magnums

Half bottles are good for trying out a wine for ordinary wines, their youngness protecting them. Great wines suffer from being in small bottles. They are better in magnum than in bottle.

Laying Away Wines

Most people feel it is better to buy wines young and lay them away for a few years. Old bottles are expensive when bought in wineshops, and the wine-drinker can make enormous savings by buying great vintages when young, before the costs of long storing must be added to the price. Even so, great wines are never cheap. There are rarely such things as bargains in wine; wines advertised for quick sale can be poor or badly stored ones, and value for your money may be slight. Reputable merchants who know their business, however, can offer through judicious buying, good wines at reasonable prices. Poor wine merchants also follow the practice of pushing cheap wines at bargain prices, always a poor value. The man who sells you the wine can be as important as the men who make it, for it is his job to select the good wine from the bad, out of all that is offered him.

Serving Wines and Opening Bottles

For red wines, which cast a deposit, care must be taken in bringing the bottle from the cellar to the table, so that the sediment is undisturbed. The wax or foil wrapping around the bottle's mouth should be removed cleanly, so that bits will not fall into the glass. The neck should be wiped clean, and the corkscrew so used that no bits of cork drop into the wine. The wine should be served at its proper temperature, white wines cooled slowly, red wines cold from the cellar and allowed to warm gradually to room temperature, so that their delicate balance will not be destroyed.

Corky Bottles

A cork is not infallible, and once in a while one will rot, particularly in old bottles. Some of the corks for wartime vintages were of poor quality. Once they are pulled, a glance will tell you if one is rotted. The wine waiter should smell the cork to see if the bottle is sound before he serves it, and he should let you smell it, too. If the cork smells of cork, it's bad; the cork should smell of the wine. A corky wine loses all its properties, and a wine

I   247

that tastes of cork is no good. Send it back and ask for another
bottle, just as you would if you were served a bad egg.

Baskets and Decanting

There is nothing wrong with sediment in an old red wine, and
in some years it is to be expected; but some wines with heavy
deposits need decanting before being served. You can tell whether
a wine should be decanted by holding the bottle up to the light.
If there is half an inch or so of sediment in the bottle, the wine
might better be decanted. Decanting is the simple process of
transferring the wine from the bottle to another container,
pouring carefully with a light behind the bottle so that you can
note when the sediment begins to come out. If poured slowly and
steadily, little of the wine is lost. When such a wine is not
decanted one must be careful when serving it.

A red wine of age and quality should stand upright for several
hours before decanting or serving, to give the sediment plenty of
time to settle to the bottom. Even when baskets are used, the
wine should stand upright before serving. In any case, baskets
are an unnecessary pretension, for they can never be a substitute
for decanting. When you stand a bottle upright, it should be
uncorked at least half an hour before serving, to allow the wine to
breathe. This is not necessary when you decant the wine, for
decanting allows the air to bring out all the imprisoned bouquet.
This is extremely important if you want to get the most out of a
fine red wine.

Many a wine-drinker has noticed that it is only when the
bottle is nearly finished that the wine seems to come into its own,
simply because it takes time for a wine to react to contact with the
air. The swirling of wine while in the glass hastens this action,
and that is why wineglasses are only half-filled, and why they
should be large. Even in small Burgundian restaurants, glasses
like large brandy snifters are used for all wines.

Service

White wines should be served cool, the sweeter the cooler, but
they lose their flavour when iced too much. A couple of hours in

the refrigerator usually serves, although a wine bucket is thought to be better. In lieu of a wine bucket, some people fill a large salad bowl with ice and allow the bottles to cool in it. Any big bowl will do. Pink wines are also served chilled, but red wines are best at room temperature. A couple of hours before serving, the red wine can be brought to the dining-table and carefully tilted upright. A wine that contains sediment should be poured in one continuous motion, not tilted repeatedly, and pouring should be stopped at the first sign of sediment. The host always pours a little of the newly-opened wine into his own glass first, in case there are any particles of cork, both tasting and smelling it to see that it is sound and not corky.

Glasses

Most people prefer clear crystal glasses for wine, unadorned, so that the sparkle of light on the wine is easily seen. The larger the glass, the better when serving fine Bordeaux and Burgundies. A tumbler is usually better than most small wineglasses, for two-thirds of the space can be left so that the wine can be swirled in the glass.

Wine is shown off by its glass, just as a girl is shown off by a pretty dress. Great wines can be ruined in small glasses, for the air cannnot get at the surface of the wine to release its aroma. Equally, a mediocre wine is shown up for what it is in a large glass, for the quality of the wine is often judged by what it looks like in a fine glass. Wineglasses, like fine wines, have always been a symbol of civilized living. The finest glasses are large and tulip-shaped, clear and thin, without markings, the bowl the size of a large orange or an apple. When less than half-filled, such a glass permits the full enjoyment of the colour, bouquet, and taste of a fine wine. France has made an art of clear crystal glasses.

Although there are many different shapes of glasses for different wines, a single glass, large thin, and clear, can serve for all, making service and replacement simpler.

STORING WINES

When serving wine at home, a cool place is desirable for storing bottles, for a wine should rest for a week or two before being served, to allow it to recompose itself. This is particularly true of old wines, and those that have a heavy sediment, which must be allowed to settle.

The worst evil that can happen to a bottle of wine is a sudden change of temperature. But wines can stand extremes of temperature if they reach such extremes gradually. For this reason summer is usually easier on wines than winter, when steam heating warms up a storage space each day, while the temperature drops quickly during the night. A month or two of such sudden changes of temperature can destroy some wines, and improper storage near heat or in strong light can ruin one. Storing wines near steam pipes is particulary injurious.

White wines should be kept in the coolest spot practicable, usually nearest the floor, for they can spoil in a matter of months. Red Bordeaux can be placed above them, Burgundies on top, while the fortified wines can stand upright on the shelf beside your spirits. All natural wines should be laid on their sides, so that the wine wets the cork, keeping it from drying and shrinking. For this reason, places for storing wine should not be too dry.

Cellars

A cellar is needed for storing extra cases of wines you like, ones that may become scarce or hard to get. There is also an immense saving with a cellar, for wines are cheaper by the case and can be bought young when prices are lower. Increase in prices of fine wines through the years of their maturing is greater than the amount of interest on the money invested in your cellar. Also, there's a delight in owning a cellar, for you have within your own home a bottled treasure of taste sensations, as full of potential pleasure as a fine library or a collection of records.

The size of a wine cellar depends on how often you serve wines. Consumed bottles should be replaced each year by new stocks, both bottles for current serving and others for laying down. A cellar gives most pleasure when there is a well-balanced stock to choose from. A cellar book in which you keep a record of your wines, with notes of your preferences, is a help when restocking, as well as a running diary for the pleasures you get from wines. With prices of wines listed in a cellar book, it is easier to replace wines of the same price category, without insisting on the identical wine, so that you may drink several wines in a certain range over a period of time, rather than one wine, which may rise in price or deteriorate. Small wine cellars are simply made in a cool corner of the house cellar, away from steam pipes and light. They should be properly ventilated, and any nearby pipes should be wrapped with insulation.

Bins and Shelves

Three compartmented shelves will hold several dozen bottles in an area only a yard long. The compartments or bins need not be large for a small cellar, and a bin not much more than a foot square will hold almost a case, although one twice that size is more practical if you have the room. The best bins are diamond-shaped, for bottles piled in a flat bin may have a tendency to roll when one is removed, unless the bottles are braced. Wines take up little room when stored in bins. A thermometer should be hung near by so that you can see that the temperature remains constant, constancy being more important than degree, although 55° F. is considered ideal. The simplest arrangment is to transfer wine to whisky cases, standing the cases on edge in a cupboard.

A MODEL CELLAR

Small Cellar

A small cellar of five to fifteen cases, as in all things concerning wine, should be based mainly on your taste. But for an adequate assortment of French wines, you might have the following

*quantities, which would cost between £125 and £170, depending
on quality and vintages, and including Champagne and brandy.
The wines alone would cost between £85 and £110.*

3 CASES OF RED BURGUNDY:

1 case of inexpensive Beaujolais of a very young vintage;
1 case at moderate price, such as estate-bottled Pommard or
Nuits-Saint-Georges, from 3 to 7 years old;
1 case of a fine estate-bottled wine such as a Richebourg,
Musigny, Chambertin Clos de Bèze, or Bonnes-Mares, from
3 to 7 years old. The more expensive the Burgundies, the
slower they will be to mature and the longer they will last.

2 CASES OF WHITE BURGUNDY:

1 case of an estate-bottled Chablis from a good vineyard,
from 2 to 5 years old, or a Pouilly-Fuissé of the same age;
1 case of estate-bottled Meursault Perrières or Blagny,
from 2 to 5 years old; or a case of Chassagne, or Puligny-
Montrachet from a good vineyard, preferably estate-bottled,
of the same age.

3 CASES OF RED BORDEAUX:

1 case of inexpensive regional wine of a good shipper, from
Margaux, Saint-Julien, Pomerol, or Saint-Émilion, 3 to 5 years
old;
1 case of château-bottled claret from the 3rd, 4th, or 5th
classified growths, 3 to 15 years old;
1 case of a fine château-bottled claret, such as the Châteaux
of Haut-Brion, Latour, Lafite, Margaux, Mouton-Rothschild,
Lascombes, Cheval-Blanc, Ausone, or Pétrus, of a good vintage,
from 3 to 20 years old, depending on how soon you will drink
it and how long you want to keep it;

1 OR 2 CASES OF WHITE BORDEAUX:

1 case of dry Graves from a good shipper, or preferably a
château-bottled white Graves such as Haut-Brion, Domaine
de Chevalier, Laville Haut-Brion, or Carbonnieux, from a
good vintage, 2 to 5 years old;

1 case of château-bottled Sauternes or Barsac (if your taste runs to sweet wines), such as Yquem, Climens, La Tour Blanche, Filhot, Coutet.

2 CASES OF MISCELLANEOUS WINES:

1 case of *rosé* from Provence or Tavel, the youngest possible, as these wines do not improve with age;

1 case of Alsace, a Gewürz-Traminer, Riesling, or Sylvaner, from 1 to 3 years old, preferably young; or

1 case of Vouvray, from 2 to 4 years old.

1 CASE OF CHAMPAGNE.

AN ASSORTMENT OF 6 BOTTLES OF COGNAC AND ARMAGNAC.

Medium Cellar

A medium cellar usually ranges in size from fifteen to forty cases, and a good case assortment of French wines might be broken up as follows:

8 CASES OF RED BURGUNDY:

3 cases from southern Burgundy, such as Beaujolais, Juliénas, Mercurey, or Moulin-à-Vent, for frequent use, from $1\frac{1}{2}$ to 5 years old;

2 cases of an estate bottling, or from a reliable shipper, of Pommard, Volnay, Chassagne-Montrachet, Beaune, Corton, Nuits-Saint-Georges, Chambolle-Musigny or Vosne-Romanée, from 2 to 7 years old;

2 cases of estate-bottled Musigny, Bonnes-Mares, Chambertin Clos de Bèze, Richebourg, or Clos Vougeot, from 3 to 7 years old, of a good vintage, for laying down until fully developed, which may take from 3 to 7 additional years;

1 case of older wines from the previous category, from 5 to 10 years old, of a good vintage, for drinking on special occasions.

5 OR 6 CASES OF WHITE BURGUNDY:

1 or 2 cases of estate-bottled Chablis from a good vineyard, from 2 to 5 years old;

1 case of Pouilly-Fuissé, from a good shipper or estate-bottled, from 2 to 15 years old;

1 case of Chassagne, or Puligny-Montrachet, estate-bottled or from a good shipper, from 2 to 5 years old;

1 case of estate-bottled Meursault-Blagny or Perrières, preferably the Clos des Perrière, or Corton-Charlemagne, of a good vintage, from 2 to 6 years old;

1 case, estate-bottled, or from a good shipper, of Bâtard-Montrachet, or Montrachet, of a good vintage, from 2 to 10 years old.

6 CASES OF RED BORDEAUX:

3 cases of a regional shipper's claret, or a *cru artisan*, or a *cru bourgeois*, from 2 to 4 years old;

1 case of château-bottled Saint-Émilion or Pomerol, or a 3rd, 4th, or 5th classified growth of a good vintage, from 3 to 10 years old;

1 case of fine claret, such as Haut-Brion, Lafite, Latour, Margaux, Mouton-Rothschild, Lascombes, Cheval-Blanc, Ausone, or Pétrus, of a good vintage, from 3 to 8 years old, for laying down for 2 years or so;

1 case of wines from the above category, of a good vintage, from 6 years of age upward or as old as possible, for present drinking.

2 OR 3 CASES OF WHITE BORDEAUX:

1 or 2 cases of dry Graves, preferably Château Haut-Brion or Domaine de Chevalier, from 2 to 4 years old;

1 case of Sauternes or Barsac, château-bottled, from 3 to 10 years old.

1 CASE OF RHÔNE VALLEY WINE:

Estate-bottled or from a good shipper, red wine from Châteauneuf-du-Pape, Hermitage, or Côte Rôtie, from 3 to 7 years for the Châteauneuf, from 6 to 15 years for the others; or a case of white Hermitage of a good vintage, from 5 to 10 years old.

2 CASES OF *ROSÉ*:

1 case from Provence, and 1 case from Tavel, from $1\frac{1}{2}$ to 4 years old.

1 OR 2 CASES OF ASSORTED WINES:

1 case of Alsatian Riesling or Gewürz-Traminer, from 1 to 5 years old; and/or
1 case of Vouvray or Saumur, from 2 to 6 years old.

2 CASES OF CHAMPAGNE:

1 medium-priced of a lesser-known brand; 1 of a well-known brand.

AN ASSORTMENT OF 9 BOTTLES OF BRANDY:

4 bottles of 3-star or VO Cognac, or inexpensive Armagnac, the balance consisting of old Cognacs aud Armagnacs, including a bottle of old Calvados and a bottle or more of "*alcool blanc*," depending on your taste.

Large Cellar

Even for a large cellar the quantities of sweet wines and minor wines would remain much the same. Quantities and varieties of Burgundies, Bordeaux, and Champagnes would increase most.

When stocking a large cellar, it is advisable to call in an expert, who will know the best buys among those wines currently available.

A portion of larger cellars should be made up of "vins de garde" wines, bought young to be kept 2 to 5 years for proper maturing.

Vintage Chart

No vintage chart is a sure guide, for great wines cannot be standardized. Wines are a product of inconstant nature and fallible man. There will be enough enjoyable bottles in any one district in any off-year to make exceptions invalidating anything so dogmatic as a vintage chart. Often overlooked, nevertheless a major factor in the purchase of wines, is the proper selection of wines that are sufficiently mature for present-day consumption. Very great years are often slow in maturing, hence your consideration of whether the wines will be consumed immediately or laid away for future consumption should be a determining factor in your selections.

EXPLANATION OF RATINGS

20, 19—exceptionally great   9, 8—fair
18, 17—very great   7, 6—low average
16, 15—great   5, 4—poor
14, 13, 12—very good   3, 2, 1—very poor
11, 10—good

N.B.: Many dry white wines may be too old for present-day consumption. All such wines are indicated by *italic figures*.

VINTAGE	RED BORDEAUX	WHITE BORDEAUX	RED BURGUNDY (Côte d'Or)	WHITE BURGUNDY	RED BURGUNDY (Beaujolais)	RHÔNE	LOIRE	ALSACE	CHAMPAGNE
1926	15	*14*	12	*12*	*11*	12	*11*	*12*	12
1927	2	6	2	*2*	*3*	7	*5*	*3*	3
1928	19	18	18	*15*	*17*	16	15	*15*	20

VINTAGE CHART

VINTAGE	RED BORDEAUX	WHITE BORDEAUX	RED BURGUNDY (Côte d'Or)	WHITE BURGUNDY	RED BURGUNDY (Beaujolais)	RHÔNE	LOIRE	ALSACE	CHAMPAGNE
1929	19	19	19	19	19	19	16	17	17
1930	0	0	4	4	4	9	6	4	4
1931	3	2	4	4	3	10	7	5	6
1932	1	1	3	4	5	11	7	5	6
1933	10	6	17	16	17	14	14	12	15
1934	17	16	17	17	17	16	13	14	15
1935	5	6	12	13	12	9	12	14	11
1936	8	8	8	6	9	14	9	10	10
1937	15	18	17	16	13	16	14	15	16
1938	9	8	14	13	10	13	9	10	12
1939	5	6	3	3	8	10	8	4	8
1940	8	9	9	9	8	9	8	11	8
1941	2	1	4	4	5	9	7	8	12
1942	12	15	12	15	14	15	11	13	15
1943	15	15	14	15	15	15	14	15	18

VINTAGE	RED BORDEAUX	WHITE BORDEAUX	RED BURGUNDY (Côte d'Or)	WHITE BURGUNDY	RED BURGUNDY (Beaujolais)	RHÔNE	LOIRE	ALSACE	CHAMPAGNE
1944	11	9	4	5	7	9	7	5	9
1945	20 [5]	19	19 [5]	16 [1]	20	19	18 [2]	17	16
1946	8	7	12	9	10	15	10	10	11
1947	19	19	19	20	19	19	19	19	19
1948	13	13	14	15	9	9	10	12	11
1949	16	18	19	17	18	16	13 [3]	16	17
1950	14	15	11	18	10	15	10	8	11
1951	9	6	8	8	7	9	7	9	7
1952	16	16 [4]	16	16	16	16	14	15	16
1953	17	16	16	17	19	14	17	17	18
1954	12	9	10	11	11	13	9	11	6
1955	18	17	15	17	18	15	15	16	16

[1] The Chablis vineyards were frozen in the Spring of 1945 and practically no wine was produced.

[2] Due to Spring frosts, the yield in this district was negligible.

[3] The quality of this vintage in this district was very spotty. Very good in the Anjou—good in Vouvray and Sancerre and very average in Pouilly-sur-Loire.

[4] Very little Barsac and Sauternes produced on account of freeze and hail.

[5] These exceptionally great wines are very slow in maturing. Too firm, the top-notch wines from these districts may be found to be disappointing if drunk when less than 12 years old. As in the 1928 Clarets, a long time will be required to allow these wines to mature properly. The lesser wines can be consumed now. The '47's have matured more rapidly than the '45's.

Bordeaux Wines

PART 1

The Official Classification of the Great Growths of the Gironde. Classification of 1855

The official production is given in tons (tonneaux), the Bordeaux standard measure, consisting of 4 barrels. A tonneau averages around 96 cases when it is bottled.

The following figures of production are approximate, varying from year to year, and an estimate has been attempted by deducting the ullage or evaporation, which usually consists of 15 per cent.

MÉDOC WINES

1st Growths or Premiers Crus

	TOWNSHIP	TONNEAUX	AVER. PROD. CASES (12 *bottles*)
Château Lafite	*Pauillac*	180	14,600
Château Latour	,,	160	13,000
Château Margaux	*Margaux*	150	12,100
Château Haut-Brion *	*Pessac Graves*	140	11,400

* This wine, although a Graves, is universally recognized and classified as one of the four First Growths of the Médoc.

MÉDOC WINES

2nd Growths or Second Crus

	TOWNSHIP	TONNEAUX	AVER. PROD. CASES (12 *bottles*)
Château Mouton-Rothschild	*Pauillac*	110	10,400
Château Lascombes	*Margaux*	90	7,100
Château Rausan-Ségla	,,	60	4,800
Château Rauzan-Gassies	,,	90	7,600
Château Léoville-Las-Cases	*St.-Julien*	170	15,500
Château Léoville-Poyferré	,,	102	9,700
Château Léoville-Barton	,,	70	6,000
Château Durfort-Vivens	*Margaux*	10	850
Château Gruaud-Larose	*St.-Julien*	185	15,000
Château Brane-Cantenac	*Cantenac*	100	8,100
Château Pichon-Longueville	*Pauillac*	78	6,300
Château Pichon-Longueville (Comtesse de Lalande)	,,	125	10,000
Château Ducru-Beaucaillou	*St.-Julien*	130	10,500
Château Cos-d'Estournel	*St.-Estèphe*	100	8,100
Château Montrose	,,	100	8,100

3rd Growths or Troisièmes Crus

Château Giscours	*Labarde*	20	1,600
Château Kirwan	*Cantenac*	100	8,100
Château d'Issan	,,	12	1,050
Château Lagrange	*St.-Julien*	100	8,100
Châtaeu Langoa	,,	75	6,100
Château Malescot-Saint-Exupéry	*Margaux*	25	2,100
Château Cantenac-Brown	*Cantenac*	90	7,100
Château Palmer	,,	100	8,100
Château Grand La Lagune	*Ludon*	20	1,600

MÉDOC WINES

3rd Growths or Troisièmes Crus [continued]

	TOWNSHIP	TONNEAUX	AVER. PROD. CASES (12 bottles)
Château Desmirail	Margaux	0	0
Château Calon-Ségur	St.-Estèphe	150	12,100
Château Ferrière	Margaux	5	450
Château Marquis-d'Alesme-Becker	,,	20	1,600
Château Boyd-Cantenac	,,	30	2,400

4th Growths or Quatrièmes Crus

	TOWNSHIP	TONNEAUX	AVER. PROD. CASES
Château Prieuré-Lichine	Cantenac-Margaux	40	3,200
Château Saint-Pierre-Bontemps	St.-Julien	40	3,200
Château Siant-Pierre-Sevaistre	,,	60	4,800
Château Branaire-Ducru	,,	100	8,100
Château Talbot	,,	140	11,400
Château Duhart-Milon	Pauillac	140	11,400
Château Pouget	Cantenac	30	2,400
Château La Tour-Carnet	St.-Laurent	70	5,600
Château Rochet	St.-Estèphe	60	4,800
Château Beychevelle	St.-Julien	100	8,100
Château Marquis-de-Terme	Margaux	130	11,000

5th Growths or Cinquièmes Crus

	TOWNSHIP	TONNEAUX	AVER. PROD. CASES
Château Pontet-Canet	Pauillac	200	16,300
Château Batailley	,,	80	6,500
Château Grand-Puy-Lacoste	,,	70	5,600
Château Grand-Puy-Ducasse	,,	35	2,800

Médoc Wines

5th Growths or Cinquièmes Crus [continued]

	TOWNSHIP	TONNEAUX	AVER. PROD. CASES (12 bottles)
Château Haut-Batailley	Pauillac	30	2,700
Château Lynch-Bages	,,	100	8,100
Château Lynch-Moussas	,,	20	1,600
Château Dauzac	Labarde	60	4,800
Château Mouton-d'Armailhacq	Pauillac	100	8,100
Château du Tertre	Arsac	100	8,100
Château Haut-Bages-Libéral	Pauillac	40	3,200
Château Pédesclaux	,,	30	2,400
Château Belgrave	St.-Laurent	150	12,100
Château Camensac	,,	70	5,600
Château Cos Labory	St.-Estèphe	45	3,600
Château Clerc-Milon-Mondon	Pauillac	35	2,800
Château Croizet-Bages	,,	50	4,000
Château Cantemerle	Macau	100	8,100

Exceptional Growths or Crus Exceptionnels

Château Villegeorge		Château la Couronne	
	Avensan		Pauillac
Château Angludet		Château Moulin-Riche	
	Cantenac		St.-Julien
Château Chasse-Spleen		Château Bel-Air-Marquis-d'Aligre	
	Moulis		
Château Poujeaux-Theil			Soussans
	Moulis		

PART 2

The *Crus Bourgeois* and *Crus Artisans*
of the Médoc

THE MINOR CHÂTEAU BOTTLINGS

Château de l'Abbaye-Skinner
Vertheuil

Château d l'Abbe-Gorsse-de-
Gorsse *Margaux*

Château Abel-Laurent
Margaux

Château Andron
St.-Seurin-de-Cadourne

Château Aney
Cussac

Château Angludet
Cantenac

Château Anseillan
Pauillac

Château Anthonic
Moulis

Château d'Arche
Ludon

Château d'Arcins
Arcins

Château d'Arsac
Arsac

Château Avensan
Avensan

Château Balac
St.-Laurent

Château Balogues-Haut-Bagès
Pauillac

Château Barateau
St.-Laurent

Château Barreyres
Arcins

Château Batailley-l'Aspic
Pauillac

Château Baury
Arsac

Château Beaulieu
St.-Germain-d'Esteuil

Château Beaumont
Cussac

Château Beauséjour
St.-Estèphe

Château Beauséjour
Listrac

Château Beauséjour-Picard
St.-Estèphe

Château Beau-Site
St.-Estèphe

Cru Beau-Site-Haut-Vignoble
St.-Estèphe

Domaine de Bécamil
Cussac

Domaine de la Bégorce-Zédé
Soussans

Château Bel-Air-Lagrave
Moulis

Château Bellegrave
Listrac

Château Bellegrave
Pauillac

Château Bellegrave-du-Poujeau
Le Pian

Château Bellevue
Macau

Château Bellevue
Pauillac

Château Bellevue-Cordeillan-
Bagès *Pauillac*

MINOR CHÂTEAUX OF MÉDOC

Château Bellevue-St.-Lambert
Pauillac

Château Bel-Orme-Tronquoy-de-
Lalande
St.-Seurin de-Cadourne

Château de Bensse
Prignac

Château Bernon
Queyrac

Château Bernonès
Cussac

Château Bichon-Bagès
Pauillac

Château Bonneau
St.-Seurin-de-Cadourne

Château Bontemps-Dubarry
St.-Julien-Beychevelle

Château Le Boscq
St.-Estèphe

Château Bouqueyran
Moulis

Château Le Bourdieu
Valeyrac

Château Le Bourdieu
St.-Médard-en-Jalles

Château Le Bourdieu
Vertheuil

Château Breillan
Blanquefort

Château Breuil
Cissac

Château Bries-Caillou
St.-Germain-d'Esteuil

Château Brillette
Moulis

Château Brouzac
Margaux

Château Brun
Le Taillan

Château de Cach
St.-Laurent

Château Cambon-la-Pelouse
Macau

Château Canteloup
St.-Estèphe

Château Capbern
St.-Estèphe

Château Cap-de-Haut
Lamarque

Château Carmeil
Macau

Château Caronne-Ste-Gemme
St.-Laurent

Grand Cru des Carruades
Pauillac

Château de Cartillon
Lamarque

Château de Castera
St.-Germain-d'Esteuil

Château Charmail
St.-Seurin-de-Cadourne

Château La Chesnaye-Ste-
Gemme *Cussac*

Château Cissac
Cissac

Château Citran-Clauzel
Avensan

Château Clarke
Listrac

Clos du Clocher
Bégadan

La Closerie
Moulis

Château du Colombier-Mon-
pelou *Pauillac*

Château La Colonilla
Margaux

Château La Commanderie
St.-Estèphe

MINOR CHÂTEAUX OF MÉDOC

Château Conseillant
Labarde

Château Constant-Bagès-Mon-
pelou *Pauillac*

Château Constant-Lesquireau
Vertheuil

Château Constant-Trois-
Moulins *Macau*

Château Corbeil
Blanquefort

Château Corconnac
St.-Laurent-de-Médoc

Château Coufran
St.-Seurin-de-Cadourne

Cru Coutelin-Merville
St.-Estèphe

Château Le Crock
St.-Estèphe

Château Cruscault
St.-Laurent

Château Cujac
Castelnau

Château Cujac
Moulis

Château de Cujac
St.-Aubin

Château Cusseau
Macau

Château La Dame-Blanche
Le Taillan

Château Daubos
Pauillac

Château Deux-Moulins
Lamarque

Château Deyrem-Valentin
Soussans

Château Dillon
Blanquefort

Château Doumens
Margaux

Château Dubignon-Talbot
Margaux

Château Dulamon
Blanquefort

Château Duplessis
Moulis

Château Duthil-Haug-Cressant
Le Pian

Château Dutruch-Grand-
Poujeaux *Moulis*

Château Dutruch-Lambert
Moulis

Château Egmont
Ludon

Château l'Ermitage
Ludon

Château d'Escot
Lesparre

Château de l'Estonnat
Margaux

Château Fatin
St.-Estèphe

Château Felletin
Lamarque

Château Felonneau
Macau

Château Fleurennes
Blanquefort

Château Fongravey
Blanquefort

Château Fonpetite
St.-Estèphe

Château Fonpiqueyre
St.-Sauveur

Château Fonreaud
Listrac

Château Fontenet
Le Taillan

Château Fontesteau
St.-Sauveur

MINOR CHÂTEAUX OF MÉDOC

Cru Fort-Médoc
Cussac

Château Fourcas-Dupré
Listrac

Château Fourcas-Hostein
Listrac

Cru Franquet Ainé
Moulis

Cru Franquet
Moulis

Château du Galan
St.-Laurent

Château Gallais
Ordonnac-et-Potensac

Château Gironville
Macau

Château Grand-Milon
Pauillac

Château Gloria
St.-Julien-Beychevelle

Château La Gombaude
Margaux

Château du Grand-St.-Julien
St.-Julien

Château Grand-St.-Lambert
Pauillac

Château du Grand-Soussans
Soussans

Château Grandis
St.-Seurin-de-Cadourne

Château Granins
Moulis

Château La Gravière
Vertheuil

Cru Gressier-Grand-Poujeaux
Moulis

Château Guitignan
Moulis

Château La Gurgue
Margaux

Château Hanteillan
Cissac

Château Haut-Bagès-Averous
Pauillac

Château Haut-Bagès-Drouillet
Moulis

Château Haut Vourdieu
Moulis

Château Haut-Breton-Lari-
gaudière *Soussans*

Château Haut-Cenot
Margaux

Château Haut-Cenot
Soussans

Cru Haut-Fourton
St.-Laurent-de-Mèdoc

Château du Haut-Moulin
Cussac

Château Haut-Pauillac
Pauillac

Château Hauterive
St.-Germain-d'Esteuil

Château Haut-St.-Julien-
Marian *St.-Julien*

Cru Haut-Tayac et Siamois
Soussans

Château La Haye
St.-Estèphe

Château Houissant
St.-Estèphe

Château La Houringue
Macau

Château de Labegorce
Margaux

Château Ladouys
St.-Estèphe

Château Laffitte
Bégadan

Château Laffitte-Canteloup
Ludon

266

MINOR CHÂTEAUX OF MÉDOC

Château Laffitte-Carcasset-St.-
Estèphe *St.-Estèphe*

Château Lafleur-Milon
Pauillac

Château Lafon
Listrac

Château Lalande
Listrac

Château Lamarque
Lamarque

Château Lamothe
Cissac

Château Lamothe-de-Bergeron
Cussac

Domaine de Lamourous
Le Pian

Château de Lamouroux
Margaux

Château Lanessan
Cussac

Château Larose-Perganson
St.-Laurent

Château Larrieu-Terrefort-
Graves *Macau*

Château Larrivaux
Cissac

Château Latour-Cantenac
Cantenac

Château Latour-Dumirail
Cissac

Château Latour-Pibran
Pauillac

Château Latour-Raúzan
St.-Sauveur

Château Laujac
Bégadan

Château Lemoyne-Lafon-
Rochet *Ludon*

Château Les Lesques
Lesparre

Château Lestage
Listrac

Château Lestage
St.-Seurin-de-Cadourne

Château Lestage-Darquier-
Grand-Poujeaux *Moulis*

Château Leyssac
St.-Estèphe

Château Listrac
Listrac

Château Listran
Jau

Château Liversan
St.-Sauveur

Château Livran
St.-Germain-d'Esteuil

Château Loudenne
St.-Yzans

Château-Ludon-Pomiès-Agassac
Ludon

Château Mac-Carthy-Raymond
St.-Estèphe

Château La Macqueline
Macau

Maison Blanche
St.-Yzans

Château Malécot
Pauillac

Château Malescasse
Lamarque

Château de Malleret
Le Pian

Château de Marbuzet
St.-Estèphe

Château Marcillan-Bellevue
St.-Laurent

Clos du Marquis
St.-Julien-Beychevelle

Château Marsac-Seguineau
Soussans

MINOR CHÂTEAUX OF MÉDOC

Château Martinens
Cantenac

Château Maucaillou
Moulis

Château Maucamps
Macau

Château Mauvesin
Moulis

Château Médoc
St.-Julien

Château Meyney
St.-Estèphe

Château Meyre-Estèbe
Avensan

Château Meyre-Vieux-Clos
Avensan

Château Monbrison
Arsac

Château Montbrun
Cantenac

Château Morin
St.-Estèphe

Château Moulin-à-Vent
Moulis

Moulin de Calon
St.-Estèphe

Cru Moulin-de-Soubeyran
Le Pian

Domaine du Moulin-du-Bourg
Listrac

Château Moulin-Riche
St.-Julien

Château Moulis
Moulis

Château Nexon-Lemoyne
Ludon

Château Nodris
Vertheuil

Château Les Ormes-de-Pez
St.-Estèphe

Château Pabeau
St.-Seurin-de-Cadourne

Château Paloumey
Ludon

Château Panigon
Civrac

Château Parempuyre
Parempuyre

Château Parempuyre-Durand-
Dassier *Parempuyre*

Cru Patache-d'Aux
Bégadan

Château Paveil
Soussans

Château Péris-de-Courcelles
Vertheuil

Château Peyrat
St.-Laurent

Château Peyrabon
St.-Sauveur

Château de Pez
St.-Estèphe

Château Phélan-Ségur
St.-Estèphe

Château Picard
St.-Estèphe

Château Pierre Bibian
Listrac

Château Plantier-Rose
St.-Estèphe

Château Pomeys
Moulis

Château Pomiès-Agassac
Ludon

Château Pomys
St.-Estèphe

Château Pontac-Lynch
Cantenac

Château Pontoise-Cabarrus
St.-Seurin-de-Cadourne

MINOR CHÂTEAUX OF MÉDOC

Château Potensac
Ordonnac-et-Potensac

Château Poujeaux-Marly
Moulis

Château Poujeaux-Thibaut
Moulis

Château Preuillac
Lesparre

Château Priban
Macau

Château Le Raux
Cussac

Cru Renouil-Franquet
Moulis

Château Reverdi
Lamarque

Château Reysson
Vertheuil

Château Le Roc
St.-Estèphe

Château Roche
St.-Estèphe

Château Romefort
Avensan

Château Romefort
Cussac

Château Rose-La-Biche
Macau

Château La Rose-Capbern
St.-Estèphe

Château Ruat
Moulis

Château St.-Estèphe
St.-Estèphe

Clos St.-Estèphe
St.-Estèphe

Château St.-Estèphe "La Croix"
St.-Estèphe

Château St.-Paul
St.-Seurin-de-Cadourne

Château Saransot-Dupré
Listrac

Château Ségur
Parempuyre

Cru Ségur-Fillon
Parempuyre

Château Sénéjac
Le Pian

Château Sénilhac
St.-Seurin-de-Cadourne

Château Sémeillan
Listrac

Château Sigognac
St.-Yzans

Château Sipian
Valeyrac

Château Siran
Labarde

Château Sociando-Mallet
St.-Seurin-de-Cadourne

Château Souley-Ste.-Croix
Vertheuil

Château du Taillan
Le Taillan

Château Tanais-Clapeau
Blanquefort

Château Tartuguière
Prignac

Château Tayac
Soussans

Château du Testeron
Moulis

Château Total
Couquèques

Château La Tour-d'Anseillan
Pauillac

Château La Tour-l'Aspic
Pauillac

Château La Tour-de-By
Bégadan

MINOR CHÂTEAUX OF MÉDOC

Château La Tour-du-Haut-
Carmail
        St.-Seurin-de-Cadourne

Château La Tour-de-Marbuzet
        St.-Estèphe

Château La Tour-de-Mons
        Soussans

Château La Tour-Marcillanet
        St.-Laurent

Château La Tour-Milon
        Pauillac

Château La Tour-de-Pez
        St.-Estèphe

Château La Tour-Pibran
        Pauillac

Château La Tour-du-Roc
        Arcins

Château La Tour-du-Roc-
Milon   *Pauillac*

Château La Tour-St.-Bonnet
        St.-Christoly-de-Médoc

Château La Tour-St.-Joseph
        Cissac

Château La Tour-Séran
        St.-Christoly-de-Médoc

Château La Tour-Sieujan
        St.-Laurent

Cru La Tour-des-Ternes
        St.-Estèphe

Château Tourteran
        St.-Sauveur

Château Tramont
        Arcins

Château des Trois-Moulins
        Macau

Château Tronquoy-Lalande
        St.-Estèphe

Château Tujan
        Blanquefort

Château Le Vallier
        Parempuyre

Château Verdignan
        St.-Seurin-de-Cadourne

Château Verdus
        St.-Seurin-de-Cadourne

Château Victoria
        Vertheuil

Château-Villambis
        Cissac

Château Vincent
        Cantenac

PART 3

SAINT-ÉMILION

1955 OFFICIAL CLASSIFICATION

In mid-1955 the best Saint-Émilion wines were officially classified by the French Institut National des Appellations d'Origine des Vins *as 1st Great Growths and Great Growths.*

The following figures of production are approximate, varying from year to year, and an estimate has been attempted by deducting the ullage or evaporation, which usually consists of 15 per cent.

1st Great Growths of Saint-Émilion

	TONS	CASES
Château Ausone	30	2,800
Château Cheval-Blanc	90	7,600
Château Beauséjour-Duffau-Lagarosse	21	2,000
Château Beauséjour-Fagouet	20	2,000
Château Belair	34	3,264
Château Canon	64	6,140
Château Figeac	100	8,100
Clos Fourtet	42	4,050
Château Gaffelière-Naudes	68	6,500
Château Magdelaine	20	2,000
Château Pavie	127	12,200
Château Trottevieille	25	2,400

Great Growths

Château l'Angélus
Château Balestard-la-Tonnelle
Château Bellevue
Château Bergat
Château Cadet-Bon
Château Cadet-Piolat

Château Canon-la-Gaffelière
Château Cap-de-Mourlin
Château Chapelle Madeleine
Château Chauvin
Château Corbin (Giraud)
Château Corbin-Michotte

271

CHÂTEAUX OF ST.-ÉMILION

Château Coutet
Château Croque-Michotte
Château Curé-Bon-la-Madeleine
Château Fonplégade
Château Fonroque
Château Franc-Mayne
Château Grand-Barrail-Lamar-
  zelle-Figeac
Château Grand-Corbin-Despagne
Château Grand-Corbin-Pecresse
Château Grand-Mayne
Château Grand-Pontet
Château Grandes-Murailles
Château Guadet-St.-Julien
Clos des Jacobins
Château Jean-Faure
Château La Carte
Château La Clotte
Château La Cluzière
Château La Couspaude
Château La Dominique
Château La Marzelle
Domaine de Larmande
Château Larcis-Ducasse
Château Laroze
Château La Serre
Château La Tour-Figeac

Château La Tour-du-Pin-Figeac
Château La Tour-du-Pin-Figeac-
  Moueix
Château le Chatelet
Château Le Couvent
Château Le Prieuré
Château Mauvezin
Château Moulin-du-Cadet
Château Pavie-Decesse
Château Pavie-Macquin
Château Pavillon Cadet
Château Petit-Faurie-de-
  Souchard
Château Petit-Faurie-de-
  Soutard
Château Ripeau
Château Saint-Georges-Côte-
  Pavie
Clos Saint-Martin
Château Sansonnet
Château Soutard
Château Tertre-Daugay
Château Trimoulet
Château Trois-Moulins
Château Troplong-Mondot
Château Villemaurine
Château Yon-Figeac

Other Principal Growths of Saint-Émilion

Château l'Arrosée
  St.-Émilion
Château Badette
  St.-Christophe-des-Bardes
Clos Badon
  St.-Émilion
Château Baleau
  St.-Émilion

Château Barde-Haux
  St.-Christophe-des-Bardes
Château Béard
  St.-Laurent-des-Combes
Château Beauséjour
  Puisseguin-St.-Émilion
Cru Bel-Air
  Puisseguin-St.-Émilion

272

CHÂTEAUX OF ST.-ÉMILION

Château Bel-Air-Ouy
St.-Étienne-de-Lisse

Château Bellefond-Belcier
St.-Laurent-des-Combes

Château Belle-Graves
Vignonet

Château Bellevue
St.-Émilion

Château Bellevue
Lussac-St.-Émilion

Château Bellevue
Montagne-St.-Émilion

Château Berliquet
St.-Émilion

Château Bertineau-Goby
Montagne-St.-Émilion

Château Bézineau
St.-Émilion

Château Bigaroux
St.-Sulpice-de-Faleyrens

Château Binet
Parsac-St.-Émilion

Clos Blanchon
Lussac-St.-Émilion

Cru La Bonnelle
St.-Pey-d'Armens

Château Bourbaine
St.-Laurent-des-Combes

Château de Boutisse
St.-Christophe-des-Bardes

Château Branne-Bragard
Montagne-St.-Émilion

Château Brun
St.-Christophe-des-Bardes

Château Calon-Montagne
Montagne-St.-Émilion

Château Calon
St.-Georges-St.-Émilion

Domaine du Calvaire
St.-Étienne-de-Lisse

Château Cantenac
St.-Émilion

Château Canterane
St.-Étienne-de-Lisse

Château Capet
St.-Hippolyte

Château Capet-Guillier
St.-Hippolyte

Château Cardinal-Villemaurine
St.-Émilion

Château Casservert
St.-Christophe-des-Bardes

Château le Cauze
St.-Christophe-des-Bardes

Domaine-de-Chantegrive-Badon
St.-Émilion

Château Le Châtelet
St.-Émilion

Château Chêne-Vieux
Puisseguin-St.-Émilion

Château Cheval-Noir
St.-Émilion

Château du Conte
St.-Hippolyte

Château Corbin
Montagne-St.-Émilion

Château Cormey-Figeac
St.-Émilion

Château Coucy
Montagne-St.-Émilion

Château Coudert
St.-Christophe-des-Bardes

273

CHÂTEAUX OF ST.-ÉMILION

Château Coudert-Pelletan
St.-Christophe-des-Bardes

Château Couperie
St.-Émilion

Domaine du Courlat
Lussac-St.-Émilion

Château Couvent-des-Jacobins
St.-Émilion

Château Cravignac-Triscos
St.-Émilion

Château Cruzeau
Sables-St.-Émilion

Château Daugay
St.-Émilion

Château Destieux
St.-Christophe-des-Bardes

Domaine Destieux
St.-Hippolyte

Château Doumayne
Sables-St.-Émilion

Château Dupuy
Parsac-St.-Émilion

Château de Ferrand
St.-Hippolyte

Château Fombrauge
St.-Christophe-des-Bardes

Château Fonrazade
St.-Émilion

Clos Font-Muret
Montagne-St.-Émilion

Château Fouguerat
St.-Émilion

Château Fourney
St.-Pey-d'Armens

Cru Fourney
St.-Pey-d'Armens

Cru Franc-Peillan
Vignonet

Château Franc-Patarabet
St.-Émilion

Château Franc-Pourret
St.-Émilion

Domaine de Garderose
Sables-St.-Émilion

Château Gaubert
St.-Christophe-des-Bardes

Château Godeau
St.-Laurent-des-Combes

Château Gontet
Puisseguin-St.-Émilion

Domaine Grand-Brousseau
St.-Hippolyte

Château Grand-Faurie
St.-Émilion

Château Grand-Pey-Lescours
St.-Sulpice-de-Faleyrens

Château Gravet
St.-Sulpice-de-Faleyrens

Château Gros
St.-Pey-d'Armens

Château Guadet-Franc-Grâce-
Dieu   *St.-Émilion*

Château Gueyrosse
Sables-St.-Émilion

Château Gueyrot
St.-Émilion

Château Guibeau
Puisseguin-St.-Émilion

Château Guibot-la-Fourvielle
Puisseguin-St.-Émilion

Château Guillou
St.-Georges-St.-Émilion

274

CHÂTEAUX OF ST.-ÉMILION

Château Haut-Cadet
St.-Émilion

Château Haut-Calon
Montagne-St.-Émilion

Château Haut-Daugay
St.-Émilion

Château Haut-Grand-Faurie
St.-Émilion

Château Haut-Lavallade
St.-Christophe-des-Bardes

Clos Haut-Mazerat
St.-Émilion

Château Haut-Monreau
St.-Christophe-des-Bardes

Château Haute-Nauve
St.-Laurent-des-Combes

Château Haut-Piquat
Lussac-St.-Émilion

Château Haut-Plaisance
Montagne-St.-Émilion

Château Haut-Pontet
St.-Émilion

Château Haut-Pourret
St.-Émilion

Château Haut-Rocher
St.-Christophe-des-Bardes

Château Haut-St.-Georges
Montagne-St.-Émilion

Château Haut-Sarpe
St.-Christophe-des-Bardes

Château Haut-Ségottes
St.-Émilion

Château Haut-Simard
St.-Émilion

Domaine Haut-Veyrac
St.-Christophe-des-Bardes

Château Jacques-Blanc
St.-Étienne-de-Lisse

Cru Jappeloup
St.-Étienne-de-Lisse

Château Jean-du-Mayne
St.-Émilion

Château Joly
Vignonet

Cru des Jouans
St.-Sulpice-de-Faleyrens

Château Jura-Plaisance
Montagne-St.-Émilion

Château Justice
St.-Étienne-de-Lisse

Clos & Château La Barde
St.-Hippolyte

Château La Bastienne
Montagne-St.-Émilion

Château La Bouygue
St.-Hippolyte

Château La Clotte-Grande-Côte
St.-Émilion

Château La Clotte
Puisseguin-St.-Émilion

Domaine de La Croix-du-Basque
Puisseguin-St.-Émilion

Château La Fleur-Pourret
St.-Émilion

Château La Gomerie
St.-Émilion

Clos La Grâce-Dieu
St.-Émilion

Clos La Madeleine
St.-Émilion

Cru La Melissière
St.-Hippolyte

CHÂTEAUX OF ST.-ÉMILION

Cru La Mouleyre
St.-Étienne-de-Lisse

Château Langlade
Parsac-St.-Émilion

Château Lanoite
St.-Émilion

Château Lapeyre
St.-Étienne-de-Lisse

Château de Laroque
St.-Christophe-des-Bardes

Château La Papeterie
Montagne-St.-Émilion

Château La Perrière
Lussac-St.-Émilion

Château La Rose-Pourret
St.-Émilion

Château La Sablière
St.-Émilion

Château Lassègue
St.-Hippolyte

Château La Tour-Baladoz
St.-Hippolyte

Château La Tour
St.-Christophe-des-Bardes

Château La Tour-de-Grenet
Lussac-St.-Émilion

Château La Tour-du-Guetteur
St.-Émilion

Château La Tour-Pourret
St.-Émilion

Château La Tour-de-Ségur
Lussac-St.-Émilion

Château des Laurets
Puisseguin-St.-Émilion

Château Lavalade
St.-Christophe-des-Bardes

Domaine-de La Vieille
Montagne-St.-Émilion

Château Le Basque
Puisseguin-St.-Émilion

Clos de l'Eglise
Parsac-St.-Émilion

Château l'Hermitage
St.-Émilion

Château Le Jura
St.-Émilion

Château Les Baziliques
St.-Christophe-des-Bardes

Château Le Sable
St.-Hippolyte

Château Le Sable
St.-Christophe-des-Bardes

Château de Lescours
St.-Sulpice-de-Faleyrens

Château Lestage
Parsac-St.-Émilion

Château Les Vieux-Chênes
Lussac-St.-Émilion

Château Le Tertre
St.-Émilion

Cru Le Touran
St.-Étienne-de-Lisse

Château Lion-Perruchon
Lussac-St.-Émilion

Domaine de Lousteauneuf-de-
Doumayne   *Sables-St.-Émilion*

Château Lucas
Lussac-St.-Émilion

Château de Lussac
Lussac-St.-Émilion

Château du Lyonnat
Lussac-St.-Émilion

CHÂTEAUX OF ST.-ÉMILION

Château Magnan-la-Gaffelière
St.-Émilion

Domaine de Maisonneuve
St.-Georges-St.-Émilion

Château Maison-Blanche
Montagne-St.-Émilion

Château Malineau
St.-Émilion

Château Mangot
St.-Étienne-de-Lisse

Château Marin
St.-Christophe-des-Bardes

Château Marquey
St.-Laurent-des-Combes

Domaine de Martet
Puisseguin-St.-Émilion

Château Martinet
Sables-St.-Émilion

Château Matras
St.-Émilion

Château Maurens
St.-Hippolyte

Domaine du Mayne
Puisseguin-St.-Émilion

Château du Mayne
Puisseguin-St.-Émilion

Château Mazerat
St.-Émilion

Domaine du Merle-St.-Emilion
St.-Hippolyte

Château Monbousquet
St.-Sulpice-de-Faleyrens

Cru Mondésir
Sables-St.-Émilion

Château Montaiguillon
Montagne-St.-Émilion

Château Mont-Belair
St.-Étienne-de-Lisse

Château Montlabert
St.-Émilion

Château Moulin-Blanc
Montagne-St.-Émilion

Château Moulin-St.-Georges
St.-Émilion

Château Musset
Parsac-St.-Émilion

Château Négrit
Montagne-St.-Émilion

Château Pailhas
St.-Hippolyte

Château Paradis
Montagne-St.-Émilion

Château Parans
St.-Étienne-de-Lisse

Château Pelletan
St.-Christophe-des-Bardes

Château Petit-Cormey
St.-Émilion

Château Petit-Mangot
St.-Étienne-de-Lisse

Domaine de Petit-Val
St.-Émilion

Château Peyrelongue
St.-Émilion

Château Peyroutas
Vignonet

Château Pindefleurs
St.-Émilion

Château Piron
Parsac-St.-Émilion

Château Pontet
St.-Émilion

Château Pressac
St.-Étienne-de-Lisse

CHÂTEAUX OF ST.-ÉMILION

Château Puisseguin
Puisseguin-St.-Émilion

Château Puy-Blanquet
St.-Étienne-de-Lisse

Château Puynormond
Parsac-St.-Émilion

Château Quentin
St.-Christophe-des-Bardes

Château Guercy
Vignonet

Château Quinault
Sables-St.-Émilion

Domaine du Rey
St.-Émilion

Château Rocher-Corbin
Montagne-St.-Émilion

Château du Rocher
St.-Étienne-de-Lisse

Château du Roc-de-Boissac
Puisseguin-St.-Émilion

Château de Roi
St.-Émilion

Château de Roques
Puisseguin-St.-Émilion

Château Roudier
Montagne-St.-Émilion

Château Roylland-Matras
St.-Émilion

Clos du Roy
Puisseguin-St.-Émilion

Château Rozier
St.-Émilion

Château Rozier
St.-Laurent-des-Combes

Château Saint-Christophe
St.-Christophe-des-Bardes

Château Saint-André-Corbin
St.-Georges-St.-Émilion

Clos Saint-Emilion
St.-Émilion

Château Saint-Georges-Macquin
St.-Georges-St.-Émilion

Château Saint-Julien
St.-Émilion

Cru Saint-Lô
St.-Pey-d'Armens

Château Saint-Martial
St.-Sulpice-de-Faleyrens

Château de Saint-Pey
St.-Pey-d'Armens

Château Sarpe-Grand-Jacques
St.-Christophe-des-Bardes

Clos des Sarrazins
St.-Hippolyte

Clos Simard
St.-Émilion

Château Souchet-Piquat
Lussac-St.-Émilion

Château Teillac
Puisseguin-St.-Émilion

Château Terrien
Lussac-St.-Émilion

Château Teyssier
Puisseguin-St.-Émilion

Château Teyssier
Vignonet

Crû Tiffray-Guadet
Lussac-St.-Émilion

Château des Tours
Montagne-St.-Émilion

Château Tourteau
St.-Georges-St.-Émilion

278

CHÂTEAUX OF ST.-ÉMILION

Domaine de Touzinat-Bragard
St.-Christophe-des-Bardes

Château Truquet
St.-Émilion

Domaine de Vachon
St.-Émilion

Château Vaisinerie
Puisseguin-St.-Émilion

Clos Valentin
St.-Émilion

Clos Verdet
Sables-St.-Émilion

Château Videlot
Sables-St.-Émilion

Château Vieux-Ceps
St.-Émilion

Château Vieux-Guinot
St.-Étienne-de-Lisse

Château Vieux-Montaiguillon
St.-Georges-St.-Émilion

Château Vieux-Pourret
St.-Émilion

Château Vieux-Sarpe
St.-Christophe-des-Bardes

Château Vignon
Lussac-St.-Émilion

Château Yon
St.-Émilion

PART 4

POMEROL

The wines of Pomerol are not officially classified. Château Pétrus is recognized as being the outstanding Great Growth, followed by the nine other wines italicized below.

The following figures of production are approximate, varying from year to year, and an estimate has been attempted by deducting the ullage or evaporation, which usually consists of 15 per cent.

Principal Growths

Château Beauchêne
Château Beauregard
Clos Beauregard
Château Bel-Air
Château Bellevue
Château Bourgneuf
Clos Bonalgue
Château Campagnac
Château Cantereau
Château Certan-Marzelle
Château du Chêne-Liége
Château Clinet
Clos du Clocher
Château Enclos-Haut-Mazeyres
Clos de l'Église-Clinet
Domaine de l'Église
Château Enclos-du-Presbytère
Château l'Évangile
    (38 tons, 3,640 cases)
Château Ferrand
Château Feytit-Clinet
Château Franc-Maillet
Domaine du Gabachot
Château Gazin
    (68 tons, 6,500 cases)

Château Gombaude-Guillot
Château Grangeneuve
Château Grate-Cap
Domaine de Grave
Château Guillot
Château Haut-Cloquet
Château Haut-Maillet
Domaine de Haut-Pignon
Château des Hautes-Rouzes
Domaine de Haut-Tropchaud
Château La Cabanne
Clos Lacombe
Domaine de Lacombe
Château La Commanderie
Château La Conseillante
    (34 tons, 3,250 cases)
Château La Croix
Château La Croix-de-Gay
Château La Croix-St.-Georges
Château Lafleur
    (10 tons, 950 cases)
Château Lafleur-Pétrus
    (17 tons, 1,600 cases)
Château Lagrange
Cru de La Nouvelle-Église

280

CHÂTEAUX OF POMEROL

Château La Patache
Château La Pointe
Château La Soulate
Château Latour-Pomerol
Château La Violette
Château Le Caillou
Château Le Carillon
Château Le Gay
Château Les Grands-Champs
Domaine Les Grands-Sillons
Château Mazeyres
Domaine de Mazeyres
Château Monregard-la-Croix
Domaine du Moulin-de-Lavaud
Château Moulinet
Château Nénin
  (85 tons, 8,100 cases)
Château Petit-Village
  (34 tons, 3,250 cases)
Château Pétrus
  (30 tons, 2,800 cases)
Château Pignon-de-Gay

Château Plince
Clos René
Château Rêve-d'Or
Château Rouget
Clos du Roy
Clos Saint-André
Château de Sales
Clos du Seigneur
Château Tailhas
Château Taillefer
Château des Templiers
Château Thibeaud-Maillet
Château Toulifaut
Château Trintin
Château Trotanoy
  (21 tons, 2,000 cases)
Château de Valois
Château Vieux-Château Certan
  (34 tons, 3,250 cases)
Château Vieux-Maillet
Château Vraie-Croix-de-Gay

PART 5

GRAVES

1953 OFFICIAL CLASSIFICATION

The vineyards of the Graves district were officially classified in 1953. Château Haut-Brion, the greatest of all Graves, is also officially classified with the great Médocs.

The following figures of production are approximate, varying from year to year, and an estimate has been attempted by deducting the ullage or evaporation, which usually consists of 15 per cent.

CLASSIFIED RED WINES OF GRAVES

	TOWNSHIP	TONS	CASES
Château Bouscaut	Cadaujac	100	8,100
Château Carbonnieux	Léognan	51	4,870
Domaine de Chevalier	Léognan	25.5	2,440
Château Haut-Bailly	Léognan	25.5	2,425
Château Haut-Brion	Pessac	100	8,100
Château La Mission-Haut-Brion	Pessac	34	3,250
Château La Tour-Haut-Brion	Talence	15	1,500
Château La Tour-Martillac	Martillac	10	1,000
Château Malartic-Lagravière	Léognan	30	2,400
Château Olivier	Léognan	20	1,600
Château Smith-Haut-Lafitte	Martillac	42	4,000

Other Principal Growths

Château Baret
Villenave-d'Ornon

Château Brown
Léognan

Château de Cabannieux
Portets

Château des Carmes-Haut-Brion
Pessac

Château La Côte-Haut-Brion
Pessac

Château Couhins
Villenave-d'Ornon

Château Fanning-La-Fontaine
Pessac

Château Haut-Gardère
Léognan

RED CHÂTEAUX OF GRAVES

Cru Larrivet-Haut-Brion
Léognan

Château Pape-Clémont
Pessac

Château Pontac-Monplaisir
Villenave-d'Ornon

Le Desert
Léognan

Château de l'Espérance
La Brède

Château Ferran
Martillac

Château Fieuzal
Léognan

Château La Garde
Martillac

Château du Grand-Laguloup
Saucats

Domaine de Grandmaison
Léognan

Château Guillaumot
La Brède

Château Haut-Madère
Villenave-d'Ornon

Château l'Hermitage
Martillac

Cru Lespaut
Martillac

Château Limbourg
Villenave-d'Ornon

Château La Louvière
Léognan

Château Lusseau
Ayguemorte-les-Graves

Château du Mejan
Ayguemorte-les-Graves

Château Millet
Portets

Château Neuf
Léognan

Château de Nouchet
Martillac

Château Le Pape
Léognan

Château Pessan
Portets

Château Pommarède-de-Haut
Castres

Château de Portets
Portets

Château de la Prâde
St.-Médard-d'-Eyrans

Château Raba
Talence

Château de Saige-Fort-Manoir
Pessac

Château Saint-Gérôme
Ayguemorte-les-Graves

Domaine La Solitude
Martillac

Château Terrefort-de-Fortissan
Villenave-d'Ornon

Château La Tour-Bicheau
Portets

Château Tourteau-Chollet
Arbanats

Château du Tuquet
Beautiran

Classified White Wines of Graves

	TOWNSHIP	TONS	CASES
Château Bouscaut	*Cadaujac*	50	4,000
Château Carbonnieux	*Léognan*	68	6,520
Domaine de Chevalier	*Léognan*	3.5	325
Château Laville-Haut-Brion	*Talence*	17	1,625
Château Olivier	*Léognan*	85	8,150

Other Principal Growths

Château d'Arricaut
Landiras
Château Baret
Villenave-d'Ornon
Château de la Brède
La Brède
Château Brown
Léognan
Château Cabannieux
Portets
Château Couhins
Villenave-d'Ornon
Château de l'Espérance
La Brède
Château de la Prâde
St.-Médard-d'Eyrans
Château Ferran
Martillac
Château Ferrande
Castres
Château Fieuzal
Léognan
Château Guillaumot
La Brède
Château Haut-Brion-Blanc
Pessac
Château Haut-Nouchet
Martillac

Château Lagravière
Toulenne
Château La Tour-Martillac
Martillac
Château Pontac-Monplaisir
Villenave-d'Ornon
Château La Louvière
Léognan
Château Lusseau
Ayguemorte-les-Graves
Château Piron
St.-Morillon
Château de Portets
Portets
Château Saint-Brice
Pont-de-la-Maye
Château Saint-Gérôme
Ayguemorte-les-Graves
Château Smith-Haut-Lafitte
Martillac
Château du Touquet
Beautiran
Château Tourteau-Chollet
Arbanats
Domaine Roland
Langon

PART 6

SAUTERNES AND BARSAC

As in the Médoc, the Sauternes vineyards were officially classified in 1855. This classification is known as the Official Classification of the Great Growths of the Gironde.

The total production from these vineyards represents approximately 25 per cent of the total Sauternes production, roughly amounting to 350,000 cases per year.

The following figures of production are approximate, varying from year to year, and an estimate has been attempted by deducting the ullage or evaporation, which usually consists of 15 per cent.

1st Great Growth

	TONS	CASES
Château d'Yquem	100	8,700

1st Growths

Château Guiraud	80	6,400
Château La Tour-Blanche	25	2,400
Château Lafaurie-Peyraguey	45	3,500
Château de Rayne-Vigneau	75	6,100
Château Rabaud-Sigalas	25	2,125
Château Rabaud-Promis	35	2,950
Clos Haut-Peyraguey	15	1,200
Château Coutet	60	4,750
Château Climens	45	3,500
Château de Suduiraut	100	8,100
Château Rieussec	70	5,500

2nd Growths

Château d'Arche	12	950
Château Filhot	50	4,000
Château Lamothe	10	750
Château Myrat	40	3,100

SAUTERNES AND BARSAC

2nd Growths [continued]

	TONS	CASES
Château Doisy-Védrines	40	3,100
Château Doisy-Daëne	25	2,400
Château Suau	15	1,200
Château Broustet	30	2,300
Château Caillou	40	3,200
Château Nairac	30	2,300
Château de Malle	40	3,200
Château Romer	15	1,200

The Crus Bourgeois or
Lesser Growths of Sauternes and Barsac

Château d'Arche-Lafaurie
Sauternes
Château d'Arche-Pugneau
Preignac
Château d'Arche-Vimeney
Sauternes
Château d'Armajan-des-Ormes
Preignac
Château Augey
Bommes
Château Barbier
Fargues
Cru Barjumeau
Sauternes
Château Bastor-Lamontagne
Preignac
Clos Batsalles
Fargues
Château Baulac
Barsac
Château Baulac-Daudijos
Barsac

Château Béchereau
Bommes
Château de Bel-Air
Preignac
Domaine Bellevue
Sauternes
Château Bergeron
Bommes
Cru Bouscla
Barsac
Château du Bouyot
Barsac
Château Brassens-Guiteronde
Barsac
Château Cadroy
Preignac
Château Cameron
Bommes
Château Cameron
Sauternes
Château Camperos
Barsac

286

MINOR CHÂTEAUX, SAUTERNES AND BARSAC

Château Cantegril	Château Grillon
Barsac	*Barsac*
Château Caplane	Château Guilhem-du-Ruy
Bommes	*Barsac*
Château de Carles	Château Guimbalet
Barsac	*Barsac*
Château du Closiot	Château Guiteronde
Barsac	*Barsac*
Cru Commet Magey	Château du Haire
Preignac	*Preignac*
Domaine de Cosse	Château Hallet
Fargues	*Barsac*
Domaine du Couité	Château Haut-Bergeron
Preignac	*Preignac*
Château Depian	Château Haut-Bommes
Barsac	*Bommes*
Château Ducasse	Château Jacques-le-Haut
Barsac	*Barsac*
Château Dudon	Château Jany
Barsac	*Barsac*
Château Farlurets	Château Jonka
Barsac	*Preignac*
Château Fleury	Château du Juge
Barsac	*Preignac*
Château de Fontebride-Boutoc	Domaine des Justices
Preignac	*Preignac*
Domaine de la Forêt	Cru La Bouade
Preignac	*Barsac*
Château Gilette	Cru Laclotte
Preignac	*Barsac*
Château Grand-Carretey	Cru Lafon
Barsac	*Preignac*
Château Grand-Mayne	Château Lafon
Barsac	*Sauternes*
Cru du Grand-Jauga	Château Lafon-Laroze
Barsac	*Sauternes*
Château des Grandes-Vignes	Cru La Gravère
Preignac	*Preignac*
Château Graves	Cru La Hourcade
Barsac	*Preignac*

K*   287

MINOR CHÂTEAUX, SAUTERNES AND BARSAC

Château Lalot		Château Mathalin
	Preignac	*Barsac*
Château Lamothe		Château Mauras
	Preignac	*Bommes*
Château Lamourette		Château du Mayne
	Bommes	*Barsac*
Cru Lanère		Château du Mayne
	Sauternes	*Preignac*
Cru Lanère		Domaine du Mayne
	Bommes	*Preignac*
Château Lapeloue		Château Mayne-Bert
	Barsac	*Barsac*
Cru La Pinesse		Château Menatte
	Barsac	*Barsac*
Château Laribotte		Château Menauta
	Preignac	*Barsac*
Château l'Aubepin		Château Mercier
	Bommes	*Barsac*
Château Laville		Château de Montalivet
	Preignac	*Barsac*
Château Le Coustet		Château du Mont
	Barsac	*Preignac*
Cru l'Haouilley		Château Monteils
	Barsac	*Preignac*
Château Le Hère		Domaine Monteils
	Bommes	*Preignac*
Château Le Mayne		Château Mont-Joye
	Barsac	*Barsac*
Château Le Mayne		Château Montjoie
	Preignac	*Preignac*
Cru Le Tucau		Cru Mothes
	Barsac	*Fargues*
Château Leyret		Château Moura
	Preignac	*Barsac*
Château Liot		Château Padouen
	Barsac	*Barsac*
Château de Luziès		Clos du Pape
	Barsac	*Fargues*
Château Massereau-Lapachère		Château Péchon
	Barsac	*Barsac*

MINOR CHÂTEAUX, SAUTERNES AND BARSAC

Château Peillon-Claverie
Fargues

Château Pernaud
Barsac

Château Petit-Mayne
Barsac

Cru Peyraguey
Preignac

Château Peyraguey-le-Rousset
Preignac

Château Peyron
Fargues

Château Piada
Barsac

Château du Pic
Preignac

Château Pierrejeu
Preignac

Château Piot
Barsac

Château de Pleytegeat
Preignac

Château Prost
Barsac

Château Raymond-Lafon
Sauternes

Château du Roc
Barsac

Château des Rochers
Preignac

Château de Rolland
Barsac

Château Roubinet
Barsac

Château Roumieu-Goyau
Barsac

Château Roumieu-Dubordieu
Barsac

Château Roumieu-Bernadet
Barsac

Château du Roy
Barsac

Clos Sahuc
Preignac

Château Sahuc-la-Tour
Preignac

Château Saint-Amand
Preignac

Château Saint-Marc
Barsac

Château Saint-Robert
Barsac

Château Simon
Barsac

Château Simon-Carretey
Barsac

Château Solon
Preignac

Château Terrefort
Sauternes

Cru Thibaut
Fargues

Château Trillon
Sauternes

Château Valmont
Barsac

Château Vigne-Vieilles
Barsac

Château Villefranche
Barsac

Cru Violet
Preignac

Château Veyres
Preignac

Bottle Sizes

BORDEAUX WINES

		BOTTLES
$\frac{1}{10}$ or 1 pint		$\frac{1}{2}$
$\frac{1}{5}$		1
Magnum		2
Double Magnum		4
Jeroboam	(*approx.*)	5
Imperial		8

All bottles containing more than the double magnum pay a higher rate of duty. Since the Second World War these large-size bottles are practically unavailable on the Bordeaux market. Recently glass-manufacturers have started remaking these large bottles.

CHAMPAGNE

Split	half pint
Pint	usual short pint, $\frac{1}{10}$ gallon, regular $\frac{1}{2}$ bottle
Quart	usual short quart, $\frac{1}{5}$ gallon, regular bottle
Magnum	two bottles
Jeroboam	four bottles
Rehoboam	six bottles

290

CHAMPAGNE BOTTLE SIZES [CONTINUED]

Methuselah (Methusalem)	eight bottles
Salmanasar	twelve bottles
Balthazar	sixteen bottles
Nebuchadnezzar	twenty bottles

Cooperage

IN VARIOUS WINE DISTRICTS
OF FRANCE

The wine-buyer throughout France is confronted with a maze of various-sized barrels, each referred to by a different name. As the wines are different, so are the barrels in which they mature. The following are some of the most useful names to retain.

Bordeaux

The production of all the châteaux is always indicated in *tonneaux* or tons. All prices are quoted in *tonneaux*. There is no barrel of this size, however. A *tonneau* consists of 4 *barriques*, containing 225 litres. A fluctuation of 2.5 per cent is permitted in content. Wines are also sold in *feuillettes* (half a *barrique*) containing 112 litres, or a *quartaut* (a quarter of a *barrique*) containing 56 litres. A *barrique* yields 24 cases of 12 bottles each. A *tonneau*, consisting of 4 *barriques*, yields 96 cases.

Burgundy

In the Côte d'Or the regular barrel, called *pièce*, contains 226 to 228 litres; a half barrel, called *feuillette*, contains 114 litres; and a quarter barrel, called *quartaut*, contains 57 litres. The old French measure called *queue* is still used in Burgundy. The bids at the auction sale of the Hospice de Beaune are made in terms of *queue*, which means 2 *pièces*. Just as with the *tonneau* in Bordeaux, there is no actual barrel of this size. A *pièce*, once bottled, yields approximately 24 to 25 cases of 12 bottles each.

Chablis

The standard barrel of lower Burgundy is a *feuillette* containing 136 litres, which is larger than the *feuillette* of the Côte d'Or.

In the *Mâconnais* the *pièce* contains 215 litres; in the Beaujolais, 216 litres.

Rhône Valley

In and around Châteauneuf-du-Pape the *pièce* contains 225 litres. This barrel is slightly smaller than the *pièce* used in the Côte d'Or.

Wines of the Loire

In the province of the Touraine the wines of Vouvray are kept in *pièces* containing 225 litres, but farther down the river the wines of Anjou, Saumur, and Layon come in slightly smaller *pièces* of 220 litres.

Champagne

The usual barrel is called *queue* and contains 216 litres. The half barrel, called *demi-queue*, contains 108 litres.

Alsace

Sales are often made, as in Germany, in huge barrels, called *foudres* in France, containing 1,000 litres. The wine is shipped, however, in barrels of various sizes, often in small barrels called *aumes* containing 114 litres, which is the same size as the *feuillettes* of the Côte d'Or.

Algeria and the Midi

Wine is quoted in hectolitres, or 100-litre units. Prices vary according to alcoholic content. The wines are stored, however, in huge barrels called *demi-muids* containing 600 to 700 litres, or, most of the time, in large glass-lined vats.

REDUCED TABLE
OF SOME OF THE MOST USEFUL
Franco-British Measures

LINEAR MEASURES

UNIT METRIC SYSTEM	COMPARISON	BRITISH EQUIVALENT
Millimetre (mm.)	——	.0394 inch
Centimetre (cm.)	10 mm.	.3937 inch
Metre (m.)	100 cm.	39.37 inches, or
		3.28 feet
Kilometre (km.)	1,000 m.	0.621 mile

British System

UNIT	COMPARISON	METRIC EQUIVALENT
Inch (in.)	——	25.4001 mm.
Foot (ft.)	12 in.	.3048 m.
Yard (yd.)	36 in.	.9144 m.
	3 ft.	
Mile (mi.)	5,280 ft.	1,609 m.
	1,760 yd.	1 km. 609 m.

UNITS OF AREA, OR SQUARE MEASURES

Metric System

UNIT	COMPARISON	BRITISH EQUIVALENT
Square millimetre (mm.²)	——	.0015 sq. in.
Square centimetre (cm.²)	.0001 m.²	155 sq. in.
Square metre (m.²)	centare	10.7639 sq. ft.
Are (a.)	100 m.²	3.9537 sq. rd.
Hectare (ha.)	10,000 m.² or	2.471 acres
	23 Burgundy *ouvrées*	
Square kilometre (km.²)	1,000,000 m.²	.3861 sq. mi.
Burgundy *ouvrée*	428 m.²	——

British System (*Square Measures*)

UNIT	COMPARISON	METRIC EQUIVALENT
Square inch (sq. in.)	——	6.4516 cm.^{2}
Square foot (sq. ft.)	144 sq. in.	.0929 m.^{2}
Square yard (sq. yd.)	1296 sq. in.	.8361 m.^{2}
	9 sq. ft.	
Acre	43,560 sq. ft.	.4047 ha.
	4,840 sq. yd.	
Square mile (sq. mi.)	27,878,400 sq. ft.	2.5900 km.^{2}
	3,097,600 sq. yd.	
	640 acres	

UNITS OF VOLUME—CUBIC MEASURES

UNIT	COMPARISON	BRITISH EQUIVALENT
Cubic metre (m.^{3})	——	35.31 cubic feet

British System

UNIT	COMPARISON	METRIC EQUIVALENT
Cubic inch (cu. in.)	——	16.3872 cm.^{3}
Cubic foot (cu. ft.)	1728 cu. in.	.0283 m.^{3}
Cubic yard (cu. yd.)	46,656 cu. in.	.7646 m.^{3}
	27 cu. ft.	

WEIGHTS

UNIT	COMPARISON	AVOIRDUPOIS
Gramme (g.)	——	.0353 ounce
Kilogramme (kg.)	1,000 grammes	2.2046 pounds
Metric ton (tn.)	1,000 kil.	.9842 ton

British System

UNIT	COMPARISON	METRIC EQUIVALENT
Ounce avoirdupois (oz. avdp.)	——	28.3495 g.
Pound (lb. avdp.)	16 ounces	.4536 kg.
Ton (tn.)	2,240 pounds	1016 kg.

295

UNITS OF CAPACITY—LIQUID MEASURE

Metric System

UNIT	COMPARISON	BRITISH LIQUID EQUIVALENT
Millilitre (ml.)	——	.0338 fluid ounce
Centilitre (cl.)	.01 l.	.3381 fluid ounce
Litre (l.)	100 cl.	1.760 pts.
Hectolitre (hl.)	100 l.	22 gallons

Liquid Measures—British

UNIT	COMPARISON	METRIC EQUIVALENT
Fluid ounce (fl. oz.)	——	29.5729 ml.
Pint (pt.)	20 fl. oz.	.568 l.
Quart (qt.)	40 fl. oz. 2 pt.	1.136 l.
Gallon (gal.)	8 pt. 4 qt.	4.54 l.

Fahrenheit and Centigrade Conversions

To convert Fahrenheit to Centigrade, subtract 32 degrees and multiply by $\frac{5}{9}$; to convert Centigrade to Fahrenheit, multiply by $\frac{9}{5}$ and add 32 degrees.

Acknowledgments

I could not have written this book without the friendly assist-
ance of a great many people—growers, cellar-masters,
shippers, and others connected with the great wine industry
of France. It is a pleasure to list some of their names here and
to offer to each of them again my grateful thanks.

Dr. Maynard A. Amerine, Department of Viticulture, Uni-
versity of California; Mignot-Aubert, President of the Growers
Association of Indre-et-Loire; J. Bavard, of Puligny-Montrachet;
James Beard, author of *The Fireside Cookbook*, of New York;
E. Besserat de Bellefon, of Ay; V. Besserat de Bellefon, of Ay;
Henri Boillot, of Volnay; Baron LeRoy de Boiseaumarié,
President of Wine Growers of France; Marc Bredif, of Vouvray;
Georges S. Chappaz, Vice-President of the Institut National des
Appellations d'Origine des Vins et Eaux-de-Vie; Pierre Damoy,
of Gevrey-Chambertin; A. Devletian, Institute National des
Appellations d'Origine des Vins et Eaux-de-Vie; M. Droin-Mary,
of Chablis, President of Chablis Growers Association; Joseph
Drouhin, of Beaune; Mme Drouhin-Laroze, of Gevrey-Cham-
bertin; The Abbé Dubaquié, Directeur Honoraire de la Station
Œnologique de Bordeaux; Roger Duclot, of Bordeaux; René
Engel, of Vosne-Romanée; Louis Eschenauer, of Bordeaux;
Henri de Fonroque-Mercié, of Bordeaux; J. Fourcaud-Laussac,
Château Cheval-Blanc, of Saint-Émilion; André Fournier,
owner of Château Canon, Saint-Émilion; Fernand Ginestet,
owner of Château Margaux, former President of the Syndicate
of Bordeaux Wine Shippers; Pierre Ginestet, Château Margaux,
Bordeaux; Jean Godet, of Cognac; Henri Gouges, President of
the Burgundy Growers Association, Nuits-Saint-Georges; Louis
Gros, of Vosne-Romanée; M. Guillaume, of Mesnil-sur-Oger;
Patrick Hennessy, of Cognac; François Hine, of Jarnac; Michel

Jaboulet-Vercherre, of Tain-l'Hermitage; U.G. Jaboulet-Vercherre, of Pommard; Alfred A. Knopf, of New York; Ed. Kressmann, of Bordeaux; Maxwell Kriendler, of the "21" Club, New York; Count and Countess Durieu de Lacarelle, Château Filhot, Sauternes (Gironde); Georges Lawton, of Bordeaux; G. Lung, of Bordeaux; René Masson, of Reims; Jean Michel, of Chablis; Julien Monnot, of Puligny-Montrachet; Duc de Montesquiou-Fenzensac, of Auch; C. Moreau, of Vosne-Romanée; Guy Moreau, of Chablis; Mme Mugnier, of Chambolle-Musigny; C. C. Phillippe, of the Waldorf-Astoria, New York; Prince de Polignac, of Reims; Claude Ramonet, of Chassagne-Montrachet; Comte de Rohan-Chabot, President of the Wine Growers Association of Provence; J. Salzmann, of Kaysersberg; Étienne Sauzet, of Puligny-Montrachet; Marcel Servin, of Chablis; Colonel Teed, of Cassis; Baron Thénard, of Givry; Nicolas Trambitsky, of Paris; J. Vidal-Fleury, of Ampuis; Seymour Weller, Château Haut-Brion, Bordeaux; P. de Wilde, of Cantenac.

Index

INDEX